Sex Differences:
Mental and
Temperamental

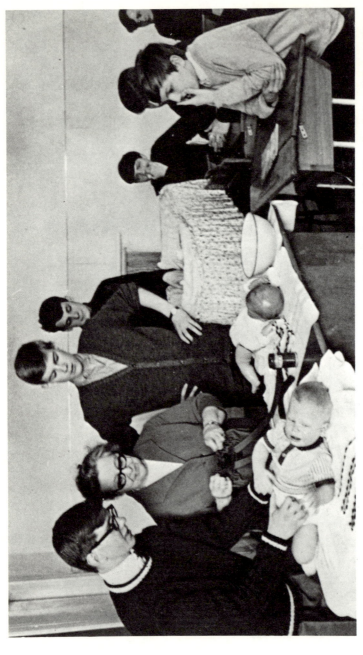

Source: S. Brun-Gulbrandsen, "Sex Roles and the Socialization Process," in E. Dahlström, ed. *The Changing Roles of Men and Women*, London: Gerald Duckworth, Ltd., 1967. Copyright 1967 by Gerald Duckworth, Ltd. Reproduced by permission.

Swedish boys in an elective course on child care.

Sex Differences: Mental and Temperamental

John P. Seward
University of California,
Los Angeles
Georgene H. Seward
University of Southern California

LexingtonBooks
D.C. Heath and Company
Lexington, Massachusetts
Toronto

Library of Congress Cataloging in Publication Data

Seward, John Perry, 1905-
  Sex differences.

    1. Sex differences (Psychology) 2. Sex differences (Psychology)—Social
aspects. 3. Sex differences. I. Seward, Georgene Hoffman, 1902-   joint
author. II. Title.
BF692.2.S45   155.3'3   79-48004
ISBN 0-669-03629-3

Published simultaneously in Canada.

Printed in the United States of America.

International Standard Book Number: 0-669-03629-3

Library of Congress Catalog Card Number: 79-48004

To Jerry

Contents

	List of Figures	ix
	Preface	xi
Chapter 1	Introduction	1
Chapter 2	Societal Setting	5
	Early Man and Early Woman	5
	Beginnings of Western Culture	7
	Later Developments	10
	Modern Times	13
	Society's Problem	25
Chapter 3	Mental Abilities	31
	Development of Differences	32
	Determinants of Differences	40
Chapter 4	Cerebral Asymmetry	59
	Specialized Hemispheres	59
	A Possible Sex Difference	60
Chapter 5	Masculinity and Femininity	75
	Theoretical Approaches	75
	Measurement	76
Chapter 6	Social Factors in Gender Development	89
	Sex and Gender	89
	Developmental Changes in Play	90
	Theories of Gender Development	92
	Modeling	95
	Children's Projected Adult Roles	98
Chapter 7	Genetic and Hormonal Deviations	103
	Homosexuals	103
	Transsexuals	107
	Hermaphrodites	110
	Identical Twins, Same Sex but Opposite Gender	114

Chapter 8   **Activity Level**   121

Course of Development   121
Aberrations   122
Origins   123

Chapter 9   **Aggressiveness and Dominance**   129

Social Factors   130
Biological Factors   134

Chapter 10   **Fear and Anxiety**   151

Chapter 11   **Compliance, Nurturance, and Affiliation**   163

Compliance   163
Nurturance   168
Affiliation   171

Chapter 12   **Need to Achieve**   183

Power, Glory, and the Need to Achieve   183
Mastery or Community?   189
Origins   193

Chapter 13   **Society's Options**   197

A Backward Glance   197
Looking Ahead   201
Eliminating Gender Differences   202
Synthesizing the Genders   203

Index   211

About the Authors   217

List of Figures

3-1   Examples of pairs of perspective line drawings presented to the subjects.   36

3-2   Part III of the Gottschaldt Embedded Figures Test.   38

4-1   Mean values of differences between verbal and spatial scores.   67

4-2   Absolute values of mean percent ear advantage in dichotic listening scores.   68

4-3   Individual changes in rod-and-frame error scores.   70

7-1   Late treated, matched pair of patients concordant for diagnosis of hermaphroditism.   112

10-1   Relative plasma concentrations of estrogen and progesterone during the menstrual cycle.   157

11-1   Preferred conversational distance.   175

12-1   Attributional model of achievement motivation.   184

Preface

Having devoted two lifetimes to seeking the determinants of motivation, we think it time to evaluate the current status of the problem. In this book the focus is on sex-related differences. Our interest in this grew out of a shared biological approach to behavior, which led us to a study of the female sex rhythm. In the course of this work it was our good fortune to meet Dr. George N. Papanicolaou, who became our mentor and lasting friend. He generously shared with us his facilities at Cornell University Medical College, where we began a series of experiments on the reproductive behavior of the guinea pig. Later Dr. Papanicolaou made it possible for us to study the effects of estrogenic hormone therapy on menopausal women.

With the onset of World War II, our paths diverged and we pursued different interests for some years. Georgene Seward accepted an opportunity to investigate the excessive menstrual absenteeism among women workers in many of the war industries. She also joined the newly organized National Council of Women Psychologists and became chairperson of the Committee on Roles of Men and Women in Postwar Society. Her book *Sex and the Social Order*, published in 1946, was an attempt to integrate the social factors with the biological factors determining behavior in that area.

In this book we have again joined forces to tackle a central issue brought to the surface by the current tussle over the status of women. Apart from physique and the physiology of reproduction, does biology play any part in how the sexes differ? If all cultural pressures were equalized from birth, would any gender differences remain? In our search for clues we have turned primarily to experimental evidence from the behavioral sciences. With the warning that such a search, as always, is likely to raise more questions than it settles, we invite the intrepid reader to share in its excitement.

Sex Differences: Mental and Temperamental

1 Introduction

How do boys and girls, men and women differ? We know the sexes differ in physique, appearance, and the parts they play in reproduction. We think they also differ in other behaviors, including attitudes, emotionality, interests, and ways of thinking. But here there is less certainty. It is well known that society expects men and women to react in certain characteristic ways, but which way does the causal sequence go? Do girls cry more than boys, and therefore society expects them to; or do they learn to act the way society expects? The question reminds us that when we talk about sex differences we must distinguish between social stereotypes and the way boys and girls really behave. It is with these observable, at least potentially measurable, psychological characteristics setting males apart from females that we are concerned.

Why should the topic attract so much attention today? In the past few decades women in our society have become intensely aware of their inferior status. The women's liberation movement has found a voice and its leaders demand a change. They challenge the outworn dogmas that have kept women "in their place." They insist that women are as well equipped as men to deal with the complex problems of survival in our industrial society. But insistence is not proof, and one effect has been to focus interest on the question: do males and females really differ in the ways social mythology has led us to believe? Aside from their procreative functions do they differ at all, except as the culture has shaped them for traditional roles?

In answer, a normal trickle of research in the area has swelled to a flood. Fortunately handbooks to the literature are available (Friedman et al. 1974; Lloyd & Archer 1976; Wittig & Petersen 1979), supplementing Maccoby and Jacklin's (1974) comprehensive treatise. What, then, can another book about sex differences add?

The basic question considered in this book is: to what extent are sex differences biologically or socially determined? Despite recent signs of a revival of interest in biological determiners, a word in defense of the project may be needed.

For some years in midcentury, social and even biological scientists branded the heredity-environment distinction as old-fashioned. Worse, it was labeled a false dichotomy, a pseudoproblem. The argument was that every activity of an organism depends on the interaction of its genetic endowment with its past and present environment. Therefore, it was held,

1

the only fruitful longitudinal inquiry is how organisms develop as a result of this or that condition, not whether they were or were not born that way.

What the interactionists lost sight of is that, although this argument applies to a single measured trait, it does not apply to a difference between two such measures. For instance, it makes no sense to ask whether muscular strength is inherited or acquired, since both alternatives are so obviously true. But it does make sense to ask if a difference in muscular strength (between girls and boys) is due to heredity or environment. To answer the question, we need only keep one set of factors constant and vary the other. This is why identical twins are so useful in dealing with this issue. The principle is sound, as are the experimental designs that embody it. Unfortunately the requirement is often exceedingly difficult to meet in practice, as every experimenter or statistician knows.

Granted that such a quest is legitimate, it is still pertinent to ask: who cares? Today the social sciences are strongly biased toward cultural as opposed to biological explanations, though the winds may be shifting. Extreme advocates of women's liberation have little patience to consider the possibility that, aside from strictly reproductive functions, women may differ from men in any important respect. Exceptions to the rule are glibly ascribed to the different roles boys and girls are trained for in most societies.

In such a charged atmosphere a statement of one's position is mandatory. Whatever our personal leanings, our purpose in this book is not to carry a torch for women's emancipation or to man the barricades against it. We believe that a lasting solution of social problems, the man-woman problem included, calls for a clear grasp of the conditions that produce them. These conditions may or may not involve chromosomes, endocrine glands, or brain centers. If and when social planning becomes a reality, it will be imperative to know what limits to acceptable sex roles are biologically set.

Inevitably our point of view has played a part in the selection of critical traits. It seems reasonable to assume that the most significant differences between the sexes should be those with an unlearned core. But how can these be identified in advance? In a few cases there is empirical evidence; for example, a suggestion of sex-linked inheritance, or prevalence in other primates. But most of the territory is uncharted, and some calculated guesswork becomes indispensable.

The following line of reasoning led to a working hypothesis. We assume that sex differences, in the human as in other species, have evolved; that is, they are to some degree the product of biological selection. We also assume that the human species, through its unprecedented (except in the dolphin [Langworthy 1932]) cerebral development, its languages and cultures, has so altered the environment as to make certain biological adaptations obsolete.

We now ask: what sex-specific characters are most likely to resist cultural change and thereby survive as biologically ingrained dispositions?

The answer is: the stablest characters will be those required by the demands of mammalian (and specifically primate) reproduction, with the division of labor it involves. John Money (1977), reducing mammalian sex differences to biological bedrock, lists impregnation by the sperm-bearing male; ovulation, gestation, and lactation by the egg-bearing female.

The aptitudes and proclivities derived from these procreative functions are more tentative. Insemination in mammals generally requires the male to take an active part, to be aggressive and competitive toward rival males, and dominant toward a possible mate (Abernethy 1974). The female on the other hand must be receptive to the male, at least when she is ovulating; after giving birth she must be willing to accept, suckle, and otherwise care for her young. Generalizing these inclinations, we should expect males, more than females, to be active, dominant, aggressive, and competitive; while females, more than males, should be compliant, timid, nurturant, and affiliative.

If this argument contains an element of question begging, our defense is that the flaw is not fatal. To point out the biological utility of such differences does not prove they exist; and where a difference is found its genetic origin must still be proved. However rationalized, the traits listed above—and discussed in chapters to follow—have the status of a hypothesis, no more and no less, to guide our search for the roots of gender.

We shall begin by considering a variety of cultures, with the question in mind: how far have the sexes proved adaptable to the demands of a given society, and to what degree have they resisted change?

References

Abernethy, V. 1974. "Dominance and Sexual Behavior: A Hypothesis." *American Journal of Psychiatry* 131:813-817.

Friedman, R.C.; Richart, R.M.; and Vande Wiele, R.L., eds. 1974. *Sex Differences in Behavior*. New York: Wiley.

Langworthy, O.R. 1932. "A Description of the Central Nervous System of the Porpoise (*Tursiops truncatus*). *Journal of Comparative Neurology* 54:437-488.

Lloyd, B., and Archer, J., eds. 1976. *Exploring Sex Differences*. London: Academic Press.

Maccoby, E.E., and Jacklin, C.N. 1974. *The Psychology of Sex Differences*. Stanford, Calif.: Stanford University Press.

Money, J. 1977. "Sex Roles and Sex-coded Roles." *Journal of Pediatric Psychology* 2:108-109.

Wittig, M.A., and Petersen, A.C., eds. 1979. *Sex-related Differences in Cognitive Functioning*. New York: Academic Press.

2 Societal Setting

Any discussion of sex differences must distinguish between social roles imposed on the individual and his underlying natural inclinations. Our task will be to search for the biological roots of sex differences, a search that will take us on a space-time journey back through the centuries and across the vast distances separating cultures. Our goal will be to find out if there are basic behaviors characterizing the sexes regardless of cultural contexts.

The question may be raised as to whether the primary biological sex differences associated with reproductive functions predispose the individuals toward psychological differences that bear on the respective roles they are expected to play in society. Cross-cultural surveys of primitive societies reveal such consistency in gender-role assignment as to suggest that the genetic and glandular differences between male and female may underlie differences in aptitude for learning certain kinds of behavior that have been exploited by most primitive peoples in establishing gender roles for the group (Minturn 1970).

Early Man and Early Woman

Hunting and Gathering Societies

Over at least a million years fundamental human social forms were forged in the hunting-gathering milieu. Cave paintings 20,000 years old fix the universal base of culture in the knowlege of the animals that men and women lived by and stalked. Early humans depended on hunting, which made it necessary for them to follow the migratory herds and, like them, to be continuously on the move. In *The Ascent of Man*, Bronowki (1973) points out that "The transhumance way of life is itself a cultural fossil now, and has barely survived. The only people that still live in this way are the Lapps in the extreme north of Scandinavia, who follow the reindeer as they did during the Ice Age" (p. 48). According to this life-style, the men killed the animals on the hoof and brought back the meat food to a group living place to share it with the women who had gathered the plant food. The female activities, which also included making pots and textiles, developing the rudiments of botany, chemistry, and medical science, and socializing the children, required skills fully as complex as those involved in the man's hunting (Reed 1971). For better or worse, division of labor between the sexes was the bedrock on which this type of society was built. The divergence between male and female increased the ease with which people performed their sex-related gender roles. The success of the hunting-gathering way of life lay in its adaptability. When men hunt and women gather, the economic reciprocity results in a system of sharing vital goods through hospitality and generous gift exchanges as the basis of human living. At the same time the development of language facilitates communication among groups of hunters who depend on close cooperation and planning to capture their prey (Washburn & Lancaster 1968).

Agricultural Revolution

As the glaciers receded about 10,000 years ago, people gave up the nomadic life and settled down to cultivate the soil. As a result of this agricultural revolution, cultures began to diversify.

With Cattle. Many of these agricultural societies depended on domesticating work animals, so that knowledge of animal husbandry became a necessary skill. Power was vested in the male because of his apparent superior strength, endurance, and motor skills. Under these circumstances, the family became institutionalized around the men, whose control of the property involved in food getting and in the economic capital derived from it gave them high prestige. A core of kin-related males tended to settle near one another, establishing residence rules centered in the father's household, and descent rules along the father's line (D'Andrade 1966). Although in these cultures sex differences in role and status were large, the emphasis on mutuality, sharing, and hospitality mitigated the harshness of raw patriarchy, and helped to maintain a good psychological balance.

Without Cattle. In cultures where subsistence was derived mainly from agriculture without the use of large animals, behavioral sex differences were less marked since food getting might be carried out by males or females. A smaller, nuclear family was typical, consisting of parents and their children, with power and authority more evenly distributed. Some of these societies were even female-centered, organized along maternal lines with residence determined by the mother and inheritance transmitted through her. Among the Hopi Indians, for example, the social unit is the clan, consisting of a group of families headed by older, active women. While the clan as a whole owns the springs, gardens, and farmlands, the children, houses, furnishings, and food belong specifically to the women. In this well-planned society, each sex has its assigned place and is integrated into the harmonious whole (Leavitt 1971).

Wherever they appear, mother-focused cultures are of special interest in showing that the sex dichotomies to which we have become accustomed, are not universal. The polarities (strong-weak, aggressive-passive, independent-dependent, instrumental-expressive, agentic-communal, and others) are not distributed by sex in these societies but are highly individualized. Whether one observes the matrifocal cultures of Indonesia, the African Ibo (Igbo) of eastern Nigeria, or the American black who originally inherited this cultural form, one is impressed by the equality of participation by women and men in the role system as well as by the dignity and competence of female work and contribution to the group. In these societies women occupy central positions in the family and may control such economic assets as houses, money, and crops. Moreover, they display the decisiveness, assertiveness, initiative, and achievement motivation usually ascribed to men. In none of these groups does a woman's identity depend on men, because from childhood on, girls are socialized to become relatively independent and active in their own right, serving as craftspersons, traders, farmers, and in other key positions in the culture (Tanner 1974).

The broad spectrum in the roles of men and women shown in an overview of Western culture provides us with an appropriate backdrop against which we may examine the scientific evidence on sex differences to which this book is centrally addressed.

Beginnings of Western Culture

Some Greek Contrasts

Minoan Crete. A culture that from modern perspective seems to have been ideally egalitarian was that of Minoan Crete. This island with its rugged shores and high mountains provided impregnable protection to its people so that both men and women were free to develop a life-style centered in peace and beauty, religion and the arts, rather than having to squander their energies in war making. Since male military leadership was not needed to preserve the society, women could share cultural values and activities with men, and were accorded an esteem comparable with that enjoyed by their sisters in the goddess-worshiping civilizations of Mesopotamia and Egypt. They mingled freely with men, unveiled and barebreasted, and could be seen together at the theater, bull dances, and other public events. They took an active part in religious ceremonials devoted to the mother goddess. The feminine role also included the more humdrum work of cultivating the fields beside the men, and of attending to the homely arts of weaving, pottery, and bread making (Glasgow 1923; Mellersh 1967).

Classical Athens. In contrast to the high status and role flexibility of their Minoan predecessors, Athenian women during the very peak of mainland

Greek culture were subjugated by the men and segregated from them. An important factor in this anomalous situation seems to have been social class. Athens, under the democracy with its middle-class standards, deprived the former aristocrats of the privileges they had previously enjoyed (Lacey 1968). In an effort to protect their children's citizenship under Pericles' stiff paternity laws, Attic males vigilantly guarded their women, who were made wards of some male relative from birth to death. On leaving her father's guardianship at marriage, a girl was at the mercy of her husband, who wielded absolute power over her property and person except for the subtler psychological influence she often had on her husband (Slater 1974). Even among the rich who could afford slaves for the menial chores, the Athenian wife was literally held under "house arrest," and restricted to special quarters at the rear of the house, safely hidden from the impertinent gaze of male visitors (Dover 1973). Her public appearances were carefully chaperoned, and limited to special religious festivals, state speeches, athletic competitions, weddings, and funerals.

Inside the house, women were primarily occupied with the care of young children, nursing the sick, making clothing, and preparing food. Outside the house, the men were responsible for buying the food and the raw wool for the women to work with. The poorer women who had to go out to earn their living were employed at jobs representing extensions of their domestic activities, such as those of housemaid or babysitter (Pomeroy 1975).

The scene changed radically during the Peloponnesian wars when women of all classes were "called up" to replace the men in many kinds of jobs such as market vendors, grape pickers, and day laborers (Richter 1971).

Roman Sex and Politics

Republican Times. For another contrast in sex roles and status paralleling the changing political scene, we turn to Rome. Although at no time did Roman women live in the semioriental seclusion of those in classical Greece, the Republic of Rome presents much the same picture of male dominance as does the Democracy of Athens. Until the third century B.C., the Roman father, like his Greek counterpart, possessed absolute power over his family. He could even have his children exposed or sold, and his wife condemned to death for a variety of offenses ranging from adultery to stealing the keys to the wine celler. During this period, the Roman woman found herself at every stage of life under the tutelage of some man: first of father or brother, then of husband who in old Roman law became "father," and finally of son or male guardian whose consent was needed to validate her property rights as well as her marital contracts (Langdon-Davies 1927).

In spite of legal subordination, the woman of republican Rome was less overprotected than in classical Athens: she was at least allowed to join her husband at table and altar and to leave the house without his permission. Within the home, as materfamilias, she became the honored madame (mea domina) rather than the slave of her household. Such minor privileges, however, did not permit much in the way of self-realization. The virtues of these early Roman women were basically inhibitory and included decorum, chastity, gracefulness, and an even temper (Finley 1968). Since spontaneity was frowned on, we have no indication of their natural bents.

Imperial Changes. As in the case of the Athenian women in wartime, the increased responsibility carried by the women of the Roman Empire while the men were away conquering the world increased their status. Marriage came to rest wholly on the formal consent of both partners, and the wife became practically independent. Patrician matrons who could afford slaves to perform the ordinary household duties were free to go to the baths; attend circuses, chariot races, or certain religious rites "for women only"; and to engage in various other activities as they liked. They spent much time beautifying their bodies with cosmetics, hair dyes, and perfumes and loading themselves with jewelry to the point of vulgarity.

Life for women in early imperial times was not all frivolous, however, but involved serious cultivation of the mind. Education of upper-class girls often extended to finishing schools, where such cultural interests as painting, singing, and playing the lyre might be pursued (Friedländer 1928). Before the end of the empire women were entering all professions. Some, gifted with literary talent, became noted verse writers, literary critics, or students of Greek and Roman poetry. The younger Pliny's wife, for example, set her husband's poems to music. Others devoted themselves to science, medicine, law, philanthropy, religion, or even politics. Those who had the temerity to challenge age-old male prerogatives brought down on themselves a storm of protest from such guardians of the establishment as Cicero and Cato.

At the low end of the social scale, slave women in Rome as in Athens were for the most part engaged in chores: making and mending clothes, cooking meals, and minding babies. Those attached to wealthy households, however, might receive special training for jobs as clerks, secretaries, hairdressers, entertainers, and other subprofessional work.

Free or freedwomen enjoyed even greater variety of vocational choice: they could become shopkeepers, waitresses in taverns, artisans, construction workers, or continue in the more traditional domestic service. It should be pointed out, however, that in spite of the overlapping of many fields open to them with those of men, there is no evidence that women were permitted to join men's craft guilds. The symbol of the feminine role was the spindle whorl often placed in women's graves to identify their sex (Pomeroy 1975).

Celtic Variations

An important variant on the man-woman theme is provided by the Celts (ancient Gauls), a far-flung, vigorous people who spread across Europe and Britain during the centuries that witnessed the rise of classical Western civilization (Tierney 1964). In this essentially rural, family-centered society, women were seen neither as sinful nor weak, but as persons in their own right, fully equal to the men who indeed shared power with them. In structure, Celtic culture was about halfway between a patriarchy, based on land ownership by the father, and a matriarchy in which the mother remained the basic link in the family (Markale 1975). Sovereignty was conceived of as a puissance or supernatural force which was female, and to which the king as sovereign must be wedded through fertility rites. The high value placed on the female is reflected in Celtic religion, in which mother earth as the central figure is surrounded by women holding babies on their laps and bearing baskets of fruit and horns of plenty.

Within the family, though the husband was the titular head, he was by no means invariably the dominant marriage partner. Authority in the home was closely correlated with the relative wealth of man and wife. In contrast to the situations in Greece and Rome, the Celtic woman had the right to select her husband and could not be married without her consent. At a feast to which all young people were invited, a daughter who was to be married expressed her decision symbolically by offering water to the man of her choice. Freedom of choice was also shown in the easy dissolution of Celtic marriages, as well as in certain admittedly temporary forms such as the "annual" marriage contracts.

Along with the apparent liberalism in attitudes toward marriage and the family went the absence of prudery and a sense of sin in sex. Sexual freedom was one aspect of the humanistic view of the Celts according to which every human being is intrinsically free, regardless of gender. The Celts saw the sexes as complementary to each other. A woman could assume social roles as varied as those of warrior, educator, prophet, or witch. Without her, a man was considered inadequate and unable to find his fulfillment. The woman was perceived as watching and protecting her man—husband, lover, or son—with an altruistic and sacrificial love. Within the broader spectrum of self-expression permitted Celtic women, the central theme seems to have been tender loving care for their men.

Later Developments

Knights, Ladies, and Courtly Love

The picture of sex differences was again altered during the Middle Ages. The freedom won at great cost by the women of imperial Rome was denounced by the early Christian Fathers. In the preachings of St. Paul, eternal salvation was threatened by the fires of hell, sexual temptation, and the wickedness of women. This attitude resulted in the degradation and irrational fear of women (Figes 1972). The evil female image personified by the devil-possessed witch contrasted with the feminine ideal of sexual asceticism. Only in rural areas such as central Sicily, far from the beaten path, could girls remain gay, happy, and natural—true *pagani*. As for the others, a degree of rehabilitation was possible through worship of the Virgin Mary who took over much of the earlier mother cult of the goddess Artemis. As the Holy Mother, she became a mediator through her Son for the salvation of sinful women (Seltman 1962). The Virgin in heaven had her earthly counterpart in the lady who shared honors in the age of chivalry with the crusading knight's most valued companion, his horse. Tutored to read poetry and play the harp, the lady, better educated than her male contemporary, was in a position to help him improve his manners. Thus woman appeared as a civilizing force with the gentling qualities of sensitivity, affection, and compassion. The developing "code of courtly love" made the lady an object of male adoration for pure friendship's sake (de Rougemont 1940) and helped transform the uncouth warrior into the gentleman.

Emphasis on the personal aspects of the man-woman relationship, though at that time considered relevant only to extramarital affairs, contributed to the ultimate love-marriage ideal. Through arranged marriages women came under the legal control of their husbands who theoretically could force their obedience. In practice, however, wives enjoyed high prestige because their domestic domain was the center of industry. This was especially notable during the long wars when, as in Roman times, much responsibility fell on their shoulders. During the protracted absences of their husbands wives were in full charge of the estates, having to attend the sick, fight lawsuits, and at times stand siege. Increased self-esteem, combined with new wealth derived by widows from rich fiefs, elevated the married woman once again to a position of power. Indeed, when the men returned from battle, it was they who became dependent and without a role.

The high privileges of the ladies of the feudal aristocracy unfortunately failed to trickle down to women of humbler social status. Continued prejudice appeared in sex inequalities within the craft guilds as well as in the professions, many of which kept their doors barred to females (Durant 1950). Nevertheless, the intelligence and administrative ability as well as the artistic talents, sensitivity, and compassion exhibited by the lady left their mark to the benefit of their gender in future generations.

"Universal Man" and Woman

With the rebirth of the classical spirit during the Renaissance the joie de vivre so long buried under the weight of the medieval Church burst forth with renewed vigor. Its infectious vitality added new zest to the relations between the sexes no less than to other areas of living. Although the romantic love introduced during the Middle Ages continued to be idealized, other dimensions were added. The feminine role, enriched through the participation of women in the revival of learning and the art of living, fostered a new intellectual comradeship between men and women. The self-actualized "universal man," bold in boudoir and battle, knowledgeable in arts, letters, and philosophy, at last found his female match. The energy, beauty, and courage of the Renaissance woman have been immortalized by Caterina Sforza for her defense of Forli, and Bianca Visconti for governing Milan. Women of the period acted not only for themselves but, like their Roman predecessors, exerted important influences on the men who still retained statutory authority over them. Even the average woman, trained for a domestic role and closely guarded before marriage, was well versed in the classics, literature, philosophy, and the arts (Durant 1953).

The spiritual love that had been set on a pedestal during the Crusades took on a more earthy cast in the new era. Since marriage as an important economic contract between famlies could not be entrusted to the caprices of desire, other sexual outlets became recognized. Adultery was widespread and unofficially condoned. Prostitution on a variety of levels again flourished, including in its ranks a class of genteel courtesans who graced Renaissance salons in Rome and Venice much as had the hetairai of ancient Athens. In France, the salon of the Marquise de Rambouillet could have challenged in brilliance and taste that of Pericles. In England, the court of Good Queen Bess was equally scintillating, inspiring the Shakespearian vision of the two sexes in complementary balance. Elizabethan man, like *l'uomo universale* of Italy, was vital and vibrant. Women, free to develop both talents and tenderness, contributed beauty, charm, and wit to the stimulating scene. They also shared with men the world of work, which at that period centered in the home.

Fallout from the Industrial Revolution

The creative spell of the High Renaissance that shed its incandescent radiance over women, as well as men, was broken by the harsh changes of the new industrial age. With the opening up of trade routes around the world following the discovery of new lands, a new middle class of commercially enterprising individuals wedged itself between nobleman and commoner. The famiy became a production unit for making articles to be sold on the international market. As long as the economic center was the home, the struggle for existence took on the air of a rough-and-ready equality among its members. The women no less than the men were trained in some skill that served as an economic asset and were allowed to display courage, initiative, resourcefulness, and wit in practicing it. In turn, the tradesman considered it his duty to be well informed on domestic affairs. Marriage became in fact a partnership, even though wives were still by law subject to their husbands (Stern 1939).

When technological advances made mass production possible, much of the manufacturing had to be moved from the home to newly established factories at a distance. The combination of family responsibility and insufficient muscular strength to operate the heavy machinery kept women from following their men to the cities to work with them as they had in the home industries. No longer sharing in production, they now had nothing to offer in exchange for their support, thereby becoming economic dependents. As a result of these changes, woman's social identity was undermined and she found herself once again captive within the four walls of her home—now in the suburbs.

While industrialization benefited the men, women's status declined until by the enlightenment it had sunk to an all-time low. Liberty, equality, and fraternity were proclaimed for all but intended for men only. The essence of feminine charm consisted of a passive docility and clinging dependence on men. The practice of female parasitism spread through all but the lowest classes, until work came to be a misfortune and disgrace instead of a source of dignity and personal worth.

In this overview of behavioral differences between the sexes throughout the early development of our culture, we have noted again, as in antiquity, their dependence on the prevailing social climate. When power is held exclusively by men, women are forced underground as the weaker sex and are treated like disadvantaged minorities, denied the rewards of the status symbols jealously hoarded by the males. In periods when male controls slacken, however, and power is more equably distributed as in Minoan Crete, the Roman Empire, and Celtic Europe, women have proved themselves as strong as men, displaying hidden talents of initiative, intelligence, courage, compassion, or whatever traits have the priorities. No characteristics that can properly be attributed to female or male nature as such can be identified from this evidence. This does not mean that, other things being truly equal, women and men might not spontaneously show different preferences.

Modern Times

Before attributing sex differences to the environmental forces shaping the individual, we need to complete our search for constancies underlying diversity by having a good look at the contemporary scene in Western culture. Since North America has been spared the violent upheavals of war and revolution, social changes including those affecting the roles of men and women have proceeded in lower key than they have in North Europe, while the feudal relic of Latin America continues as a baseline of near-zero movement. To evaluate the critical issues in sex differences with which this book is mainly concerned, we need perspective from national subcultures undergoing more definitive changes than in our own. To this end we shall present the situation in West Germany, the Soviet Union, the slower but surer advances of Sweden, and the kaleidoscopic picture of the Israeli kibbutz.

Changing Sex Roles in Germany

Under the Reichs. In Germany under the kaiserreich, authoritarianism permeated the culture, including the social roles played by males and females. In the hierarchical power structure women were relegated to the kinder-kuche-kirche role that made them as powerless as were the Jews and the blacks who had been branded as inferiors. The fall of the kaiser at the end of World War I was followed by the Weimar Republik which recognized women as equal partners with men in every phase of life, from family to university (Puckett 1930). This new life-style, however, was short-lived, undermined by the media which continued to propagate the old German values of military might supported by traditional gender roles. When the Nazis came to power, they set up the Third Reich, which systematically reinforced all the repressive and regressive influences designed to reestablish the authoritarian pecking order. The strong-weak dichotomy was again invoked, with the male at the strong pole and the female at the weak one. Masculinity as the badge of natural superiority and the display of attributes presumably expressing it were applauded. Germany was once more a man's world, with a steep gradient between men and women.

Under the Postwar Republics. After Germany's defeat in World War II, a prostrate people rose from the ashes of the burnt-out Third Reich to rebuild their county on a new model.

In the eastern sector, which became part of the Russian-dominated bloc, a socialist model was adopted, the German Democratic Republic. In the west, the more conservative German Federal Republic developed and has been selected as a middle-of-the-road model of gender-role patterning for our consideration. Here the stereotypes had been so deeply embedded that the duality in gender imagery continued in the writings of leading German scientists. According to this view (Lersch 1947), man is the rational, active agent mainly oriented toward the outer world, in contrast to woman who is by nature sensitive, emotional, and passive, creating the intimate climate within the home. The little girl in her earliest years learns to adapt to the world in a caring way, while the boy finds a world of resistance to be aggressively overcome through achievement goals. This contrasting picture of the two sexes has strongly influenced the educational objectives and methods throughout the Federal Republic. In an effort to meet their feminine needs women were steered toward jobs providing an opportunity for caring within an intimate, friendly atmosphere simulating their natural sphere, the home. Such restrictions made it difficult for women to find employment in the industrial world which was presumably alien to them. The prevailing incompatibility between the values of full-time mothering and outside work demands has made general acceptance of a dual home-career role for mothers very difficult.

Today, under social pressures toward egalitarian attitudes women are seeing themselves as more than caretakers. Within the home there seems to be a tendency for husbands to relinquish their traditional dominance and for wives to give up their submissiveness (Lehr & Rauh 1970).

A blurring of sex-role differentiation carried over to the following generation is suggested by the increasing similarity in the rearing of sons and daughters (Devereux et al. 1962). In spite of the leveling of parental expectations for their male and female children, however, the children themselves apparently have continued to follow traditional interests, the boys expressing preferences for sports and technology, while the girls choose as their favorite fields social welfare, music, and crafts. Ideals also show some consistent sex differences over the generation from the 1930s to the 1960s. Boys idealized achievements, especially in public life, while girls concentrated on physical attributes like beauty and clothes. The stability of the sex-role patterning was indicated by selection of the same masculine and feminine ideals in the 1960s as in the 1930s. Even life goals of girls and boys projected into the next century showed the same sticky traditionalism: boys still focused on their future work, while girls' thoughts revolved around their husbands and families.

The picture of social sex roles in the German Federal Republic is obviously complex. On the level of overt activity, women's rights have triumphed both in the outside world of work and in the inside world of home. Under the surface, however, there still lurk the old sex differences in orientation which persist despite pressures of war and peace, of politics and education, and of successive generations. It is this persistent core, this ultimate distillate, that cannot be ignored, and remains what may be the essential substance of a basic difference between the sexes, indicating at the bottom line an achieving male and a caring female.

Soviet Men and Women

In sharp contrast to Germany, Russia after the revolution broke down the role dichotomy between the sexes. Through the socialization of industry power was shifted from the owners of the means of production to all workers, female as well as male. Even more important for women than the external changes in status were the new personal independence and dignity accorded them. They were treated as adults whose behavior was left to their own discretion in all areas, including the most intimate one of sexual relations (Field & Flynn 1970).

At Home and Work. In no way have recent trends diminished the central importance of the child whose rearing is geared to collective living. But as in other socialist countries, full-time mothering is neither demanded nor desired (Safilios-Rothschild 1975). Crèche and nursery school extend the family circle and provide identification with collective ideals and subordination of personal needs to group welfare from the earliest years (Bronfenbrenner 1968, 1970). Role play, as in the game of "taking care of baby," helps to prepare the child for social responsibility, which is constantly emphasized by training in *vospitanie*, or communist morality. Because of the disproportionate number of females in the population, girls as well as boys are taught such traditionally masculine skills as metalworking. A boom in day-care facilities during the past few years has made it possible to transfer many of the functions formerly performed in the home to the larger community. In spite of these trends, the Soviet family has remained a private source of strength and stability within a radically changing world (Geiger 1968).

In the occupational sphere, the wartime decimation of the male population has made it difficult to predict the future, but Field and Flynn (1970) suggest the likelihood of a redistribution of occupations between the sexes not unlike that of other Western industrialized countries. This would mean that women will be shifted from heavy industry, construction, and the more arduous agricultural work to jobs in the developing household-servicing industries which will bring them full circle back to the housework from which they seemed so eager to escape. It is important to bear in mind that training of males and females in the Soviet Union was not aimed at blurring sex identities and differences: on the contrary, the goal was to make fuller use of the complementary qualities of the two sexes even in the performance of similar types of work. For women the accent was still on modesty, tenderness, and maternal warmth (Fogarty et al. 1971).

A New Double Sex Standard? Although the Soviet Union has set up a model of sex equality by allowing women access to most areas of public life, the new freedom has not meant the substitution of a single role for a double standard. In fact, it has introduced a new form of double standard according to which women are given the dubious privilege of carrying the burden of two worlds: while enjoying equality with men outside the home, they still have the greater responsibility within it. This is in part due to the persistence of male domination but more importantly because the women themselves maintain a division of labor within the home. According to interview results reported by Mandel (1975), men are expected to help with such chores as washing floors, repair work, and even marketing, while women cook and mend. When there are children, the task of rearing falls chiefly on mothers who accept it as an outgrowth of bearing and nursing them. An example of their attitude was the response of one woman to the question, "Who stays home to care for a sick child?" She answered, "The mother, of course. Women are warmer—there's something in their nature causing this." This belief in basic qualitative sex differences has created a dilemma for the Soviet woman. It provides a convenient rationale or at least a rationalization for the men to refuse their fair share of household responsibilities.

According to Field and Flynn (1970), women, like men, are expected to put in a full day's work at the office, in the plant, or in the field, but Soviet men are defensive of their masculinity and consequently are reluctant to reciprocate by helping their wives with household duties. They are embarrassed by what the neighbors might say if they were caught washing dishes or making beds. Needless to say, Soviet women find this situation extremely frustrating and have even gone so far as to take their complaints to the newspapers where they have decried the injustice of their having to work as hard as men on the job while their husbands refuse to lift a finger to help at home.

One Woman's View. A dispassionate evaluation of the situation of Soviet women makes one wonder whether the propagandistic pressure to utilize their talents and training in the technology of the work world may not violate deeper needs. Vera Dunham (1968) cites a poem by one Soviet girl who confesses that she wants to give up her work and fall in love, craving a "woman's simple happiness" and the full life through love and motherhood.

One wonders for how many of the others this young woman is speaking, and one wonders about her meaning of a full life. Perhaps this represents merely the outcry of a single girl who deviates from her fellow female compatriots. But even if only a few or perhaps one lone voice is expressed, it is valid and may signify basic trends submerged by the current cultural overlay.

Now, with more than a half century of struggle behind, reformism and yearning for the good life, or perhaps for "the good old days" of conventional gender roles, seem to bespeak the prevailing mood, and the idle wife rather than the feminist has become a status symbol. Is the new feminine ideal just the old self-sarificing woman at heart, represented by the new writers as a secular Virgin Mary who demands nothing for herself? Barring unpredictable changes, the inevitable pressures noted above and found, throughout the history of Western culture, to push women back to more traditional ways will become stronger as the sex ratio evens up at last, and women's labor is no longer crucial to the national economic growth (Rosenthal 1975).

Scandinavian Models

Emancipation of Women. Sweden, which had to a large extent escaped the convulsions of war and revolution, could enjoy the luxury of more gradual changes. This is nowhere clearer than in the shift from the traditional European male-dominated family to one based on equality between spouses. A decade-long debate on women's two roles—home and work—culminated in the famous Report to the United Nations on the Status of Women, urging their absolute emancipation and equality with men (Dahlström 1971). Sex differences in personality and behavior were regarded as secondary to the primary biological functions of reproduction, thus not justifying casting men and women in different social roles. It was pointed out that new, flexible human roles should be created in which the same possibilities would be opened to members of either sex within the family, on the labor market, and indeed in all other social situations.

Emancipation of Men. The threat to family cohesion in the industrializing nations occasioned by the removal of men from the formerly self-sufficient economic unit of the home has been much reduced in Sweden. Here the men have continued to share with the women family concerns within the home just as the women share with the men work outside the home. The new equality not only frees women from their traditional roles but, as former Prime Minister Palme pointed out (1972), has resulted in the emancipation of men. Guided by personal preference rather than social pressure, a man is now free to choose even the role of househusband, which enjoys legal status in Sweden, just as a woman may still choose to be a housewife. The new freedom of both sexes might be expected, in time, to bring about a redistribution of their vocational and domestic activities.

Implementing equality between men and women requires support at all levels of society. New school curricula with updated textbooks giving boys as well as girls the same opportunities to learn cooking, child care, and sewing, and girls as well as boys analogous opportunities for shop, mechanics, and electronics are primary prerequisites (Linnér 1971). Such basic changes in school programs obviously need to be reinforced by parents and public opinion in order to take firm root.

Practice versus Theory. The model Sweden has evolved throughout the current century has gone well beyond the attempts of Germany or even of the Soviet Union to resolve the conflict of gender roles. This gradual process, however, is notoriously slow and there may be wide gaps between statutory equality and equality in practice. No better Scandinavian example of such a discrepancy can be found than Holter's (1970) survey of over 1,000 Oslo blue-collar and white-collar workers' attitudes toward sex-differentiating norms in major sectors of Norwegian life. Results showed that in spite of the respondents' general disavowal of such differentiation their answers to specific questions revealed tacit acceptance. Thus, though a large majority of the employees sampled agreed that women ought to have as many chances for occupational advancement as men, 53 percent expressed the opinion that women should stick to the care of home and children. In passing it might be noted that the male subjects held more traditonal attitudes than did the female.

Swedish studies bear out these tendencies, since even after the removal of many outside obstacles, there remain the more formidable inner, deeply rooted ideas and conventional role expectancies of employers, fellow workers, husbands, and women themselves. In the mid-1960s the vocational choices of adolescent boys and girls in one typical Swedish town still showed the traditional cleavage, with boys leaning toward technical, mercantile, legal, and administrative fields, and girls toward language, teaching, and service occupations (Thorsell, cited by Liljeström 1970).

Below the level of conscious awareness lie the most powerful blocks to full acceptance of equality in gender roles. A number of studies in both Sweden and Norway early in the debate indicate discrepancies between verbal attitudes and behavior (Brun-Gulbrandsen 1971). In interviews with Oslo mothers in 1958, 95 percent of the respondents expressed a general intention of raising their boys and girls alike, but in dealing with specific behaviors they applied sanctions reflecting their own deeply ingrained gender-role prejudices; for example, that girls should have more training in domestic science than boys and that boys should have more carpentry instruction than girls. Other studies from the same time and places indicated that schoolchildren themselves had internalized parental sex-role stereotypes at least as early as 8 years of age, even though the parents were unaware of having influenced them. Adolescents accepted a dichotomy of interests: it was appropriate for boys to see films about war and crime while romantic ones were suitable for girls. Likes and dislikes of certain activities correlated with the stereotypes. The sex-role dichotomy was again apparent in the traits representing masculine and feminine ideals: independence, daring, courage, wisdom, physical strength, technical knowledge, and skill for boys; kindness, meekness, helpfulness, sentimentality, and good nature for girls.

Evidence of this sort suggests that the early internalization of behavioral gender norms makes it very difficult to eradicate them later. Parents in spite of their intellectual convictions are themselves caught in the bind so that they are not free to give complete and unconflicted home backup to the school in imparting new attitudes. The children, in their confusion about the issue, tend to cling to the old, more "natural" models.

The Special Case of the Israeli Kibbutz

For additional perspectives, we may observe the passing scene in the Israeli kibbutzim, or collective settlements established to meet the exigencies of pioneering conditions in the new Jewish homeland. To free adults for the community work necessary for survival, the family was drastically restructured (Rabin 1970). Children lived apart from their parents in a special children's house and were mainly socialized from early infancy by especially trained female nurses (*metaplot*). Daily contacts with their parents were limited to a "children's hour" at the parents' apartment where they enjoyed tea and talk with one another.

Growing up in a Kibbutz. In the kibbutz sex differences have been deliberately played down: boys and girls eat, sleep, and play together. Consequently few personality differences appear and sex-linked play has not been fostered. Nevertheless, certain types of spontaneous play parallel those found in traditional society: boys choosing the more strenuous locomotor and mechanical activities involving climbing and running, while girls preferred verbal, fantasy, and artistic expression (Spiro 1965).

Disenchantment. Theoretically, sex dedifferentiation gave husband and wife equal rights to hold independent jobs. Collectivistic child rearing made possible the elimination of the double sex standard without the specter of child neglect. The new sexual freedom was to be counterbalanced by voluntary self-abnegation and ascetic dedication to the kibbutz way of life. At first, the women expressed enthusiasm for their newly won equality with men by reaction formations against the "feminalia" of frills, jewelry, cosmetics, and flirtatious ways, as well as by great reserve and seriousness regarding sexuality.

As the kibbutz movement took shape, however, there emerged the familiar sex division of labor, with the men maintaining power in the high-income-producing management spots, while the women, as in the old order, found themselves in such nonproductive service jobs as baby nurses, kindergarten teachers, cooks, and similar low-echelon types of work from which they had expected to be liberated. Specializing in the uninspiring duties of cooking, mending, *or* baby-sitting in the children's house for other peoples' children proved even more boring than the traditional female lot of cooking, mending, *and* baby-sitting in their own homes with their own babies.

Today, the feminism of the West is actually reversing itself in the kibbutz, where the women want less of work and more of family rather than more of work and less of family. Occupational roles have become more traditional than ever, with women working inside and men outside the home (Schlesinger 1977). Female responsibilities include the usual stereotypical kitchen and child-care services; male, production activities on farm and in factory. One might be tempted to conclude that this reversal of Western feminism is a response to continuing patriarchism, intensified perhaps by the continuing threat to the survival of the state were it not for the fact that the pressure to return to the earlier family and gender roles has come not from the old timers, but from the young *sabra* or native Israeli mothers (Beit-Hallahmi & Rabin 1977; Endleman 1977). Since the decision to classify many service branches including child care as female specialties was made jointly by men and women, their reemergence in the old categories can hardly be attributed to male chauvinism.

Counterrevolution. Spiro (1979) in a crucially significant book on gender and culture in the kibbutz compares the attitudes of the now adult residents of the kibbutz, Kiryat Yedidim, with their former records as children obtained twenty-five years ago. Anticipating that the new evidence would confirm the prevailing culturist bias of attributing sex differences to social pressures, Spiro was surprised to find that the recent sex differences could not be adequately accounted for in that way but demanded a precultural explanation. The new material showed dramatic shifts in attitudes toward marriage and the family, with reversals at every level—emphasis on a wedding ceremony, private apartment living, opposition to divorce— and other signs of prerevolutionary trends, initiated and supported by the women themselves. The mother role emphasizing baking, crocheting sweaters for the children, preparing their meals, putting them to bed, and similar acts of maternal devotion had become major sources of personal fulfillment for these wives. A desire for more children and for more time to spend with them on the part of the kibbutz husbands, reinforced the accent on private home life.

Spiro's further analysis of a six-kibbutz sample of sixty more *sabras* selected from the three main federations, confirmed the counterrevolutionary trends found in Kiryat Yedidim. These data were also characterized by a retreat from the sex-role uniformity of the pioneer radical feminism to the more traditional femininity-masculinity (M-F) stereotypes of the generation that followed. Although males and females were considered equal in talents and abilities, and of equal worth as human beings, they were not seen as alike. In fact they developed important differences in interests and needs that were equally valuable to kibbutz living, in the absence of environmental support or training. Under the circumstances, *sabra* women are willing to accept role equivalence as the more appropriate sign of equality than identity with men as feminist ideology teaches.

Future Prospects. Beyond the domestic domain, women as well as men have problems of vocational choice. In the kibbutz the range of opportunities has been frustratingly limited. As the industrialization of the country at large expands, there will be more opportunity for participation of the kibbutzim in that larger division of labor. Then the question will inevitably arise as to whether the specific identity of the kibbutz as a separate institution can survive or whether indeed it has outlived its usefulness.

*The Sexes in Latin America: Will the
Old Order Change?*

At the opposite extreme from Scandinavia and other northern cultures of Europe and America, with their trends toward sex equality and free choice of social roles, stands the hacienda life of Latin America that takes us back to a feudal past. This atavistic scene originated in the relative isolation of the Spanish peninsula, where Moorish influence blocked the forward thrust of the Renaissance until today the sexes diverge more in Latin America than anywhere else in Western culture (Williamson 1970).

Machismo. The peculiar fabric of Latin American sex roles resulted from the Spanish conquerors' imposing their form of male dominance on the patriarchal tradition of the indigenous Indians. The hybrid was machismo, a boisterous masculine protest by the conquered against their feelings of "castration" following losses of lands and women. Vengeance on the women, whom they despised for having betrayed them in favor of the powerful Spaniards, lent to the exaggerated masculinity a strongly sadistic quality (Cappon 1975). The masculine ambivalence toward women was intensified by the Paulist image of "woman as temptress." The Latin-American man, like the medieval knight, resolved this conflict by splitting his concept of woman into good and bad. His wife, like his mother on earth and Holy Mother in heaven, must be pure and faithful and bear his children, while his mistress or prostitute served as an outlet for his sexual needs. In his fantasy projection of the good woman, the man obviously invented qualities for her that were specifically designed to counterbalance his faults and vices.

Marianismo. The other face of machismo, sometimes called "marianismo," is a mother cult derived in part from the ancient mother-goddess cults that flourished in the Aegean area. In the Latin-American form, however, the feminine superiority was limited to the spiritual domain and could coexist with inferiority in general social status. Here the goddess appears as Our Lady of Guadalupe, a condensation of Mary, mother of Jesus, and the Aztec Serpent Woman, mother of the gods. She is a model of moral strength and saintliness shown in her self-abnegation and sacrifice (Stevens 1973). According to this criterion, the ideal woman is quiet and prudent, avoiding any expression of friendliness that could be interpreted as flirtatiousness, or worse still, bewitchment. She is as closely chaperoned as any girl from classical Athens in order to ensure her virginity at marriage.

Role Shaping in the Family. The heart of Latin-American life is the family, which traditionally includes a variety of godparents, along with parents, grandparents, aunts, uncles, and cousins. The divine parents, God the Father and the Virgin Mother, are the prototypes of the earthly father as supreme judge, authority, and protector, and the mother as a symbol of purity, self-sacrifice, and comfort. In structure the family is hierarchical, with the father at the apex, demanding from the other members appropriate respect, according to their rank (Peck & Díaz-Guérrero 1967). At the core is the mother who, with her intense maternal devotion, is the chief source of warmth in her children's lives and often the actual authority in spite of her ritual deference to the father.

Different role patterns are instilled in boys and girls: the boy must grow up to fit the machismo concept of masculinity; the girl, to accept her destiny of superlative femininity centered in home and motherhood. To achieve these diverse ends, separate and segregated training begins in earliest infancy. Guns, swords, military helmets, and horses serve the little boy as playthings while he is learning such manual skills as fishing and riding. The little girl is taught modesty in toilet habits and decorum in manners (Lewis 1951).

At adolescence the young man is allowed much greater freedom than the young lady. He is expected to meet the macho demands of his peers by joining a gang and acting out sexually with a variety of partners. The sexual role for the male is seen more as an eliminative function than as a social relationship. During this phase of life the boy is also looking for a girl to marry, who, like his mother, is saintlike, chaste, delicate, sweet, dreamy, religious, homey, and maternal.

For the adolescent girl formal schooling customarily ceases, since it is not feminine to have an advanced education, and she is returned to household chores. A romantic courtship, in which she is idealized in serenades and poems, ends abruptly with marriage and the menial down-to-earth services expected of her.

The classical picture of the sexes in the old social order of Latin America is ever so gradually changing. Trends toward modernization are reflected in the new literature and are clearly evident in the upper echelons of educational and professional groups. Colombia's Caldas University provides a recent example. Between 1974 and 1976, female students in a course on human sexuality were questioned concerning their sex practices (Alzate 1978). In spite of the deeply entrenched virginity cult throughout Latin America, over one-third of this sample admitted having had premarital coitus, a substantal figure though lower than comparable data obtained from Colombian male medical students or American college women. Isolated as this shift may seem, it could be the start of a more general change of sex mores in the culture as a whole.

In the area of occupational choices shifting attitudes are also becoming apparent. According to a survey of women in Peru, Argentina, Mexico, Ecuador, and Uruguay, they were no longer limiting their goals to the domestic scene but were becoming responsive to the social and financial attractions of outside employment (Geist 1975). Although still few and far between, studies revealing such trends toward modernization, however slight, are significant signs pointing to the twilight of the machismo mystique.

Cuba: The Exception

Against the current tide of political reactionism in South America, Communist Cuba stands out in bald relief. In setting up its revolutionary goals the new regime mandated equality between women and men. The result is that women are no longer only consumers in the society but also contribute to its production by serving as cane cutters, citrus packers, automotive mechanics, and even traffic officers. At the professional level one may find dentists, doctors, and engineers.

The effort to mobilize Cuban women for the labor force from above, however, without the support of a strong grass-roots liberation movement, has met with strenuous resistance from both sexes (Aguirre 1976). Although Cuba is more egalitarian than other Spanish-American countries, the fact remains that males and females do not enjoy equal status. The double standard still persists, accompanied by male domination at home and sexist discrimination at work. But the chief block has come from the women themselves whose low aspiration levels prevent their taking advantage of the opportunities now open to them. In spite of the extraordinary new child-care facilities, they still see their primary responsibility as in the home. Traditional stereotypes are reinforced even by *Mujeras*, the official journal of the Federation of Cuban Women, created by Castro himself. In its pages women are advised on the care of sick children, how to make children's toys, or how to beautify their bodies (Purcell 1973).

On a broader base, one answer to the social sex-role problem in Cuba might be recognition and reward by the society not only for work contributing to the gross national product, but also for work involving the nurturant and human-caring tasks that may be in essence feminine but are equally vital to good community living and are crucial for tempering the depersonalizing process of modernization (Chaney 1975).

Society's Problem

Our intercomparisons of gender roles in Western culture from the egalitarian to the reactionary extreme have consistently shown that when men call the plays, women comply with the demands, but that when men are not at the controls, women meet the situation by exhibiting whatever behavior is appropriate, independently of gender. This is not all there is to it, however, because it fails to take account of a basic divergence between the sexes: males tilting toward achievement in work, sports, technology, and public life; females, toward affiliation, often expressed in the private domain through service, caring, teaching, and art. This difference in orientation asserts itself even when women are not treated like oppressed minorities. The outstanding case in point is that of the Israeli kibbutz, with its female-initiated counterrevolutionary movement back to the family and the femininity earlier abandoned for feminism. In other less definitive examples such as Sweden, the Soviet Union, and Cuba, the trend was less conspicuous but could be read between the lines.

If this overview has served to state society's problem regarding the genders, the following chapters, analyzing sex differences in terms of their origins and development, should help to clarify the issues involved as a first step toward solution.

References

Aguirre, B.E. 1976. "Women in the Cuban Bureaucracies: 1968-1974." *Journal of Comparative Family Studies* 7:23-40.

Alzate, H. 1978. "Sexual Behavior of Colombian Female University Students." *Archives of Sexual Behavior* 7:43-54.

Beit-Hallahmi, B., and Rabin, A.I. 1977. "The Kibbutz as a Social Experiment and as a Child-rearing Laboratory." *American Psychologist* 32:532-541.

Bronfenbrenner, U. 1968. "The Changing Soviet Family." In D.R. Brown, ed. *The Role and Status of Women in the Soviet Union*. New York: Teachers College Press, pp. 98-124.

_____. 1970. *Two Worlds of Childhood: U.S. and U.S.S.R.* New York: Russell Sage Foundation.

Bronowski, J. 1973. *The Ascent of Man*. Boston: Little, Brown.

Brun-Gulbrandsen, S. 1971. Sex Roles and the Socialization Process." In E. Dahlstrom, ed. *The Changing Roles of Men and Women*. Boston: Beacon Press, pp. 59-78.

Cappon, J. 1975. "Masochism: A Trait in the Mexican National Character." *International Mental Health Research Newsletter* 17:2 and 8-10

Chaney, E.M. 1975. "The Mobilization of Women: Three Societies (Chile, Cuba, Vietnam)." In R. Rohrlich-Leavitt, ed. *Women Cross-culturally: Change and Challenge*. The Hague: Mouton, pp. 471-489.

Dahlström, E. 1971. "Analysis of the Debate on Sex Roles." In E. Dahlström, ed. *The Changing Roles of Men and Women*. Boston: Beacon Press, pp. 170-205. Originally published, London: Duckworth, 1967.

D'Andrade, R.G. 1966. "Sex Differences and Cultural Institutions." In E.E. Maccoby, ed. *The Development of Sex Differences*. Stanford, Calif.: Stanford University Press, pp. 174-204.

Devereux, E.C., Jr.; Bronfenbrenner, U.; and Suci, G.J. 1962. "Patterns of Present Behavior in the United States of America, and the Federal Republic of Germany: A Cross-national Comparison." *International Social Science Journal* 14:488-506.

Dover, K.J. 1973. "Classical Greek Attitudes to Sexual Behavior." *Arethusa* 6:59-73.

Dunham, V. 1968. "Changing Image of Women in Soviet Literature." In D.R. Brown, ed. *The Role and Status of Women in the Soviet Union*. New York: Teachers College Press, pp. 60-97.

Durant, W. 1950. *The Story of Civilization: The Age of Faith*. New York: Simon & Schuster.

_____. 1953. *The Story of Civilization: The Renaissance*. New York: Simon & Shuster.

Endleman, R. 1977. "Familistic Social Change in the Israeli Kibbutz." *Annals of the New York Academy of Sciences* 285:605-611.

Field, M.G., and Flynn, K.I. 1970. "Worker, Mother, Housewife: Soviet Woman Today." In G.H. Seward and R.C. Williamson, eds. *Sex Roles in Changing Society*. New York: Random House, pp. 257-284.

Figes, E. 1972. *Patriarchal Attitudes: Women in Society*. London: Pantheon Books.

Finley, M.I. 1968. *Aspects of Antiquity*. New York: Viking Press.

Fogarty, M.P.; Rapoport, T.; and Rapoport, R.N. 1971. *Sex, Career and Family, Including an International Review of Women's Roles*. London: Allen & Unwin.

Friedländer, L. 1928. *Roman Life and Manners under the Early Empire*. Magnus, trans., 4 vols. London: Routledge.

Geiger, K. 1968. *The Family in Soviet Russia*. Cambridge: Harvard University Press.

Geist, H. 1975. "Comparison of Reasons for Occupational Choice in Women of Five Spanish-speaking Latin American Countries." *Revista Latino-americano de Psicologia* 7:87-95.

Glasgow, G. 1923. *The Minoans*. London: Jonathan Cape.

Holter, H. 1970. *Sex Roles and Social Structure*. Oslo: Universitetsforlaget.

Lacey, W.K. 1968. *The Family in Classical Greece*. London: Camelot Press.

Langdon-Davies, J. 1927. *A Short History of Women*. New York: Literary Guild of America.

Lapidus, G.W. 1978. *Women in Soviet Society: Equality, Development, and Social Change*. Berkeley: University of California Press.

Leavitt, R.R. 1971. "Women in Other Cultures." In V. Gornick and B.K. Moran, eds. *Women in Sexist Society: Studies in Power and Powerlessness*. New York: Basic Books, pp. 276-301.

Lehr, U., and Rauh, H. 1970. "Male and Female in the German Federal Republic." In G.H. Seward and R.C. Williamson, eds. *Sex Roles in Changing Society*. New York: Random House, pp. 220-238.

Lersch, P. 1947. *Vom Wesen der Geschlechter*. München: Erasmus.

Lewis, O. 1951. *Life in a Mexican Village: Tepozlán Restudied*. Urbana, Ill.: University of Illinois Press.

Liljeström, R. 1970. "The Swedish Model." In G.H. Seward and R.C. Williamson, eds. *Sex Roles in Changing Society*. New York: Random House, pp. 200-219.

Linnér, B. 1971. "What Does Equality between the Sexes Imply?" *American Journal of Orthopsychiatry* 41:747-756.

Mandel, W.M. 1975. *Soviet Women*. Garden City, N.Y.: Anchor Books.

Markale, J. 1975. *Women of the Celts*. A. Mygind, C. Hauch, and P. Henry, trans. London: Gordon Cremonesi.

Mellersh, H.E.L. 1967. *Minoan Crete*. London: Evans.

Minturn, L. 1970. "A Survey of Cultural Differences in Sex Role Training and Identification." In N. Kretschmer and D.N. Walcher, eds. *Enviromental Influences on Genetic Expression: Biological and Behavioral Aspects of Sexual Differentiation*. Bethesda, Md.: National Institutes of Health.

Palme, O. 1972. "The Emancipation of Men." *Journal of Social Issues* 28:237-246.

Peck, R.F., and Diáz-Guérrero, R. 1967. "Two Core-Culture Patterns and the Diffusion of Values across Their Border." *International Journal of Psychology* 2:275-282.

Pomeroy, S.B. 1975. *Goddesses, Whores, Wives, and Slaves: Women in Classical Antiquity*. New York: Schocken Books.

Puckett, H.W. 1930. *Germany's Women Go Forward*. New York: Columbia University Press.

Purcell, S.K. 1973. "Modernizing Women for a Modernizing Society: The Cuban Case." In A. Pescatello, ed. *Female and Male in Latin America*. Pittsburg: University of Pittsburg Press.

Rabin, A.I. 1970. "The Sexes: Ideology and Reality in the Israeli Kibbutz." In G.H. Seward and R.C. Williamson, eds. *Sex Roles in Changing Society*. New York: Random House, pp. 285-307.

Reed, E. 1971. *Problems of Women's Liberation*. New York: Pathfinder Press.

Richter, D.C. 1971. "The Position of Women in Classical Athens." *Classical Journal* 69:1-8.

Rosenthal, B. 1975. "The Role and Status of Women in the Soviet Union: 1917 to the Present." In R. Rohrlich-Leavitt, ed. *Women Cross-culturally: Change and Challenge*. The Hague: Mouton.

de Rougemont, D. 1940. *Love in the Western World*. M. Belgion, trans. New York: Harcourt.

Safilios-Rothschild, C. 1975. "A Cross-cultural Examination of Women's Marital, Educational and Occupational Options." In M.T.S. Mednick, S.S. Tangri, and L.W. Hoffman, eds. *Women and Achievement: Social and Motivational Analyses*. New York: Wiley, pp. 48-70.

Schlesinger, Y. 1977. "Sex Roles and Social Change in the Kibbutz." *Journal of Marriage and the Family* 39:771-779.

Seltman, C. 1962. *Women in Antiquity*. New York: Collier.

Slater, P.E. 1974. "The Greek Family in History and Myth." *Arethusa* 7:9-44.

Spiro, M. 1965. *Children of the Kibbutz*. New York: Schocken Books.

_____ . 1979. *Gender and Culture: Kibbutz Women Revisited*. Durham, N.C.: Duke University Press.

Stern, B.J. 1939. "The Family and Cultural Change." *American Sociological Review* 4:199-208.

Stevens, E.P. 1973. "Marianismo: The Other Face of Machismo in Latin America." In A. Pescatello, ed. *Female and Male in Latin America*. Pittsburg: University of Pittsburg Press, pp. 90-101.

Tanner, N. 1974. "Matrifocality in Indonesia and Africa and among Black Americans." In M.Z. Rosaldo and L. Lamphere, eds. *Woman, Culture, and Society*. Stanford, Calif.: Stanford University Press, pp. 129-156.

Tierney, J.J. 1964. "The Celts and the Classical Authors." In J. Raftery, ed. *The Celts*. Cork: Irish Republic: Mercier Press, pp. 23-33.

Washburn, S.L., and Lancaster, C.S. 1968. "The Evolution of Hunting."
    In S.L. Washburn and P.C. Jay, eds. *Perspectives on Human Evolu-
    tion*, vol. 1. New York: Holt, Rinehart, & Winston, pp. 213-229.
Williamson, R.C. 1970. "Role Themes in Latin America." In G.H. Seward
    and R.C. Williamson, eds. *Sex Roles in Changing Society*. New York:
    Random House, pp. 177-199.

3 Mental Abilities

Where shall we begin? Our introduction touched mainly on temperamental traits. But people also differ in aptitudes, in what things they can most readily learn and what levels of performance they may eventually reach. Skills are easier to measure than temperaments and perhaps no less important in comparing the sexes. Besides, such measures are available on children from kindergarten through college. Since the scores are fairly objective, any sex differences that appear can be more clearly related to genes and hormones on the one hand and to society's give and take on the other. One thing is important to bear in mind as we proceed: most if not all known cases of psychological sex difference involve a difference between the averages of two overlapping groups. This means that a sizable portion of the inferior group, depending on the degree of overlap, exceeds the average performance of the superior one and vice versa. In such cases it takes a large sample from each sex to establish a real (significant) difference.

A number of approaches are available. At this point we may take note of a different path from the one we have chosen. Diane McGuinness (1975) starts from her own comparisons of auditory and visual acuity in young men and women. Briefly, she found women superior in tests of hearing, men in tests of seeing. Some support for her results came from surveys of children and adults (Burg 1966; Hull et al. 1971; Roberts & Duvan 1972), though not as yet from infants (Maccoby & Jacklin 1974). Assuming these simple sensory differences to be inborn, McGuinness contends that they bias the development of perception and behavior: in males toward exploring and restructuring the environment, in females toward communication with others. Though we shall not pursue her provocative argument here, the reader may wish to test its usefulness in raising new questions as well as interpreting facts already known.

Our own starting point is with mental abilities. We do not, of course, question the recognized advantage of men in height, weight, and muscular development. In sensory equipment, despite McGuinness' assertion, sex differences seem quite inconspicuous (Maccoby & Jacklin 1974). On the motor side it has long been accepted doctrine that girls excel in fine coordinations, like threading a needle, while boys do better with gross ones, like rotary pursuit, that is, keeping a stylus in contact with a small disk on a turntable. But a review of recent studies (Fairweather 1976) permits no such simple dichotomy. Besides, we shall find the intellectual abilities challenging enough.

Development of Differences

Intelligence

Odd as it may seem, we shall find little use for the concept of intelligence or IQ here. Of the many definitions offered none has been widely accepted, and attempts to measure pure intelligence have failed. Tests covering a variety of skills have proved more useful. As to sex differences, girls do consistently better on a few subtests, boys on a few others, while both do about equally well on the rest. By general consensus, therefore, no sex difference in overall mental ability has been established.

Naturally interest shifts to the subtests. Wechsler's (1955) widely used Adult Intelligence Scale (WAIS) contains six verbal tests and five performance tests. In his standardizing groups women outscored men on two verbal tests—Vocabulary and Similarities (for example, In what way are wood and alcohol alike?)—and one performance test (substituting symbols for digits by a code). Men scored higher than women on three verbal tests: Information (What is the population of the United States?), Comprehension (Why does the state require people to get a marriage license?), and Arithmetic Reasoning; and two performance tests: Picture Completion and Block Designs.

It would be interesting to know how early such differences emerged. Wechsler designed two tests for children: the WISC (years 7 to 15) and the WPPSI, for the preschool and primary levels (years 4 to 6½). Herman (1968) took the data of the 1,200 boys and girls on whom the WPPSI was standardized and analyzed them for sex differences. Here the girls did better on three of the five performance tests, including Block Designs, and one verbal (Sentences).

Not much can be learned from two such widely separated cross sections. But other questions intrude. Perhaps the most urgent one is: what do these tests and others like them measure? What can we learn about an adult's mental powers by giving him problems in arithmetic to solve, or about a child by giving him a maze to trace? In particular, what do the results tell us about sex differences that is of more far-reaching significance than the tests themselves? There is no simple answer, but a powerful tool is available in the statistical techniques of factor analysis.

Essentially factor analysis is a strategy designed to extract, from the intercorrelations of many specific tests, a few common traits or skills that presumably have combined to produce them. A factor analyst, for example, might well define intelligence as a general factor (*g*) common to all the positively correlated tests in a standard battery. We shall encounter this approach again in chapter 5. Without exploring its intricacies (for which the interested reader should consult an introductory text [Comrey 1973]), we may at least profit by some of its discoveries.

Special Abilities

For one thing, we find that among the most frequent and stable factors to emerge from countless investigations are the verbal, the numerical, and the spatial, to which we direct our attention. For another, we learn something about how these factors develop. According to the differentiation hypothesis (Garrett 1946; Burt 1958), what starts out as a highly generalized ability becomes increasingly specialized in the course of childhood. Anastasi (1970) cited considerable evidence to support this view. She also martialed an impressive array of studies—some experimental, others comparing school curricula, social classes, and ethnic cultures—pointing to the enormous effect of experience in shaping individual patterns of ability.

Of special concern to us are the studies that take account of sex differences in factorial structure. Another point made by Anastasi sharpens our interest: it appears that the salience and complexity of an ability in the factor pattern tends to go with a high level of its tested performance. Thus Werdelin (1961), studying high school boys and girls in Sweden with a variety of tests, was able to extract two space factors from the boys' results but only one from the girls'. Though the girls were superior to the boys in verbal ability, they were inferior in most geometrical and spatial tests. At the college level Very (1967) found one spatial factor in women, three in men. Again women led men in the verbal area but trailed in the spatial and mathematical areas. On the other hand, in tests of primary school children the girls' performance called for two verbal factors to the boys' one (Lindsey 1967).

These findings suggest that two areas in particular (verbal and spatial) should repay closer inspection. A third factor, the numerical, has a more indirect interest, chiefly because of its contribution to skill in mathematics.

Verbal Ability. The first clear sex difference to appear is in the verbal area. Girls have a way with words that starts early in life. A pioneering study (McCarthy 1930) of preschool children found girls responding at greater length, and more intelligibly, than boys. Even before the first word, they "vocalize" excitement more consistently (Kagan 1969). In itself this last finding may seem trivial, but longitudinal studies give it weight. At Berkeley, Cameron et al. (1967) discovered a vocalization factor in the test performance of infants during their first 18 months, that correlated significantly with the girls' IQs between 13 and 26 years of age. For boys the corresponding correlations were mostly negative and too small to be reliable.

After starting school, girls keep ahead of boys in word play for several years. Studies in Britain and the United States show girls are better readers until about 10 years of age; thereafter the difference is no longer significant (Thompson 1975). Even during this early period exceptions occur. In one study of first graders (Avakian 1961), three verbal tests showed a sex difference, all in favor of the boys. Avakian had a plausible explanation in the testing materials: pictures of a lantern, hatchet, or camera; words like airplane, spear, bugle, and baseball glove. But she also added the surprising result of factor analysis: the girls relied primarily on a factor of verbal comprehension; the boys, more than the girls, depended on a factor of spatial perception.

Eighth-grade children (age 13 to 15) gave some interesting results (McCall 1955). About 450 boys and girls took thirty-one subtests from three intelligence tests. McCall found that the same three factors (verbal, numerical, and spatial) took care of most of the variance in both sexes. In this case the boys did significantly better in fifteen subtests, eleven of which were nonverbal. But the more interesting difference between the sexes was the way in which they went about the various tasks (as shown by the "loadings" of a test by one or more factors). The girls relied on their verbal ability to deal with numbers and shapes as well as words. The boys, on the other hand, brought their mathematical and spatial skills to bear on linguistic problems. These results suggest that boys' and girls' mental functions, though apparently similar, actually diverge in subtle ways as they mature; the girls continuing to rely on verbal facility, the boys finding more use for visual-spatial processes.

Do we have any clues as to the nature of these factors? The verbal factor probably includes both receiving and transmitting, since many more cases of reading disability and speech disorder (such as stammering) occur among males than females (Eisenberg 1966; Peckham 1973). A study by Coltheart et al. (1975) suggests that women depend more on subvocal speech, men on visual imagery, in doing verbal tasks. In one experiment, for example, seventy-four college students, half men and half women, were told to consult a mental alphabet twice: once in order to count the number of letters containing the sound *ee*; once to count the letters with a curve in their printed form. The women did better on the first task, the men on the second.

It appears that some of the most interesting sex differences in mental process may fail to show up in scores. As to the latter, though quite a few investigations of verbal capacity show nonsignificant differences between the sexes (one reviewer, Fairweather [1976], finds the evidence "not compelling"), the overall balance remains tilted in favor of females.

Numerical Ability. As to dealing with numbers, there is little to choose between girls and boys during the first ten years; what significant differences there are favor the girls. Thereafter boys increasingly move ahead (Maccoby & Jacklin 1974). In one longitudinal study of numerical aptitude involving more than 20,000 high school students (Droege 1967), first-year girls led boys, but by the senior year the boys had closed the gap. We shall have more to say about mathematics in the next section.

Spatial Ability. A sex difference in coping with visual space is more widely acknowledged than in either verbal or numerical aptitude. At least after age 14 evidence of male superiority is relatively clear and consistent (Maccoby & Jacklin 1974), withstanding even Fairweather's (1976) diligent uncovering of exceptions.

What is spatial ability? Factor analysts disagree about the number and nature of its components. Macfarlane Smith (1964) defined its essence as "the perception, retention, and recognition (or reproduction) of a figure or pattern in its correct proportions" (p. 96). Guilford distinguished a factor for "spatial relations and orientation" from one for "visualization," the latter involving the mental manipulation of visual objects (Michael et al. 1957).

How do sex differences fit into this unclear picture? Werdelin (1961) found that boys were better than girls at grasping the organization of a visual structure but not at manipulating it. The latter restriction, however, is open to question. Shepard and Metzler (1971) prepared pictures showing a pair of solid objects seen from different perspectives. The difference was produced by rotating one object of the pair between 20 and 180 degrees (figure 3-1). Subjects were then asked to judge whether the two objects were the same or different. The result was remarkable. Reaction time increased in direct proportion to the angle of rotation, suggesting that the subjects mentally rotated the objects to make the required judgment.

The Shepard-Metzler Mental Rotations Test (modified for group testing) was one of a battery used in a large-scale family study in Hawaii (Wilson et al. 1975). About 3,000 individuals (1,000 families), ranging in age from 14 to 60, took the tests. Scores for a spatial factor showed a marked sex difference in favor of males at all ages ($p < .001$), and in mental rotations the difference was even more pronounced.

Two small-scale experiments reported by Metzler and Shepard (1974) may yield some insight into the latter difference. Sixteen young adults, eight males and eight females selected for high spatial ability, were tested with the rotated pairs. Both sexes showed a linear increase of reaction time with increasing angle of rotation, but the women were slower and their times increased more steeply than the men's. If this finding is verified, it may prove to be crucial for the theories considered in chapter 4 (Harris 1978).

But a sex difference comes out in other, quite simple performances. Wolf (1973), for example, questioned several hundred doctors and their wives about their personal orientation in space. Of those replying, twice as many wives as husbands acknowledged that they frequently confused right and left ($p < .001$, meaning that the probability of such a number occur-

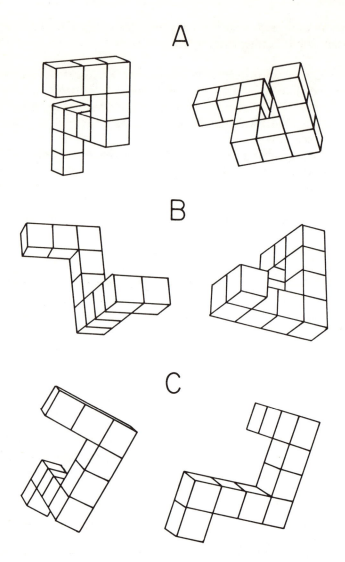

Source: R. N. Shepard and J. Metzler, "Mental Rotation of Three-dimensional Objects," *Science* 171(1971):701-703. Copyright 1971 by the American Association for the Advancement of Science. Reproduced by permission.

Figure 3-1. Examples of pairs of perspective line drawings presented to the subjects. (A) A "same" pair, which differs by an 80° rotation in the picture plane; (B) a "same" pair, which differs by an 80° rotation in depth; and (C) a "different" pair, which cannot be brought into congruence by any rotation.

ring by chance is less than one in a thousand). Sandström (1953) found college women less able than men, in total darkness, to hit a point of light with
a single thrust.

Quite surprising are the results of the Water-level Test, involving the
rule that the surface of a liquid stays horizontal no matter how far the con-
tainer is tilted. The Swiss psychologist Piaget, renowned for his illuminating
studies of children's thinking, held that a child can learn the rule only after
achieving the concept of horizontality, which occurs between ages 7 and 11
(Piaget & Inhelder 1956). Piaget's view has received some support under
controlled conditions (Smedslund 1963; Barna & O'Connell 1967). But according to other investigators many university students, mostly women, do
not grasp the principle (Rebelsky 1964; Willemsen & Reynolds 1973) and
may even fail to "catch on" after being shown (Thomas et al. 1973). One
study found males ahead of females at every age level from nursery school
through college (Thomas & Jamison 1975).

The Question of Cognitive Style

So far, sex differences in mental ability seem to hinge on which subject matter is involved: words, numbers, or objects in space. But behind this
assumption lurks a doubt: do males and females also differ in the way they
handle problems, in their cognitive style; and if so, how?

Let us start with the meaning of cognitive style most commonly
recognized. It grew out of Witkin's early work on spatial orientation
(Witkin et al. 1954). In a typical test, the Rod and Frame Test (RFT), the
subject was seated in a pitch-dark room facing a luminous rod in a frame,
the rod movable, the frame fixed and tilted. His task was to adjust the rod
to be vertical. Witkin's discovery, frequently though not always confirmed
by others, was that women's adjustments deviated farther from the true vertical than men's. Another measure, even more widely adopted because more
convenient, was the Embedded Figures Test (EFT), in which the object was
to discern, in the shortest possible time, a simple design presented as part of
a more complex one (figure 3-2). Here, too, men generally proved superior.

Interpreting these results, Witkin and his group proposed that men are
better able than women to disregard the visual surroundings that deflect or
conceal the critical object. In a word, women are more field dependent in
perception than men. But if that were so, was it likely that such a difference
would be confined to perception? Witkin thought not; on the contrary, he
suggested that the tilted rod and embedded figures might be tapping
something as basic to development as differentiation itself. This central
process would determine behavior at many levels, and not only in response

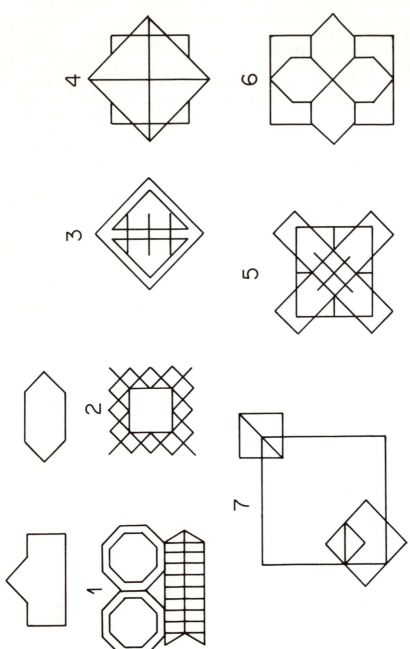

Source: L.L. Thurstone, "A Factorial Study of Perception," *Psychometric Monographs*, no. 4, 1944. Copyright 1944 by The University of Chicago Press. Reproduced by permission.

Figure 3-2. Part III of the Gottschaldt Embedded Figures Test (Thurstone version). The task is to detect which of the two figures above is contained in each numbered design below.

to objects in a laboratory but to other people in daily life. Applied to sex difference in cognitive style, the theory predicted that males would prove to be more analytic, females more global, in thinking as well as perception.

Witkin's theory has been a center of controversy from the start, with the healthy result of stirring up a great deal of valuable research. The battle still goes on, with many basic questions as yet unsettled. A crucial issue is the relation between field independence and the so-called primary mental abilities. Sherman (1967) took the position that sex differences attributed to cognitive style could all be due to the recognized difference in spatial ability. She herself found that among college students RFT and EFT scores were as closely correlated with a test of spatial relations as with each other (Sherman 1974). Vernon (1972) came to much the same conclusion by factor analyzing test scores of high school students. It has even been shown that, when sex differences in spatial tests were statistically removed, differences in the RFT and EFT were no longer significant (Hyde et al. 1975; Wolf 1969).

On the other hand, Witkin's group has gathered much evidence for his view (Witkin et al. 1962) and there is more besides. An impressive number of experiments, mostly done on college students in the 1950s and 1960s, showed males to be better problem solvers than females. This finding suggests that we take a different approach: discover some aspect of reasoning that is related to field independence, then see if males and females differ in that aspect.

Take, for example, the "productive thinking" needed to solve a mystery story. This path proved to be a cul-de-sac when Saarni (1973) gave such problems to children 10 to 15 years old and found no relation between their ability to solve them and to detect the true vertical in the RFT.

Much earlier, however, Luchins (1942) had called attention to a property of "rigidity" in reasoning and devised a way to measure it. He asked adult subjects to imagine three plain water jars holding, say, seven, four, and two quarts, and to figure out how to get exactly five quarts of water. As to sex differences, he found—and Cunningham (1965) confirmed for children—that males shifted more readily than females from a familiar but complicated strategy to a simple one in order to reach the goal. In other words they were less rigid, better at "set breaking" or restructuring the problem. It could be argued that restructuring need be stretched only a little to include an analytic or field-independent style.

Some qualified support can be mustered for this idea, qualified because the water-jars test as a valid measure of rigidity has been severely attacked (Levitt 1956). To measure set breaking Guetzkow (1951) used both Luchins' test and another well-known device in which the subject, armed only with a pliers, has to tie together two strings hanging too far apart to reach. (Solution: Use the pliers as the bob of a pendulum.) Not only did more males than females solve each problem, but success in both problems was associated with high scores on the EFT.

At this juncture the game of anagrams has proved a useful tool of inquiry. Rearranging letters to make meaningful words certainly involves restructuring, but is strictly verbal and therefore possibly female territory. If boys were found to beat girls at this game, it would argue strongly for the notion that they are better set breakers in general. Results to date indicate otherwise (Maccoby & Jacklin 1974); if anything, girls more than hold their own with boys. Given the proper materials, they can be as analytic as the masters of space. The case, however, is not yet closed. In one experiment with college women (Gavurin 1967), solving anagrams was found to correlate with spatial ability, but only if the letters were glued down. In another experiment (Mendelsohn & Covington 1972) a sex difference in favor of men was found, but only when the anagram had to be rearranged *after* being removed from view.

Maccoby and Jacklin's thoughtful discussion of the whole issue leaves open the possibility of a sex difference in restructuring. The only note we can add at this point comes from a study of 201 English schoolboys (Satterly 1976). Analyzing the results of a broad range of tests, Satterly unearthed a factor tentatively labeled "flexible thinking," with a high loading on the EFT, clearly distinct from both spatial and verbal-mathematical factors. All we lack is a replication on 201 English schoolgirls.

How, then, do we answer the question of cognitive style? We are strongly tempted to abstain for lack of evidence, but that would not be altogether excusable. We can say with some confidence, borrowing a term from Gardner, that people vary in the abilty, or inclination, to articulate a perceptual field (Gardner et al. 1960). It also appears that males are more likely or able to do so than females. But whether this tendency goes beyond dealing with visual space, and if so what form it takes, have not been securely established. At this point the conservative position is to consider the RFT and EFT as measuring related aspects of spatial ability.

Determinants of Differences

We come now to the heart of the matter: how to explain the differential abilities that have come to light. Again we remind ourselves we have to do with two basic sets of conditions. These are sometimes referred to as environmental and hereditary, but for our purposes the terms *social* and *biological* are more appropriate. Abilities themselves, as products of development, depend inescapably on both sets of conditions. But differences in abilities may depend on one factor or the other or, as in most cases, both. We are entitled to ask to what extent a specific sex difference stems from biological roots and how much is shaped by society.

Social Factors

Verbal Ability. If word artistry is primarily a social product, its prevalence in the two sexes might be expected to vary from one culture to another. The noted anthropologist Margaret Mead (1958) claimed that in every society studied women surpass men in linguistic behavior (p. 47). That would imply that women talk more or better than men simply by virtue of being female. But no anthropologist would draw that conclusion, of course, unless an intensive search for social causes had failed.

Despite the verbal advantage commonly granted to preadolescent females, there is some evidence for cross-national differences. Tests of reading ability in schoolchildren of four English-speaking countries (Johnson 1974) showed girls ahead in the United States and Canada, boys ahead in England and Nigeria. An earlier study (Preston 1962) had measured the prowess of young readers in the United States and West Germany and found a similar reversal of sex difference, with American girls and German boys in the lead.

Why should this be? It happens that in Canada and the United States most grade school teachers are women, while in England, Nigeria, and West Germany the majority are men. Sex of teacher, by itself, may be unimportant (Dwyer 1973), but it may contribute to a feminine atmosphere in the American schoolroom, of which even second- and third-grade children seem well aware (Kagan 1964). This atmosphere in turn may have carried over to influence the large proportion of high school boys, and their fathers, who labeled reading a "mostly feminine" activity (Mazurkiewicz 1960).

Whatever feminine bias exists in elementary school apparently fails to include arithmetical problems; one wonders why. Perhaps girls, more than boys, are predisposed to find satisfactions in reading. Support for this idea comes from several sources. A study of fifth graders (Bing 1963) compared children high and low in verbal ability and found that the verbal group came from homes that provided more stimulation to all sorts of word play.

Do girls get more of such stimulation than boys? It seems so. Even as early as two days postpartum, mothers talked to their first-born daughters more than to their sons (Thoman et al. 1972). To judge from repeated tests, they continue to do so for at least two years (Cherry & Lewis 1976). We have already seen that infant girls vocalize more than boys.

These observations raise a ticklish point: do girl babies babble more because they are girls or because their mothers more often reinforce their vocal efforts by babbling back, as they have been found to do (Moss 1967)? Again does a mother talk more to her girl baby than her boy baby because the girl is more likely to respond, as observed (Lewis 1972), or for some other reason? Here we find ourselves as baffled as ever by the claims to priority of hen and egg.

Numerical Ability. Here the same question provides a starting point: how does the male advantage in mathematics hold up across cultures? The best answer we could find was in a comparison of twelve nations sponsored by UNESCO (Husen 1967), covering western Europe, the United States, Australia, Israel, and Japan. Several thousand students in each country, 13 and 17 to 18 years old, took mathematical achievement tests and filled out attitude scales. The outcome was surprisingly uniform. Boys scored higher than girls almost throughout (the one exception was at age 13 in Israel); the difference was greater in reasoning problems than in mere computation; and the boys were also more interested in mathematics. Such a sweeping result does little to help explain it; whatever the cause, it seems to hold good over most of Western culture.

Could it be that boys do better with numbers simply because they have taken more courses in mathematics? Not likely, since the sex difference shows up before students have been given much freedom to choose. Moreover, in one longitudinal study of high school students with number of mathematics courses controlled, the usual sex difference emerged (Hilton & Berglund 1974).

Is it just that boys like mathematics more, or dislike it less, than girls? (If so, we should still have to ask why.) Hilton and Berglund reported that more girls than boys found mathematics boring. But when more than 1,300 pupils from second to twelfth grades were asked to rank four subjects from most liked to least, mathematics (or arithmetic) was ranked equally by boys and girls (Ernest 1976). Evidently there is nothing about numbers as such that attracts or repels one sex more than the other.

The most widely held view on this issue boils it down to a matter of motivation. Girls are bored by mathematics because they see no future in it. For boys on the other hand it is a password, indeed a prerequisite, to careers ranging from accountant to astronaut. Two examples, both from Ernest's 1976 paper, will suffice to show how pervasive is the stereotype of mathematics as a male prerogative. First, Lucy Sells, a sociologist, writes as follows: "in a . . . sample of freshmen admitted to Berkeley in Fall 1972, 57 percent of the boys had taken four full years of mathematics, including the trigonometry-solid geometry sequence, compared with 8 percent of the girls" (p. 9).

Second, schoolchildren of both sexes were asked whom they went to for help with their homework. Between fifth and ninth grades a dramatic switch occurred in the percentages of youngsters calling on their mothers as compared with their fathers for help in mathematics. The curve for mother fell from about 45 percent to 10 percent, while father's curve rose from 20 percent to almost 50 percent (p. 4).

The role of the father model is shown clearly by what happens when it is missing. Carlsmith (1964) matched a group of Harvard freshmen whose early life had been fatherless against a matched group of normally fathered controls. Comparing their aptitude scores on college entrance examinations, he found that a decided majority of the father-absent group scored higher in verbal than mathematical aptitude, while almost all the controls did better in mathematics. Furthermore, the earlier in life the father had been absent and the longer he had stayed away, the lower was the mathematical compared with the verbal score. Similar results came from a sample of high school boys and, interestingly, high school girls.

Sex-role stereotyping, granted its undeniable effects on motivation and learning, may or may not account for all the sex differences in numerical ability. We shall return to that issue in a later section.

Spatial Ability. Here the cross-cultural approach yields richer returns. For a starter we have Porteus' (1965) account of results with his well-known Maze Test. Over a span of fifty years the test has been given to children and young adults of both sexes in many lands. Since it is practically nonverbal, subjects could be drawn not only from such advanced cultures as the Chinese, Japanese, Australian, and American, but from primitive tribes in South Africa, Central Australia, and islands of the South Pacific.

In 105 comparisons between the sexes males outscored females in 99. Though few of the differences were tested for significance, the chance probability of such a box score is vanishingly small. The largest differences were found in the least cultured societies. Since these were the groups with the most rigid division of sex roles, the finding strongly suggests a cultural origin. Porteus, however, impressed by wide differences in performance between the males of two groups from similar environments, and vice versa, preferred to leave open the social-biological question.

More clear-cut data on cultural and social factors are available. Berry (1971) theorized that spatial ability should distinguish hunting from farming populations. Further, since wives and children are more strictly controlled in agricultural than in hunting communities, a female inferiority in spatial skills should be more conspicuous among food gatherers than hunters. Berry gave spatial tests to samples of four primitive peoples in West Africa (Sierra Leone), New Guinea, Australia, and Canada (Baffin Island), and to Scottish samples for comparison with Western culture. His main hypothesis was confirmed. Most interesting to us are the results for the two samples farthest apart in way of life, the farming Temnes of Sierra Leone and the hunting Eskimos of Baffin Island (Berry 1966). These two groups stood lowest and highest, respectively, in all four spatial tests. Moreover, while the Temnes revealed a clear difference in favor of males, the Eskimos showed no sex difference. (The only other sex differences occurred in one rural New Guinea sample and in the Edinburgh control group, both favoring males.)

Not so readily explained are the cross-cultural findings of Dawson et al. (1974). They studied improvement with age in the use of cues to the third dimension by Chinese children of Hong Kong. Along with sex differences in favor of boys over 8, they presented comparable data on Alaskan Eskimo children and on European and African children living in South Africa. As expected, the Eskimo children scored higher than the Hong Kong Chinese in three-dimensional perception of drawings and photographs. But unexpectedly, the Chinese sample scored well above the Europeans, who, one would suppose, enjoyed the more varied environment and less rigid restraints. We are left with one more puzzle to solve.

The idea that males owe their spatial superiority to experience rather than heredity has not gone unchallenged. In an earlier generation Smith (1948), finding Scottish boys better than girls in spatial tests, suggested that the opposite outcome was just as likely; girls, for example, had more experience than boys in cutting and drafting sewing patterns. Munroe and Munroe (1971) in the course of a year spent among the Logoli of western Kenya, put the matter to a test. They guessed that the Logoli boys were better at spatial relations because they wandered farther from home in their spare time. In a test with matched boy-girl pairs their hunch proved to be correct.

In answer to Smith's objection, it could be argued that sex roles might affect performance on a test of spatial ability even with equal opportunities for learning. Women's scores might suffer merely because they felt that angles and arcs were not for housewives but for architects and engineers. This hypothesis, too, has been tested (Castore & Stafford 1970). Three groups of male and female college students took the same test of spatial visualization. To vary sex-role relevance it was presented to one group as revealing aptitude for draftsmanship; to a second group, talent for fashion design; to a third (neutral) group, promise in pattern development. The results gave no support to the hypothesis; they favored the men by about the same amount in all three groups.

Sex roles may still contribute to male priority in visualizing space, provided they induce boys to spend more time than girls in related activities. What such activities may be, however, is largely unknown.

Biological Factors

Genes and Intelligence. Males and females certainly inherit differences in such physical features as body build, sex organs, chromosomes, and hormones. Whether they also inherit different ways of thinking, feeling, and doing is less certain. With respect to mental abilities the question becomes exceedingly hard to handle. Though less inflammatory than the parallel issue of racial inequalities of IQ, it stirs prejudices that make it hard to stick to the evidence. But an even greater obstacle is the complexity of the problem itself. Before taking up possible sex differences we should therefore deal briefly with the role of heredity in intellectual skills.

General intelligence has been the concept most thoroughly explored, though expert opinion has it that the surface has been barely scratched (Lewontin 1975; McAskie & Clarke 1976). Measurements of family resemblance make up the bulk of the research. One review of fifty-two widely assorted studies showed an impressive relation between closeness of kinship and correlation of test scores (Erlenmeyer-Kimling & Jarvik 1963). But it must be admitted that similarity of environment usually goes with closeness of kinship and may therefore be responsible for at least part of that relation.

Studies of adopted children deserve more serious attention. Theoretically they permit the investigator to separate the effects of heredity and environment. Skodak and Skeels (1949) found evidence of both. On the side of heredity, foster children's IQs correlated significantly with their own mothers' IQs and educational levels, but not with the educational levels of their foster mothers. On the other hand, their average IQ was twenty points higher than that of their own mothers, clearly the result of a superior environment. A pitfall of the method is that the correlation with foster parent may represent, to some degree, selective placement by the agency for adoption rather than environmental influence on the child.

A second technique for distinguishing genetic effects from experience is the comparison of identical twins with fraternal twins. Identical twins come from a single egg and are called monozygotic (MZ); fraternal twins come from two separately fertilized ova and are called dizygotic (DZ). MZ twins have the same genes, while DZ twins are no more alike genetically than ordinary siblings. So the mental-test scores of MZ pairs should be more highly correlated than those of DZs; indeed, the difference between the two correlations is typically used to measure the heritability of a trait (Vandenberg 1976). A summary of some twenty studies of MZ and DZ twins showed median correlations of .87 and .57, respectively (Nichols 1969).

Even this attractive method has a serious defect: it assumes that the two types of twin are exposed to equally similar environments. Some critics consider this assumption untenable (Lewontin 1975), but there are indications that the flaw need not be fatal (Freedman & Keller 1963; Scarr 1969; Vandenberg & Johnson 1968). It seems fair to conclude that heredity plays a part in producing differences in intelligence, though how large a part, compared with environment, can seldom be estimated with confidence.

Special Abilities. Turning to special abilities with this reservation in mind, we find a respectable body of data pointing toward heritability. MZ twins have proved significantly more alike than DZ twins of the same sex in a variety of tests, including reading achievement (Matheny & Dolan 1974), sentence structure (Munsinger & Douglass 1976), arithmetic achievement (Husén 1960), and spatial ability (Osborne & Gregory 1966; Vandenberg 1969). It is not unreasonable to suppose that sex differences in the capacities tapped by such tests may be to some degree inherited.

Before starting we must choose the most promising aptitudes for the purpose. Some headway has already been made in revealing heritable factors underlying mental tests; it was done by multivariate analysis of the scores of MZ and DV twins. Bock and Vandenberg (1968) applied the method to the results of high school twins on the Differential Aptitudes Test (Bennett et al. 1947), treating males and females separately. The first component for both sexes looked like a general test-taking factor. The second component, stronger in boys than girls, involved pictures and diagrams rather than letters or numbers. Bock (1973) made similar use of the Primary Mental Abilities Tests (Thurstone 1938); these yielded three significantly heritable dimensions in both sexes. The first and second, for both males and females, had heaviest loadings in Verbal Meaning and Space; the third, in Number for boys and Word Fluency for girls. (Space showed a highly significant sex difference in favor of boys; Word Fluency, a similar advantage for girls; no sex difference appeared in Number or Verbal Meaning.) Disregarding the last negative finding, we shall consider evidence bearing on biological sex differences in numerical, verbal, and spatial abilities.

Numbers. A study by Stafford (1972) offers a good introduction to research in the whole area. He tested quantitative reasoning in 200 pairs of MZ and DZ twins from 12 to 18 years of age, using such problems as "how many pencils can you buy for 50 cents if they are 2 for 5 cents?" A sex difference in favor of the boys became significant after age 15. Stafford's question was whether any of this difference was hereditary.

First he examined the differences between DZ twins to see if they varied more than those between MZ twins, as they should if heredity was important. They did and they didn't: the pertinent DZ/MZ ratio was significantly above 1:1 for males but not for females.

Next Stafford tested the hypothesis that quantitative reasoning might be a sex-linked recessive ability. Here a word of explanation may help (for a fuller discussion see Lerner & Libby [1976]). A trait is sex-linked if it depends on a gene in the sex chromosome, of which females carry a pair (XX) while males have but one, paired with a Y chromosome (XY). Some genes come in two forms, or alleles, one dominant, the other recessive. A recessive character is expressed in behavior only if its allele is *not* paired with a dominant one; otherwise it is suppressed. (More than 120 such traits have been discovered; the two best known examples are red-green color blindness and hemophilia.) The hypothesis is attractive, partly because it implies a sex difference and partly because it offers some specific predictions to be tested. Stafford demonstated two ways of testing it. Finding, as expected, signs of a bimodal distribution, he was able to predict the proportions of high and low scorers among DZ twins and to compare these with the actual results. Here again the boys supported the theory but the girls did not.

A better known prediction is the order of correlations to be expected between members of a family. For example, a sex-linked recessive gene can be transmitted from father to daughter but not from father to son; therefore the correlation of fathers with daughters may be substantial, but with sons must approximate zero. Stafford presented the results of three studies, including one of his own, showing correlations between family members in arithmetic reasoning. Their loose adherence to the predicted order was interesting but hardly convincing, especially in view of a weak relation between father and daughter. In general, as his study indicates, a genetic sex difference in numerical reasoning is suggested but as yet unproved.

Words. Earlier we noted fairly solid evidence for female superiority in the use of language. Just now studies were cited indicating strongly that skill with words has a hereditary component. It does *not* follow from these premises that the proposed sex difference is even partly inherited; it might be altogether environmentally induced.

There is, however, a striking example of a sex-related verbal disorder with a presumably hereditary root: specific reading disability (at one time called congenital word blindness and more recently developmental dyslexia). The diagnosis is usually invoked when a child has extreme difficulty in learning to read though normal in intelligence and other aptitudes. Symmes and Rapoport (1972) phrased the concept neatly as "unexpected reading failure." It occurs, as typically estimated, in 5 to 10 percent of schoolchildren in the United States (DeFries et al. 1976b).

More boys than girls are disabled readers, reported sex ratios varying around 3 or 4:1 (Klasen 1972). Most authorities agree that the condition is hereditary. Genealogies show high proportions of cases among the relatives of handicapped readers, ranging from 11 to 70 percent (Klasen 1972). Familial statistics rarely take account of the environment; twin studies do better. Of twelve MZ pairs examined, both twins were nonreaders in all twelve; of thirty-three DZ pairs this was true of only eleven: 100 percent concordance against 33 percent (Hermann 1959). Such data, as Klasen warns, may not be "sufficient proof of genetic origin," but they are certainly impressive.

When it comes to the mechanism of inheritance there is still plenty of room for speculation. Perhaps the most radical proposal was offered by Symmes and Rapoport (1972), who found their almost exclusively male sample of dyslexics well above the norms in tests of visualizing three-dimensional space. They suggested that the same sex-linked recessive process advanced to account for spatial competence might also involve the reading failure sometimes associated with it. Most investigators, however, find this hypothesis at odds with the familial data. Hallgren (1950), for example, found too many dyslexic fathers with dyslexic sons to support sex linkage, and the large number of affected parents and siblings suggests a dominant mode of transmission rather than a recessive one. Sladen (1970) favored a single autosomal (not sex-linked) locus with "variable dominance in males" and "largely recessive in females" (p. 30). This theory among others was rejected by Lewitter, who studied eighty-four pairs of matched families (DeFries et al. 1976b). He could not reject a "polygenic . . . model with different thresholds in males and females" (p. 202).

And so it goes. For us the dispute has a side effect: it lends a touch of reality to the idea of a probably hereditary sex difference in an intellectual endeavor.

Space. Of all the special abilities, the question of an innate male superiority in dealing with space has attracted the most attention. Much of it started with Johnson O'Connor's (1943) report that in spatial tests 25 percent of women attained the score made by 50 percent of men. His finding is what would be expected if the tests were tapping a sex-linked recessive trait.

As we have seen, this hypothesis predicts the exact within-family correlations that would be produced, other things being equal, by the estimated frequency of the "spatial gene." Of course, other things never are equal, but at least the predicted rank-order of correlations should be within reach. Stafford (1961) was the first to put the hypothesis to a formal test. He gave a test called Identical Blocks to over 100 families with teenage sons or daughters. The correlations he obtained between parent and child were remarkably close to those predicted. For example, the predicted correlations (r) for father with daughter and mother with son were both .41; the actual r's were both .31. For mother with daughter the expected figure was .17; the obtained, .14. As predicted, there was no correlation between mothers and fathers or fathers and sons.

Unfortunately, later attempts to confirm the theory by correlating parents with children have been less encouraging. Two of them (Hartlage 1970; Bock & Kolakowski 1973) gave limited support. But a large-scale study of about 1,000 families in Hawaii (DeFries et al. 1976a) gave none. On the other hand, the prospect for sibling r's looks a bit better at this writing. Theoretically sisters should correlate more closely than brothers, and these in turn more closely than brothers with sisters. Yen (1975) gave some 380 pairs of high school siblings four tests of spatial ability and obtained the expected order in three of the tests, as well as in the two "principal components" derived from them.

The theory of a single gene on the sex chromosome implies something about the distribution of scores within each sex; namely, instead of the normal curve of probability, a large enough sample should contain two overlapping curves, one for subjects possessing, the other for those not possessing, the recessive form of the gene. This implication has been tested. Bock and Kolakowski (1973) showed that their data, properly treated, met the bimodal requirement. Moreover, the boys' upper and lower curves contained about half of the subjects apiece, while the girls' upper curve was much smaller, as the theory implied. Yen (1975) put her data through a similar test and was able to confirm the two-curve hypothesis for some of her tests, but not all.

Summing up the evidence so far, we see enough on the positive side to suggest that a sex-linked gene may be necessary to superior spatial ability, but enough on the negative side to suggest that it may not be sufficient. A striking example of its inadequacy appears in Turner's syndrome. A person with this condition has only one sex chromosome, an X. Female in body build, short in stature, she has no ovaries and pubertal changes depend on injections of estogen. From our standpoint the most interesting thing about girls with Turner's syndrome is their difficulty in coping with spatial relations. Though normal in general intelligence, they fall well below the norms in such tests as Wechsler's Block Design and Object Assembly (Money 1963), PMA Space (Money & Alexander 1966), figure drawing, and using a road map. Money (1963) called this deficiency "space-form blindness."

At first this finding seems to bear out the sex-linkage theory, but on second thought it poses a paradox. If the X chromosome carries a recessive gene for space-form vision, why should not Turner's cases (X0) do as well in that department as males (XY)? Evidently the lack of an X is not equivalent to a Y; a piece is missing (Garron 1970).

Gonadal hormones come readily to mind. Estrogen must probably be rejected, since treatment with it at puberty has not been shown to improve spatial performance. That leaves androgen as the most likely candidate. Two other clinical anomalies of prenatal development are of special interest here. (For further treatment see chapter 7; also Money & Ehrhardt [1972].)

In the adrenogenital syndrome (AGS) the adrenal cortex releases, instead of cortisol, an androgenlike substance. The condition may occur in a fetus of either sex, but our question is how it affects a genetic female. We know that with the aid of cortisone and corrective surgery such cases may be accepted as physically normal girls. Do they also take feminine directions in mental growth?

Early studies of AGS patients had consistently reported IQs above normal or higher than control groups. But when Baker and Ehrhardt (1974) matched patients against their own parents and unaffected siblings, the control IQs proved to be equally elevated. As for special abilities, neither verbal nor spatial tests produced any significant difference.

In the androgen-insensitivity syndrome an obscure inherited defect makes the genetic male unable to use the androgen secreted by his testes. As a result, the external genitals are feminized, so the child is usually brought up as a girl. Masica et al. (1969) reported the results of testing fifteen patients between 5 and 27 years old. Wechsler IQs were significantly higher on the verbal than on the performance tests, suggesting that high spatial ability depends on androgen. But the argument evaporates when we recall that the subjects had all been raised as girls.

Fortunately we do not have to depend entirely on clinical material. As Petersen (1976) pointed out, sex hormones and spatial ability seem to run parallel to each other in the course of life. And Petersen herself did a most interesting study to clarify that relationship. From the files of the Fels Research Institute she secured complete data on thirty-five males and forty females at 13, 16, and 18 years of age. The data included tests of spatial visualization and "fluent production" on the one hand and ratings of secondary sex characteristics (muscles, body shape, genital or breast size, pubic hair) on the other. Petersen found the males superior in spatial tests, the females in fluency. But she was more concerned about the relation between mental and physical measures within each sex. What she found was that by age 18 spatial ability was related to physical masculinity *in both sexes*. Surprisingly, the relationship was positive in females but *negative* in males.

If this result seems to demolish the spatial superiority of men over women, Maccoby (1966), in a different connection, pointed out a way for us to reconcile the two findings. Suppose the mental and physical effects of androgen were related in a curvilinear fashion, such that spatial competence reached its peak at a midpoint of masculinity, then declined. Then if, as seems likely, girls' spatial scores fell mainly below that midpoint and boys' scores above it, we should have the gist of Petersen's data. The more masculine girls and the less masculine boys would be the best dealers in space.

References

Anastasi, A. 1970. "On the Formation of Psychological Traits." *American Psychologist* 25:899-910.

Avakian, S.A. 1961. "An Investigation of Trait Relationships among Six-Year-Old Children." *Genetic Psychology Monographs* 63:339-394.

Baker, S.W., and Ehrhardt, A.A. 1974. "Prenatal Androgen, Intelligence, and Cognitive Sex Differences." In R.C. Friedman, R.M. Richart, and R.L. Vande Wiele, eds. *Sex Differences in Behavior*. New York: Wiley.

Barna, J.D., and O'Connell, D.C. 1967. "Perception of Horizontality as a Function of Age and Stimulus Setting." *Perceptual and Motor Skills* 25:70-72.

Bennett, G.K.; Seashore, H.G.; and Wesman, A.G. 1947. *The Differential Aptitude Tests*. New York: Psychological Corporation.

Berry, J.W. 1966. "Temne and Eskimo Perceptual Skills." *International Journal of Psychology* 1:207-229.

———. 1971. "Ecological and Cultural Factors in Spatial Perception Development." *Canadian Journal of Behavioral Science* 3:324-336.

Bing, E. 1963. "Effect of Childrearing Practices or Development of Differential Cognitive Abilities." *Child Development* 34:631-648.

Bock, R.D. 1973. "Word and Image: Sources of the Verbal and Spatial Factors in Mental Test Scores." *Psychometrika* 38:437-457.

Bock, R.D., and Kolakowski, D. 1973. "Further Evidence of Sex-linked Major-Gene Influence on Human Spatial Visualizing Ability." *American Journal of Human Genetics* 25:1-14.

Bock, R.D., and Vandenberg, S.G. 1968. "Components of Heritable Variation in Mental Test Scores." In S.G. Vandenberg, ed. *Progress in Human Behavior Genetics*. Baltimore: Johns Hopkins.

Burg, A. 1966. "Visual Acuity as Measured by Dynamic and Statistical Tests: A Comparative Evaluation." *Journal of Applied Psychology* 50:460-466.

Burt, C. 1958. "The Inheritance of Mental Ability." *American Psychologist* 13:1-15.

Cameron, J.; Livson, N.; and Bayley, N. 1967. "Infant Vocalizations and Their Relationship to Mature Intelligence." *Science* 157:331-333.

Carlsmith, L. 1964. "Effect of Early Father Absence on Scholastic Aptitude." *Harvard Educational Review* 34:3-21.

Castore, C., and Stafford, R.E. 1970. "The Effect of Sex Role Perception on Test-taking Performance." *Journal of Psychology* 74:175-180.

Cherry, L., and Lewis, M. 1976. "Mothers and Two-Year-Olds: A Study of Sex-differentiated Aspects of Verbal Interaction." *Developmental Psychology* 12:278-282.

Coltheart, M.; Hull, E.; and Slater, D. 1975. "Sex Differences in Imagery and Reading." *Nature* 253:437-440.

Cunningham, J.D. 1965. "Einstellung Rigidity in Children." *Journal of Experimental Child Psychology* 2:237-407.

Comrey, A.L. 1973. *A First Course in Factor Analysis*. New York: Academic Press.

Dawson, J.L.; Young, B.M.; and Choi, P.P. 1974. "Developmental Influences in Pictorial Depth Perception among Hong Kong Chinese Children." *Journal of Cross-cultural Psychology* 5:3-22.

DeFries, J.C.; Ashton, G.C.; Johnson, R.C.; Kuse, A.R.; McClearn, G.E.; Mi, M.P.; Rashad, M.N.; Vandenberg, S.G.; and Wilson, J.R. 1976a. "Parent-Offspring Resemblance for Specific Cognitive Abilities in Two Ethnic Groups." *Nature* 261:131-133.

DeFries, J.C.; Vandenberg, S.G.; and McClearn, G.E. 1976b. "Genetics of Specific Cognitive Abilities." *Annual Review of Genetics* 10:179-207.

Droege, R.C. 1967. "Sex Differences in Aptitude Maturation during High School." *Journal of Counseling Psychology* 14:407-411.

Dwyer, C.A. 1973. "Sex Differences in Reading: An Evaluation and a Critique of Current Theories." *Review of Educational Research* 43:455-468.

Eisenberg, L. 1966. "The Epidemiology of Reading Retardation and a Program for Preventive Intervention." In J. Money and G. Schiffman, eds. *The Disabled Reader*. Baltimore: Johns Hopkins.

Erlenmeyer-Kimling, L., and Jarvik, L.F. 1963. "Genetics and Intelligence: A Review." *Science* 142:1477-1478.

Ernest, J. 1976. "Mathematics and Sex." Preprint. *American Mathematical Monthly*.

Fairweather, H. 1976. "Sex Differences in Cognition." *Cognition* 4:231-280.

Freedman, D.G., and Keller, B. 1963. "Inheritance of Behavior in Infants." *Science* 140:196-198.

Gardner, R.W.; Jackson, D.N.; and Messick, S.J. 1960. "Personality Organization in Cognitive Controls and Intellectual Abilities." *Psychological Issues* II (4, whole no. 8).

Garrett, H.E. 1946. "A Developmental Theory of Intelligence." *American Psychologist* 1:372-378.

Garron, D.G. 1970. "Sex-linked, Recessive Inheritance of Spatial and Numerical Abilities and Turner's Syndrome." *Psychological Review* 77:147-152.

Gavurin, E.I. 1967. "Anagram Solving and Spatial Aptitude." *Journal of Psychology* 65:65-68.

Guetzkow, H. 1951. "An Analysis of the Operation of Set in Problem-solving Behavior." *Journal of General Psychology* 45:219-244.

Hallgren, B. 1950. "Specific Dyslexia (congenital word blindness): A Clinical and Genetic Study." *Acta Psychiatrica Scandinavica*, supplement 65.

Harris, L.J. 1978. "Sex Differences in Spatial Ability." In M. Kinsbourne, ed. *Asymmetrical Function of the Brain*. Cambridge: Cambridge University Press.

Hartlage, L.C. 1970. "Sex-linked Inheritance of Spatial Ability." *Perceptual and Motor Skills* 31:610.

Herman, D.O. 1968. "A Study of Sex Differences in the Wechsler Preschool and Primary Scale of Intelligence." *Proceedings of the 76th Annual Convention of the American Psychological Association* 3:455-456.

Hermann, K. 1959. *Reading Disability*. Copenhagen: Munksgaard.

Hilton, T.L., and Berglund, G.W. 1974. "Sex Differences in Mathematical Achievement: A Longitudinal Study." *Journal of Educational Research* 67:231-237.

Hull, F.M.; Mielke, P.W.; Timmons, R.J.; and Williford, J.A. 1971. "The National Speech and Hearing Survey: Preliminary Results." *ASHA* 3:501-509.

Husén, T. 1960. "Abilities of Twins." *Scandinavian Journal of Psychology* 1:125-135.

Husén, T., ed. 1967. *International Study of Achievement in Mathematics: A Comparison of Twelve Countries*. New York: Wiley.

Hyde, J.S.; Geiringer, E.R.; and Yen, W.M. 1975. "On the Empirical Relation between Spatial Ability and Sex Differences in Other Aspects of Cognitive Performance." *Multivariate Behavioral Research* 10:289-309.

Johnson, D.D. 1974. "Sex Differences in Reading across Cultures." *Reading Research Quarterly* 9:67-86.

Kagan, J. 1964. "The Child's Sex Role Classification of School Objects." *Child Development* 35:1051-1056.

———— . 1969. "On the Meaning of Behavior: Illustrations from the Infant." *Child Development* 40:1121-1134.

Klasen, E. 1972. *The Syndrome of Specific Dyslexia*. Baltimore: University Park Press.

Lerner, I.M., and Libby, W.J. 1976. *Heredity, Evolution, and Society*, 2d ed. San Francisco: Freeman.

Levitt, E.E. 1956. "The Water-Jar Einstellung Test as a Measure of Rigidity." *Psychological Bulletin* 53:347-370.

Lewis, M. 1972. "Parents and Children: Sex-Role Development." *School Review* 80:229-240.

Lewontin, R.C. 1975. "Genetic Aspects of Intelligence." *Annual Review of Genetics* 9:387-405.

Lindsey, J.M. 1967. "The Factorial Organization of Intelligence in Children as Related to the Variables of Age, Sex, and Subculture." *Dissertation Abstracts* 27 (10-B):3664-3665.

Luchins, A.S. 1942. "Mechanization in Problem Solving: The Effect of Einstellung." *Psychological Monographs* 54 (6, whole no. 248).

Maccoby, E.E. 1966. "Sex Differences in Intellectual Functioning." In E.E. Maccoby, ed. *The Development of Sex Differences*. Stanford, Calif.: Stanford University Press.

Maccoby, E.E., and Jacklin, C.N. 1974. *The Psychology of Sex Differences*. Stanford, Calif.: Stanford University Press.

Masica, D.N.; Money, J.; Ehrhardt, A.A.; and Lewis, V.G. 1969. "IQ, Fetal Sex Hormones, and Cognitive Patterns: Studies in the Testicular Feminizing Syndrome of Androgenic Insensitivity." *Johns Hopkins Medical Journal* 124:34-43.

Matheny, A.P., and Dolan, A.B. 1974. "A Twin Study of Genetic Influences in Reading Achievement." *Journal of Learning Disability* 7:99-102.

Mazurkiewicz, A.J. 1960. "Social-Cultural Influences and Reading." *Journal of Developmental Reading* 3:254-263.

McAskie, M., and Clarke, A.M. 1976. "Parent-Offspring Resemblances in Intelligence: Theories and Evidence." *British Journal of Psychology* 67:243-273.

McCall, J.R. 1955. *Sex Differences in Intelligence: A Comparative Factor Study*. Washington, D.C.: Catholic University Press.

McCarthy, D.A. 1930. *The Language Development of the Preschool Child*. Minneapolis: University of Minnesota Press.

McGuinness, D. 1975. "The Impact of Innate Perceptual Differences between the Sexes on the Socializing Process." *Educational Review* 27:229-239.

Mead, M. 1958. "The Childhood Genesis of Sex Differences in Behavior." in J.M. Tanner and B. Inhelder, eds. *Discussions on Child Development*. New York: International Universities Press.

Mendelsohn, G.A., and Covington, M.V. 1972. "Internal Processes and Perceptual Factors in Verbal Problem Solving: A Study of Sex and Individual Differences in Cognition." *Journal of Personality* 40:451-471.

Metzler, J., and Shepard, R.N. 1974. "Rotation of Tri-dimensional Objects." In R.L. Solso, ed. *Theories in Cognitive Psychology: The Loyola Symposium*. New York: Wiley.

Michael, W.B.; Guilford, J.P.; Fruchter, B.; and Zimmerman, W.S. 1957. "The Description of Spatial-Visualization Abilities." *Educational and Psychological Measurement* 17:185-199.

Money, J. 1963. "Cytogenetic and Psychosexual Incongruities with a Note on Space-Form Blindness." *American Journal of Psychiatry* 119:820-827.

Money, J., and Alexander, D. 1966. "Turner's Syndrome: Further Demonstration of the Presence of Specific Cognitional Deficits." *Journal of Medical Genetics* 3:47-48.

Money, J., and Ehrhardt, A.A. 1972. *Man and Woman, Boy and Girl*. Baltimore: Johns Hopkins University Press.

Moss, H.A. 1967. "Sex, Age, and State as Determinants of Mother-Infant Interaction." *Merrill-Palmer Quarterly* 13:19-36.

Munroe, R.L., and Munroe, R.H. 1971. "Effect of Environmental Experience on Spatial Ability in an East African Society." *Journal of Social Psychology* 83:15-22.

Munsinger, H., and Douglass, A. 1976. "The Syntactic Abilities of Identical Twins, Fraternal Twins, and Their Siblings." *Child Development* 47:40-50.

Nichols, R.C. 1969. "The Inheritance of General and Specific Ability." In M. Manosevitz, G. Lindze, and D.D. Thiessen, eds. *Behavioral Genetics: Method and Research*. New York: Appleton-Century-Crofts.

O'Connor, J. 1943. *Structural Visualization*. Boston: Human Engineering Laboratory.

Osborne, R.T., and Gregory, A.J. 1966. "The Heritability of Visualization, Perceptual Speed, and Spatial Orientation." *Perceptual and Motor Skill* 23:379-390.

Peckham, C.S. 1973. "Speech Defects in a National Sample of Children Aged Seven Years." *British Journal of Disorders of Communication* 8:2-8.

Petersen, A.C. 1976. "Physical Androgyny and Cognitive Functioning in Adolescence." *Developmental Psychology* 12:524-533.

Piaget, J., and Inhelder, B. 1956. *The Child's Conception of Space*. London: Kegan Paul.

Porteus, S.D. 1965. *Porteus Maze Test: 50 Years' Application*. Palo Alto, Calif.: Pacific Books.

Preston, R.C. 1962. "Reading Achievement of German and American Children." *School and Society* 90:350-354.

Rebelsky, F. 1964. "Adult Perception of the Horizontal." *Perceptual and Motor Skill* 19:371-374.

Roberts, J., and Duvan, K.R. 1972. "Binocular Visual Acuity of Children: Demographic and Socioeconomic Characteristics." *Vital and Health Statistics*. Series 11, no. 112.

Saarni, C.I. 1973. "Piagetian Operations and Field Independence as Factors in Children's Problem-solving Performance." *Child Development* 44:338-345.

Sandström, C.I. 1953. "Sex Differences in Localization and Orientation." *Acta Psychologica* 9:82-96.

Satterly, D.J. 1976. "Cognitive Styles, Spatial Ability, and School Achievement." *Journal of Educational Psychology* 68:36-42.

Scarr, S. 1969. "Environmental Bias in Twin Studies." In M. Manosevitz, G. Lindzey, and D.D. Thiessen, eds. *Behavioral Genetics: Method and Research*. New York: Appleton-Century-Crofts.

Shepard, R.N., and Metzler, J. 1971. "Mental Rotation of Three-dimensional Objects." *Science* 171:701-703.

Sherman, J.A. 1967. "Problem of Sex Differences in Space Perception and Aspects of Intellectual Functioning." *Psychological Review* 74:290-299.

———. 1974. "Field Articulation, Sex, Spatial Visualization, Dependency, Practice, Laterality of the Brain, and Birth Order." *Perceptual and Motor Skill* 38:223-225.

Skodak, M., and Skeels, H.M. 1949. "A Final Follow-up Study of 100 Adopted Children." *Journal of Genetic Psychology* 75:85-125.

Sladen, B. 1970. "Inheritance of Dyslexia." *Bulletin of the Orton Society* 20:30-40.

Smedslund, J. 1963. "The Effect of Observation on Children's Representation of the Spatial Orientation of a Water Surface." *Journal of Genetic Psychology* 102:195-201.

Smith, I.M. 1948. "Measurement of Spatial Ability in School Pupils." *Occupational Psychology* 22:150-159.

———. 1964. *Spatial Ability: Its Educational and Social Significance.* London: University of London Press.

Stafford, R.E. 1961. "Sex Differences in Spatial Visualization as Evidence of Sex-linked Inheritance." *Perceptual and Motor Skill* 13:428.

Stafford, R. 1972. "Hereditary and Environmental Components of Quantitative Reasoning." *Review of Educational Research* 42:183-201.

Symmes, J.S., and Rapoport, J.L. 1972. "Unexpected Reading Failure." *American Journal of Orthopsychiatry* 42:82-91.

Thoman, E.; Leiderman, P.; and Olson, J. 1972. "Neonate-Mother Interaction during Breast-feeding." *Developmental Psychology* 6:110-118.

Thomas, H., and Jamison, W. 1975. "On the Acquisition of Understanding That Still Water Is Horizontal." *Merrill-Palmer Quarterly* 21:31-44.

Thomas, H.; Jamison, W.; and Hummel, D.D. 1973. "Observation Is Insufficient for Discovering That the Surface of Still Water Is Invariantly Horizontal." *Science* 181:173-174.

Thompson, G.B. 1975. "Sex Differences in Reading Attainments." *Educational Research* 18:16-23.

Thurstone, L.L. 1938. "Primary Mental Abilities." *Psychometric Monographs*, no. 1.

———. 1944. "A Factorial Study of Perception." *Psychometric Monographs*, no. 4.

Vandenberg, S.G. 1969. "A Twin Study of Spatial Ability." *Multivariate Behavioral Research* 4:273-294.

———. 1976. "Twin Studies." In A.R. Kaplan, ed. *Human Behavior Genetics.* Springfield, Ill.: Charles C Thomas.

Vandenberg, S.G., and Johnson, R.C. 1968. "Further Evidence on the Relation between Age of Separation and Similarity in IQ among Pairs of Separated Identical Twins." In S.G. Vandenberg, ed. *Progress in Human Behavior Genetics*. Baltimore: Johns Hopkins University Press.

Vernon, P.E. 1972. "The Distinctiveness of Field Independence." *Journal of Personality* 40:366-391.

Very, P.S. 1967. "Differential Factor Structures in Mathematical Ability." *Genetic Psychology Monographs* 75:169-207.

Wechsler, D. 1955. *Manual for the Wechsler Adult Intelligence Scale*. New York: Psychological Corporation.

Werdelin, I. 1961. *Geometrical Ability and the Space Factors in Boys and Girls*. Lund, Sweden: CWK Gleerup.

Willemsen, E., and Reynolds, B. 1973. "Sex Differences in Adults' Judgments of the Horizontal." *Developmental Psychology* 8:309.

Wilson, J.R.; DeFries, J.C.; McClearn, G.E.; Vandenberg, S.G.; Johnson, R.C.; and Rashad, M.N. 1975. "Cognitive Abilities: Use of Family Data as a Control to Assess Sex and Age Differences in Two Ethnic Groups." *International Journal of Aging and Human Development* 6:261-276.

Witkin, H.A.; Dyk, R.B.; Faterson, H.F.; Goodenough, D.R.; and Karp, S.A. 1962. *Psychological Differentiation*. New York: Wiley.

Witkin, H.A.; Lewis, H.B.; Hertzman, M.; Machover, K.; Meissner, P.B.; and Wapner, S. 1954. *Personality through Perception: An Experimental and Clinical Study*. New York: Harper.

Wolf, S.M. 1973. "Difficulties in Right-Left Discrimination in a Normal Population." *Archives of Neurology* 29:128-129.

Wolf, V.C. 1969. "A Study of the Embedded Figures Test in Relation to Sex Differences and Some Primary Mental Abilities." Doctoral dissertation, University of Chicago, Department of Education.

Yen, W.M. 1975. "Sex-linked Major Gene Influences on Selected Types of Spatial Performance." *Behavior Genetics* 5:281-298.

4

Cerebral Asymmetry

A biological chain of causality has at least three links: chromosomal, hormonal, and neural. We know that the male and female hormones act early to modify physical growth in characteristic ways. The central nervous system is hardly immune to such influences. Therefore, if men and women typically differ in certain intellectual traits, it may well be due in part to subtle differences in structure between male and female brains. The question arises whether this argument applies to the traits discussed in chapter 3: verbal and spatial aptitudes, perhaps variants of cognitive style.

Specialized Hemispheres

Over the last twenty years or so, increasing attention has been paid to signs of a division of labor between the hemispheres of the human cerebral cortex (Milner 1971). Since Broca's epochal discoveries over a century ago, it had been known that with few exceptions the left hemisphere was in charge of both sending and receiving verbal messages. If brain damage impaired either of these functions, as in aphasia, the lesion was almost invariably found somewhere in the left hemisphere. As a result, the left brain was labeled major, or dominant, and held responsible for most of an individual's intentional activities.

At first the minor (or silent) hemisphere was given no distinctive character, aside from relaying sensory and motor impulses to and from its busy counterpart. But this picture changed in our own century as more and more cases were reported in which spatial deficiencies—in getting dressed, reading a map, tracing a maze—accompanied lesions in the minor (usually right) hemisphere (Hécaen 1962).

These reports were followed by a flood of experiments with normal subjects. A few will serve as examples. In dichotic listening, a favorite method, different sounds are presented simultaneously, one to each ear, and the subject reports all he hears. The right ear, serving primarily the opposite hemisphere, is consistently more accurate when the stimuli are digits (Kimura 1967) but trails the left ear when they are melodies or "environmental" sounds (Knox & Kimura 1970).

Parallel results are found for vision. Each hemisphere receives impressions from the opposite half of the visual field. Of nonsense words flashed briefly from one side or the other, more are correctly recognized from the right visual field than from the left; but for sloping lines the results are reversed (Fontenot & Benton 1972). If the off-center target is a matrix of letters, subjects identify them better on the right but *locate* them better on the left (Robertshaw & Sheldon 1976).

But the spark that kindled the most excitement came from the work of Sperry and others on "split brains" (Gazzaniga 1970). The hemispheres are connected by commissures, large bundles of nerve fibers running in both directions with no other apparent function. These tracts enable the hemispheres to work together as a unit, or better perhaps as a well-practiced dance team. But in so doing they make it extremely difficult to discover what each partner contributes to the final performance. If only that bridge of fibers could be severed, allowing each half to react independently of the other!

This operation, first used experimentally with monkeys and later to control epileptic seizures in humans, has fulfilled its promise (Nebes 1974). The results in daily living are not dramatic; in fact they are hardly noticeable. But in carefully devised experiments they are indeed remarkable (Sperry 1972). In a typical experiment the split-brained subject sits facing a screen with his left hand hidden and holding a pencil. While he stares straight ahead two geometrical forms appear for a fraction of a second: a square on the left of the fixation point, a triangle on the right. The subject is asked to draw what he has just seen; he draws a square. Asked what he is drawing, he says, "a triangle."

In a still more mystifying experiment (Levy et al. 1972) commissurotomized patients were briefly shown a picture of a composite face; that is, the right half of one face joined at the midline with the left half of a different face. (In this situation each hemisphere "sees" a single, complete face.) Asked to point out the face in a "rogues' gallery" of pictures, subjects selected the one of which half had been projected to the right hemisphere. Asked to name or describe the face, they indicated the other half. As we might expect, split-brained subjects found it unusually difficult to associate names with faces.

These and other findings support the idea that the major (usually left) hemisphere is specialized to deal with words and their meanings, the minor one for dealing with spatial relations. Not all researchers are satisfied with this interpretation. But before looking more closely we need some assurance that we are on the track of a possible sex difference. Do males and females differ in hemispheric specialization, and if so, how?

A Possible Sex Difference

Earlier we found reason to suspect that males are superior in spatial skills, while females excel in verbal fluency. Now it appears that the hemispheres have evolved toward a division of labor between verbal and spatial functions. It would not be surprising therefore to find that men and women differ in cerebral asymmetry; that is, the relative specialization of the hemispheres. There is evidence that they do, but not enough to say just how. As Marshall (1973) pointed out, the facts left room for two opposing theories of lateralization in male and female brains.

Two Theories. Both theories make use of the probable, but by no means perfect, relationship between the left-side control of language and the predominance of right-handedness in the population. True, in almost all dextrals, making up about 90 percent of people, the left hemisphere is in charge of speech as well as manual skill. But among the other 10 percent, the sinistrals and ambidextrals, this is true of only 55 to 65 percent; the rest are right-dominant or bilateral for speech (Milner et al. 1964; Levy 1974). The evidence is fairly impressive, drawn from the same sorts of clinical and experimental studies cited above, that control of language is less one-sided, or lateralized, in left-handed than right-handed persons.

Returning to our theories, we find Buffery and Gray (1972) taking the position that linguistic skills are heightened if the "control tower" is located in the dominant hemisphere. Spatial skills, on the other hand, are held to profit from broad, bilateral representation. Female rhetoric and male orientation can be at least partly explained by showing that the female brain is more strongly lateralized both for speech and spatiality than the male.

Here is where handedness enters the picture. Some surveys (Oldfield 1971) have shown that more men than women are left-handed, implying that men's hemispheres are also less differentiated and thus supporting the Buffery-Gray hypothesis. Other surveys, however, have found little if any difference in hand preference between the sexes (Annett 1967; Briggs & Nebes 1975; Falek 1959).

Now let us consider the rival theory. Its author, Jere Levy, working on split-brain experiments with Sperry, had acquired a healthy respect for the potentialities of the mute hemisphere. She assumed that hemispheric specialization had evolved and was biologically adaptive. The advantage, as she saw it, was to reduce competition between the reception of speech and the perception of the environment (Levy 1969). Like Buffery and Gray, she found indirect support for her thesis in results on handedness. Since sinistrals are supposed to be less lateralized than dextrals (and therefore more subject to interference between verbal and nonverbal inputs) they might be expected to show some deficit in tests of mental aptitudes. Comparing left-handed with right-handed male students on the Wechsler scale, she found the left-handers slightly higher on the verbal tests but markedly inferior on the performance tests ($p < .0002$). Presumably their right hemispheres were to some degree "wired for speech" and therefore less free to handle nonverbal problems. If we made the same assumption about females, Levy suggested, we could explain women's inferiority to men in spatial tests. (The left-handers' deficiency is still not proved. James et al. [1967] and Miller [1971] agreed with Levy's finding, but one large-scale study by Newcombe and Radcliffe [1973] found no difference in Wechsler performance scores between dextrals and sinistrals.)

Some Evidence and a Box Score. How have these contending theories fared under more direct experimental tests? The pertinent question here is how sharply verbal and spatial functions are lateralized. Are the hemispheres more specialized, that is, the left for language and the right for space, in females, as Buffery and Gray would claim, or in males, as Levy argues? It must be admitted that both theories can muster noteworthy support.

Consider, for example, experiments using subjects' right and left hands to compare the opposite, that is, controlling, hemispheres. Buffery (1971) had dextral children close their eyes and draw a square with one hand while drawing a circle with the other. Girls, more than boys, drew better squares with their left hands than with their right, contrary to what Levy might have predicted.

On the sensory side indications are otherwise. In one experiment Witelson (1976) tested dextral children for visual recognition of meaningless shapes after feeling them with either the right or left hand. Girls did equally well with either hand, but boys scored higher with the left; that is, hemispheric asymmetry seemed greater in the male. When Flanery and Balling (1979) did an essentially similar experiment substituting tactual for visual recognition, the same sex difference in asymmetry showed up, but only among adult subjects.

The Braille system for blind readers raises an arresting question. Braille letters are patterns of raised points read by feeling them with the index finger. Since these letters make words they should be more readily learned by the left hemisphere, but since they are also tactile forms they might be easier for the right one. Which is the case, and is it the same for both sexes?

When sighted dextrals, 7 to 14 years old, were taught Braille letters by touch alone (Rudel et al. 1974), the younger ones learned faster with their right hands and the older with their left, in both sexes. Does this mean that the right hemisphere matures more slowly than the left? Perhaps, but in any case it is interesting that the shift occurred earlier and more decidedly in boys than in girls.

Hemispheric rivalry in hearing and vision has attracted more attention than in touch, but with no increase in consistency of result. Among studies of dichotic listening we find two that appear quite comparable. Each one used about 150 undergraduate subjects equally divided by sex and handedness. The only obvious difference in procedure was that Lake and Bryden (1976) used consonant-vowel syllables as stimuli, while McKeever and Van Deventer (1977*b*) used digits. The former experiment found a stronger right-ear advantage in males than females ($p < .05$); in the latter whatever slight difference there was favored the females.

Turning to work on vision, we find two related studies that merit a more detailed description.

1. Hannay's (1976) experiment, with thirty male and thirty female undergraduates as subjects, had to do with the recognition of visual form. A nonsense shape was flashed briefly in the subject's right or left visual field. Ten seconds later a similar form was presented for the subject to look at directly and signal same or different. Besides this task all subjects took a test of spatial ability, the Wechsler Block Design Test.

About half of the women scored higher when the shape was seen by the right hemisphere, the other half when seen by the left. On the Block Design Test the former, right-hemisphere group was unquestionably superior to the latter, left-hemisphere one ($p < .001$). For the men as a whole the left hemisphere was better at form recognition than the right ($p < .05$). There was no relation between scores on that task and the Wechsler test.

These results present a problem. The women's data fit Buffery and Gray's idea of female specialization quite nicely. But the men's suggest a kind of reverse specialization, with the speech hemisphere taking the lead in dealing with visual space. Some light is shed when we learn that the shapes used were quite simple, with an averge association value of 39 percent; that is, 39 percent of observers were reminded of something. It seems likely that many subjects resorted to verbal associations to bridge the ten-second interval between shapes. Perhaps more men than women were able to do so. The missing piece of the puzzle is what the subjects were doing during those ten seconds.

2. Metzger and Antes (1976) took steps to supply the missing piece. Their method was to measure the difference between the hemispheres in speed of response to visual stimuli. Their subjects, male and female college students, were shown a pair of words followed a few seconds later by a single word flashed to left or right of the fixation point. The subjects had to indicate whether the single word was one of the preceding pair or not. Half of the subjects were advised to rehearse the paired words throughout the interval; the other half were advised to hold in mind a picture of the words. The only significant sex difference was in the effects of the two instructions on reaction time: the females reacted faster when advised to rehearse; the males, when advised to visualize.

In a second experiment, instead of recognizing the words themselves subjects had to recognize drawings of the objects named, when these were flashed to either hemisphere. Accordingly, the visualizing instruction advised the subject to form a mental picture of the object. In this case instructions to rehearse produced faster reactions by way of the left hemisphere;

instructions to visualize shifted the advantage to the right. They failed to produce a significant sex difference (there were only five subjects of each sex). But the women were plainly more affected than the men: their right-hemisphere responses were especially retarded by instructions to rehearse, as were their left-hemisphere responses by instructions to visualize. The trend favored Buffery and Gray.

Lest our examples create a false impression of the general trend of data, let us cite two more experiments comparing visual half-fields. In both cases the subjects, college men and women, had to recognize a stimulus flashed briefly to right or left of center and to press the correct button with all possible speed. In one (Rizzolatti & Buchtel 1977) the stimuli were photographs of faces. These produced faster responses when seen in the left visual field, and projected to the opposite hemisphere, than in the right visual field. The other experiment (Bradshaw et al. 1977) involved words and nonwords (*kirl, gote*). Here responses were faster to the right visual field than to the left. For our theories the important finding is that in both experiments the males were responsible for the difference between fields; in the females the hemispheres were virtually equipotential.

The experiments cited should give some idea of the hazards to be encountered in this field of inquiry. A survey by Harshman and Remington (1976) covered clinical, experimental, anatomical, and brain-wave data but was limited to verbal and visuospatial functions and adult subjects. Of the twenty-two reports included, six showed no sex difference, but sixteen found men more strongly lateralized than women. In a masterly discussion citing over 300 studies, Harris (1978) also defends Levy's position as the basis for a further elaboration of his own. Subject to future developments, the bulk of evidence suggests that women's hemispheres are probably more symmetrical than men's in the activities explored.

A more interesting question has to do with the inner core of Levy's theory. She holds that women's inferiority in dealing with visual space is due to competition between verbal and nonverbal processes within the same (right) hemisphere. From the clinic comes a bit of evidence (McGlone & Kertesz 1973) that Levy's assumption may be true. Patients with injuries to either the right or left hemisphere were given a battery of tests for aphasia and, for spatial ability, Wechsler's Block Design Test. In males damage to the right hemisphere impaired performance with the blocks. In females damage to the left hemisphere determined the degree of impairment in both kinds of test. The latter finding suggests that the female right hemisphere is able to process both verbal and nonverbal material. But the question is: how well can it do both jobs? Since the use of brain-damaged patients makes it hard to answer that question, the data fall short of a crucial test.

McGlone and Davidson (1973) designed a more conclusive experiment. Their ninety-nine subjects were high school and college students about equally divided between right-handed and left-handed males and females. Two tests of spatial ability were given and a dichotic listening test with words. The results confirmed Levy's prediction: females fell below males in spatial performance, and the lowest scores were made by females whose left ears (right hemispheres) were superior in dichotic listening.

But even this slender prop has not been left unshaken. McKeever and Van Deventer (1977a) replicated the McGlone-Davidson study with sixty male and seventy-one female college students. As before, females were inferior to males in mentally manipulating odd shapes, but this time it made no difference which ear heard more digits.

Dyslexia Revisited. As stated, Levy's hypothesis is one-sided: it says only that a verbal "blueprint" may efface a spatial one in the same hemisphere. The victim of this abrasive process is the verbal female who frequently confuses left with right. Inevitably the question arises: does hemispheric competition ever work the other way, with the spatial system encroaching on the free play of the verbal? Sandra Witelson (1977) claims that it does, and in this case at the expense of the male.

She bases her assertion on an intensive study of developmental dyslexia, the severe form of reading disability which afflicts many more boys than girls. Her experimental group consisted of eighty-five right-handed dyslexic boys between 6 and 14 years old. (There were also fifteen dyslexic girls, a typical ratio, but the results were too scant for inclusion.) She had a control group of 156 boys, right-handed normal readers in the same age range. To throw light on hemispheric handling of spatial relations, she tested recognition of objects after feeling them with either hand; in one test the objects were meaningless shapes, in another they were letters. To reveal linguistic dominance, she tested dichotic listening for digits. From the results Witelson inferred two cerebral factors in dyslexia: a bilateral arrangement for dealing with spatial relations, and impaired functioning of the linguistic center in the left hemisphere. It seems quite plausible that the first factor might be responsible for the second.

As to sex differences, even if we accept both Levy's and Witelson's interpretations, the basic question remains: in the integration of the hemispheres, why should disharmony be largely confined to the right hemisphere in females and the left hemisphere in males?

A Growth Factor? Longitudinal studies of the development of cerebral asymmetries of function might well yield clues to sex differences. Within the scope of this chapter we can hardly do better than call attention to Deborah Waber's (1976) stimulating work on rate of maturation. Waber's achievement was to see a connection between the widely suspected sex differences in verbal and spatial ability and the fact that females reach sexual maturity several years before males. She speculated that the hemispheres become lateralized for verbal and spatial functioning under the influence of the gonadal hormones, with the result that early maturation favors linguistic skill and late maturation, spatial. Hemispheric asymmetry, she conjectured, is promoted by late maturation.

To test these hypotheses Waber apportioned eighty subjects, from 10 to 16 years old, to eight groups so as to permit independent comparisons between girls and boys, early and late maturers, and younger and older children. All subjects took three verbal and three spatial tests, and a dichotic listening test for lateral bias in perceiving speech.

The results were trenchant, both in their agreements and disagreements with theory. First, as shown in figure 4-1, the early maturers of both sexes were better at verbal than spatial tasks, while for later maturers the reverse was true. But the difference scores in the figure do not tell the whole story; actually the early and late maturers were equal in verbal performance, the entire reversal being due to the spatial superiority of late over early maturers. Second (figure 4-2), the relative ear advantage in dichotic listening was larger for late than early maturers of both sexes, but only in the older subgroups; the younger ones were equal in asymmetry.

Third, sex differences in the verbal and spatial tasks were insignificant. At first glance this negative result would seem to render the whole project trivial. On second thought, however, it is just what would be expected if Waber's hypothesis was correct. Since the effect of sex was measured in groups equated for rate of maturation, a zero difference suggests that this factor may account for *all* the sex difference usually obtained. The truth is never so simple, but if Waber's finding is verified its importance is undeniable.

Cognitive Style and the Hemispheres. As already noted, some students of behavior are not content to assign control of speech to one hemisphere and matters of space to the other. Words and shapes, they hold, must be translated into processes more appropriate to neurophysiology. In other words, what distinguishes language, spoken or written, from spatial relationships in a way that might require different mechanisms for efficient handling?

A number of paired properties have been suggested for the left and right hemispheres, respectively: focal-diffuse (Semmes 1968), serial-parallel (Cohen, 1973), analytic-synthetic (Levy-Agresti & Sperry 1968). The dimension that emerges from these labels strongly resembles Witkin's concept of cognitive style, first described as varying between field independence and field dependence, later from analytic to global (Witkin et al. 1962).

Evidence from the clinic supports this view. Russo and Vignolo (1967) gave Gottschaldt's Embedded Figures, the test most frequently used to

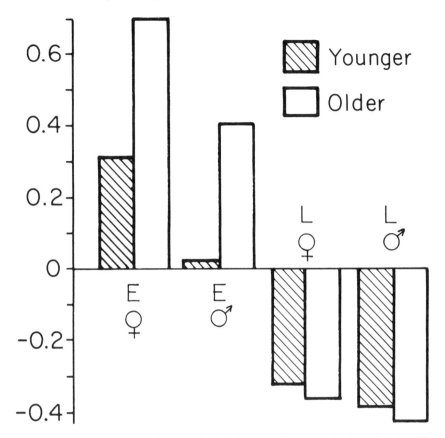

Figure 4-1. Mean values of differences between verbal and spatial scores for each grouping of sex (♀ ♂), maturation (Early, Late), and age level (Younger, Older). Positive values indicate that the verbal score is greater than the spatial score; negative values indicate the reverse.

measure field independence, to ninety-five patients with unilateral brain lesions and forty control subjects. The poorest performers were those with lesions in the left hemisphere who also suffered from aphasia; nonaphasics did no worse than the controls. Patients with right-hemisphere lesions were also impaired on the test, though not so severely as the aphasic group. The authors concluded that finding embedded figures depended, not on the speech mechanism itself, but on a discriminative ability essential to its use, together with a spatial factor.

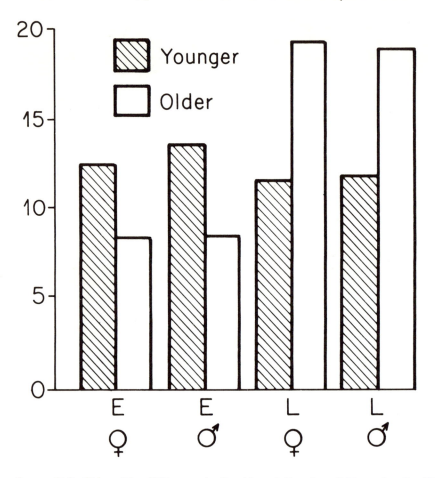

Source: D.P. Waber, "Sex Differences in Cognition: A Function of Maturation Rate?" *Science* 192 (1976):572-573. Copyright 1976 by the American Association for the Advancement of Science. Reproduced by permission.

Figure 4-2. Absolute values of mean percent ear advantage in dichotic listening scores for each grouping of sex, maturation, and age level.

Easier to interpret is some evidence supplied by Witkin's original measure, the Rod and Frame Test. Cohen et al. (1973) gave the test to female patients before and after a unilateral electroconvulsive shock treatment (ECT) for depression. Twelve patients were shocked in the left hemisphere, twelve in the right, and twelve received no shock. The results were remarkably clear-cut (figure 4-3). After treatment all left-shocked subjects made larger errors in adjusting the rod; all right-shocked subjects made more accurate adjustments; the controls changed little if at all.

With cognitive style in mind, we may infer that shock to the left hemisphere lowered the subject's ability to concentrate on the rod apart from the frame; in short, to analyze the complex. Right-hemisphere shock, on the other hand, presumably weakened the field; that is, it reduced the power of the frame to deflect the rod from the true vertical.

A Tentative Solution. Assuming a sex difference in cognitive style, we are finally ready for the question: what part, if any, does cerebral asymmetry play in producing it? No sooner do we ask the question than we find ourselves in trouble. As we have seen, the indications are that males tend to be more field independent or analytic, females more field dependent or global. Evidence just cited shows that field independence as tested relies more on the left hemisphere than the right. It follows that dominance of the left over the right hemisphere should be stronger in males than females, at least in tests of cognitive style. But this conclusion does not mesh easily with other findings we have noted. Females lead males in verbal skills, generally conceded to the left hemisphere, while male superiority is in spatial relationships, where the right hemisphere presides. How can these inconsistencies be reconciled?

First, we may provisionally agree with the bulk of evidence (Harshman & Remington 1976; Harris 1978). Cerebral asymmetry is more pronounced in males than females, in the sense that the male right hemisphere is normally more highly specialized for global, or integrative, perception. Essentially this is Levy's position. Second, it would be hard to doubt that both differentiation and integration, in varying amounts, are required by tests of cognitive style.

Third, following Levy, we assume that such tasks can be handled better if both cooperating hemispheres are highly specialized for their respective functions than if one is only partly specialized. Buffery and Gray (1972) suggested that males excelled in spatial affairs because both hemispheres were relatively free to cope with them. We think Buffery and Gray were correct in stressing the advantage of bilateral strategy, but not for the reason given.

Evidence bearing directly on this question is scarce indeed. We found one such experiment, making use of the electroencephalogram (EEG); that is, brain waves recorded at the surface of the cranium. Tucker (1976) compared EEGs from the right and left hemispheres of male and female undergraduates while taking three tests: (1) the Mooney Closure Faces Test (Mooney 1957), calling for integration of odd shapes into a face; (2) the Gottschaldt EFT, calling for perceptual analysis; and (3) a vocabulary test from the Wechsler scale.

The women showed a positive correlation between the Mooney and Gottschaldt tests that was hardly significant ($p < .10$) but reliably different from the negative trend of the men. As to the EEG, brain waves were more

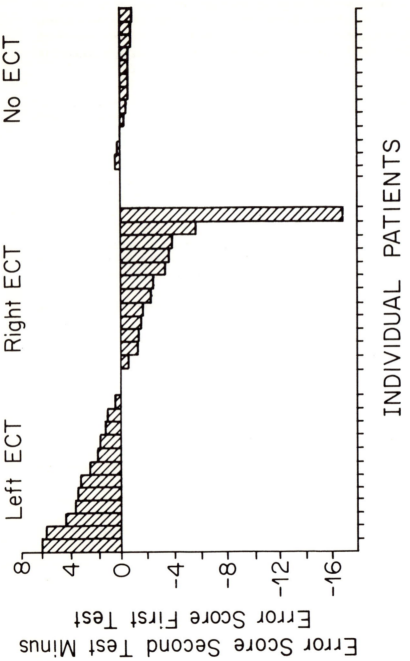

Figure 4-3. Individual changes in rod-and-frame error scores (degrees deviation from vertical) from first, or pre-ECT, to second, or post-ECT, tests. Increases in error are shown by positive scores and decreases by negative scores.

Source: B.D. Cohen, S. Berent, and A.J. Silverman, "Field-dependence and Lateralization of Function in the Human Brain," *Archives of General Psychiatry*, 28 (1973):165-167. Copyright 1973 by the American Medical Association. Reproduced by permission.

closely related to test performance in men than in women. While taking the Mooney test, men showed a significant correlation between relative right-hemisphere involvement and test scores. During the vocabulary test the corresponding correlation with left-hemisphere activity fell just short of significance. For women none of the correlations reached an acceptable level. As far as they go, Tucker's results are in keeping with Levy's hypothesis. They encourage us to believe that a difference in cerebral asymmetry may prove to be partly responsible for a sex difference in cognitive style.

References

Annett, M. 1967. "The Binomial Distribution of Right, Mixed, and Left Handedness." *Quarterly Journal of Experimental Psychology* 19:327-333.

Bradshaw, J.L.; Gates, A.; and Nettleton, N.C. 1977. "Bihemispheric Involvement in Lexical Decisions: Handedness and a Possible Sex Difference." *Neuropsychologia* 15:277-286.

Briggs, G.G., and Nebes, R.D. 1975. "Patterns of Hand Preference in a Student Population." *Cortex* 11:230-238.

Buffery, A.W.H. 1971. "Sex Differences in the Development of Hemispheric Asymmetry of Function in the Human Brain." *Brain Research* 31:364-365.

Buffery, A.W.H., and Gray, J.A. 1972. "Sex Differences in the Development of Spatial and Linguistic Skills." In C. Ounsted and D.C. Taylor, eds. *Gender Differences: Their Ontogeny and Significance*. Edinburgh: Churchill Livingstone.

Cohen, B.D.; Berent, S.; and Silverman, A.J. 1973. "Field-dependence and Lateralization of Function in the Human Brain." *Archives of General Psychiatry* 28:165-167.

Cohen, G. 1973. "Hemispheric Differences in Serial versus Parallel Processing." *Journal of Experimental Psychology* 97:349-356.

Falek, A. 1959. "Handedness: A Family Study." *American Journal of Human Genetics* 11:52-62.

Flanery, R.C., and Balling, J.D. 1979. "Developmental Changes in Hemispheric Specialization for Tactile Spatial Ability." *Developmental Psychology* 15:364-372.

Fontenot, D.J., and Benton, A.L. 1972. "Perception of Direction in the Right and Left Visual Fields." *Neuropsychologia* 10:447-452.

Gazzaniga, M.S. 1970. *The Bisected Brain*. New York: Appleton-Century-Crofts.

Hannay, H.J. 1976. "Real or Imagined Incomplete Lateralization of Function in Females?" *Perception and Psychophysics* 19:349-352.

Harris, L.J. 1978. "Sex Differences in Spatial Ability." In M. Kinsbourne, ed. *Asymmetrical Function of the Brain*. Cambridge: Cambridge University Press.

Harshman, R.A., and Remington, R. 1976. "Sex, Language, and the Brain: Part I. A Review of the Literature on Adult Sex Differences in Lateralization." *UCLA Working Papers in Phonetics 31*, March.

Hécaen, H. 1962. "Clinical Symptomatology: Right and Left Hemispheric Lesions." In V.B. Mountcastle, ed. *Interhemispheric Relations and Cerebral Dominance*. Baltimore: Johns Hopkins University Press.

James, W.E.; Mefferd, R.B., Jr.; and Wieland, B. 1967. "Repetitive Psychometric Measures: Handedness and Performance." *Perceptual and Motor Skills* 25:209-212.

Kimura, D. 1967. "Functional Asymmetry of the Brain in Dichotic Listening." *Cortex* 3:163-178.

Knox, C., and Kimura, D. 1970. "Cerebral Processing of Nonverbal Sounds in Boys and Girls." *Neuropsychologia* 8:227-237.

Lake, D.A., and Bryden, M.P. 1976. "Handedness and Sex Differences in Hemispheric Asymmetry." *Brain and Language* 3:266-282.

Levy, J. 1969. "Possible Basis for the Evolution of Lateral Specialization of the Human Brain." *Nature* 224:614-615.

———. 1974. "Psychobiological Implications of Bilateral Asymmetry." In S.J. Dimond and J.B. Beaumont, eds. *Hemisphere Function in the Human Brain*. London: Paul Elek.

Levy, J.; Trevarthen, C.; and Sperry, R.W. 1972. "Perception of Bilateral Chimeric Figures Following Hemispheric Deconnexion." *Brain* 95:61-78.

Levy-Agresti, J., and Sperry, R.W. 1968. "Differential Perceptual Capacities in Major and Minor Hemispheres." *Proceedings of the National Academy of Sciences* 61:1151.

Marshall, J.C. 1973. "Some Problems and Paradoxes Associated with Recent Accounts of Hemispheric Specialization." *Neuropsychologia* 11:463-470.

McGlone, J., and Davidson, W. 1973. "The Relation between Cerebral Speech Laterality and Spatial Ability with Special Reference to Sex and Hand Preference." *Neuropsychologia* 11:105-113.

McGlone, J., and Kertesz, A. 1973. "Sex Differences in Cerebral Processing of Visuospatial Tasks." *Cortex* 9:313-320.

McKeever, W.F., and Van Deventer, A.D. 1977a. "Failure to Confirm a Spatial Ability Impairment in Persons with Evidence of Right Hemisphere Speech Capability." *Cortex* 13:321-326.

_____ . 1977*b*. "Visual and Auditory Language Processing Asymmetries: Influences of Handedness, Family Sinistrality, and Sex." *Cortex* 13:225-241.

Metzger, R.L., and Antes, J.R. 1976. "Sex and Coding Strategy Effects on Reaction Time to Hemispheric Probes." *Memory and Cognition* 4:167-171.

Miller, E. 1971. "Handedness and the Pattern of Human Ability." *British Journal of Psychology* 62:111-112.

Milner, B. 1971. "Interhemispheric Differences in the Localization of Psychological Processes in Man." *British Medical Bulletin* 27:272-277.

Milner, B.; Branch, C.; and Rasmussen, J. 1964. "Observations on Cerebral Dominance." In A.V.S. DeRueck and M. O'Connor, eds. *Disorders of Language*. London: Churchill.

Mooney, C.M. 1957. "Age in the Development of Closure Ability in Children." *Canadian Journal of Psychology* 11:219-226.

Nebes, R.D. 1974. "Hemispheric Specialization in Commissurotomized Man." *Psychological Bulletin* 81:1-14.

Newcombe, F., and Radcliffe, G. 1973. "Handedness, Speech Lateralization, and Spatial Ability." *Neuropsychologia* 11:399-407.

Oldfield, R.C. 1971. "The Assessment and Analysis of Handedness: The Edinburgh Inventory." *Neuropsychologia* 9:97-113.

Rizzolatti, G., and Buchtel, H.A. 1977. "Hemispheric Superiority in Reaction Time to Faces: A Sex Difference." *Cortex* 13:300-305.

Robertshaw, S., and Sheldon, M. 1976. "Laterality Effects in Judgment of the Identity and Position of Letters: A Signal Detection Analysis." *Quarterly Journal of Experimental Psychology* 28:115-121.

Rudel, R.G.; Denckla, M.B.; and Spalten, E. 1974. "The Functional Asymmetry of Braille Letter Learning in Normal Sighted Children." *Neurology* 24:733-738.

Russo, M., and Vignolo, L.A. 1967. "Visual Figure-ground Discrimination in Patients with Unilateral Cerebral Disease." *Cortex* 3:113-127.

Semmes, J. 1968. "Hemispheric Specialization: A Possible Clue to Mechanism." *Neuropsychologia* 6:11-26.

Sperry, R.W. 1972. "Mental Unity Following Surgical Disconnection of the Cerebral Hemispheres." In S.L. Washburn and P. Dolhinow, eds. *Perspectives on Human Evolution 2*. New York: Holt, Rinehart, & Winston.

Tucker, D.M. 1976. "Sex Differences in Hemispheric Specialization for Synthetic Visuospatial Functions." *Neuropsychologia* 14:447-454.

Waber, D.P. 1976. "Sex Differences in Cognition: A Function of Maturation Rate?" *Science* 192:572-573.

Witelson, S.F. 1976. "Sex and the Single Hemisphere: Specialization of the Right Hemisphere for Spatial Processing." *Science* 193:425-427.

_____ . 1977. "Developmental Dyslexia: Two Right Hemispheres and None Left." *Science* 195:309-311.

Witkin, H.A.; Dyk, R.B.; Faterson, H.F.; Goodenough, D.R.; and Karp, S.A. 1962. *Psychological Differentiation*. New York: Wiley.

5 Masculinity and Femininity

Theoretical Approaches

So far we have focused on intellectual differences between the sexes. When we ask how men and women differ in dynamics, we are likely to think first of certain temperamental qualities loosely lumped together as masculine and feminine. This tendency provides a natural frame of reference for extending our inquiry into the realm of personality.

The belief that sex differences go beyond the requirements of reproduction can be traced to earliest times. As Bakan (1966) reminds us, nature worship recognized male and female principles. In the divine partnership of heaven and earth, heaven was almost invariably personified as male, earth as female (though in ancient Egypt the relationship was reversed). In a school of Chinese philosophy Yin was the feminine passive, negative principle; Yang the masculine, active, positive principle. Interestingly, the Hindu school of Shakti, teaching transcendence through repose, made the female principle active and creative, the male principle quiescent.

In our own time attempts are still made to capture the essence of a masculine-feminine dichotomy. The well-known sociologist Talcott Parsons finds it in the sex roles of the typical family (Parsons & Bales 1955). The father's function is instrumental, maintaining favorable relations with the outer world. The mother takes care of the inner harmony of the group, strengthening bonds of affection among its members; hers is the expressive role.

Bakan proposes a more far-reaching duality, agency and communion, infusing all levels of life from the single cell to human society. Agency stands for the properties that make for self-preservation, separateness, mastery; communion, for oneness with others, contact, and cooperation. Their significance for us is that males are held to be more agentic, less communal than females. In developing his provocative thesis Bakan cites evidence from psychological tests, statistics on mortality (more males than females commit suicide), and human sexuality (for women, but not men, according to Kinsey, love is more important than sex). As a bonus, anyone looking for a defense of marriage can find plenty of ammunition here.

Freud's theorizing has led to related views. David Gutmann (1965) formulated his around the concept of ego strength. He held that the male and female egos were not strictly comparable; they could be equally strong but each in its own way. When Gutmann asked adults of 40 to 70 years to interpret pictures, they revealed a characteristic difference between the sexes. The men looked at the pictures objectively, as puzzles to be solved; the women responded emotionally, as if they were personally concerned. But other measures indicated that the women's egos were not necessarily weaker. Gutmann concluded that the two sexes have learned to adapt to two distinct environments, or milieus. The male milieu he calls allocentric, that is, externally regulated, impersonal, unpredictable. To survive in such a habitat calls for rationality and careful planning. The female milieu is autocentric. This means that it is largely composed of familiar persons in the same setting, so that adjustment depends mainly on sympathetic interaction with others.

The reader who mistrusts speculative theorizing may be reassured to learn that deductions form Bakan's and Gutmann's theories have been tested against empirical data, and strikingly confirmed (Carlson 1971). It will also be interesting to compare Gutmann's ideas with those of Erik Erikson, discussed in chapter 6. But now it is time to turn to the inductive explorations that account for most of what we know about the nature of masculinity (M) and femininity (F).

Measurement

Social Stereotypes

We do not have to rely on the educated guesses of scholars to reveal the nature of masculinity-femininity (M-F). All of us, in the course of growing up, have picked up a rough idea of how boys and girls, men and women are expected to behave in our society. We learn these guidelines partly through personal observation, partly by being told; and it is generally agreed that they exert a powerful impact in shaping our development. The picture they provide should therefore prove quite useful.

But first, do sexual stereotypes actually exist? That is, do most people agree on the traits, aside from sexuality itself, that distinguish women from men? Sherriffs and Jarrett (1953) had about 350 males and 500 female college students check fifty-eight items as more characteristic of men or women (for example, more likely to hold a grudge, or most faithful in marriage). Although the authors had included twenty-four doubtful items, all but a few were agreed upon by both male and female subjects. (The sexes disagreed on whether men or women are more creative, fearful of pain, insightful, poor at losing, and stubborn.) On another occasion 390 of the subjects rated the items for social value: the sexes differed significantly in their ratings on only two out of fifty-eight. Interestingly, the women consistently assigned more extreme values, positive or negative, than the men.

Granting the prevalence of stereotypes, we need to describe them. To this end Sherriffs and McKee (1957) gave fifty male and fifty female undergraduates a list of 200 adjectives with instructions to go through it twice, once checking those that were true of men in general, then checking for women in general. They were not obliged to check every adjective.

It will suffice to consider only those terms yielding significant sex differences agreed on by subjects of both sexes. Men in general emerge as easygoing and frank, steady and rational, bold and assertive, with the faults that come of carrying these virtues to excess; that is, they are also boastful, hardheaded, and reckless. Women in general are described as tactful, affectionate, and sensitive, but on the debit side as submissive, touchy, and highstrung.

It may occur to the reader that these portraits are limited by the adjectives that happen to be included in the list. With this objection in mind the authors tried an open-end procedure: they asked other students to list ten traits characteristic of each sex. After sorting more than 1,400 suggestions into twenty-six categories, they found only two new trait clusters—aside from physical attributes—not provided by the checklist. Both were assigned predominantly to women: oriented to home and hearth, and talkative (talks too much, chatterers, or senseless prattle).

At this point it might appear that M and F are fairly simple concepts, generally thought to consist of a few traits, some more prevalent in men, others in women. But when researchers tried to measure these attributes more precisely, they ran into difficulties. Early workers seemed to assume that M and F were at opposite poles of a continuum, such that an increment of M implied a decrement of F, and vice versa. Later it was recognized that this bipolar hypothesis conflicted with an equally likely one: that an individual might be masculine in some respects and feminine in others (Constantinople 1973).

An inquiry by Jenkin and Vroegh (1969) posed a direct challenge. They had twenty-five men and twenty-five women check adjectives to describe six different versions of M-F: most males, most females, the most masculine person and the most feminine person imaginable, and the least masculine and least feminine person imaginable.

The results were provocative. "Most males" were described as usual (active, competitive, ambitious) and so were "most females" (sociable, gentle, motherly). But the crucial comparison is between the terms chosen for "least M" and "most F," and vice versa. "Most masculine imaginable" brought out such words as strong, confident, athletic, humane. "Most feminine imaginable" evoked charming, gracious, thoughtful, along with many others. Surprisingly, quite a few terms were checked for both concepts; for example, affectionate and emotionally stable (though affectionate ranked 1st for "most feminine" and 42d for "most masculine," while emotionally stable ranked 23d and 2d, respectively). At the opposite extreme there was less overlapping. "Least masculine" elicited terms like weak, cowardly, immature, and indecisive, while "least feminine" prompted arrogant, crude, and hard. Clearly the concepts "most masculine" and "least feminine" bore little resemblance to each other, and the contrast between "least masculine" and "most feminine" was equally sharp. These impressions were borne out by significant negative correlations between the paired concepts.

Jenkin and Vroegh's results lend no support to the bipolarity hypothesis. The authors concluded that masculine and feminine traits vary along separate dimensions related by a common gradient of social desirability: "most masculine" and "most feminine" seem to be good concepts; "least masculine" and "least feminine" seem bad. It would seem that the subjects were biased against feminine ("least masculine") men and masculine ("least feminine") women.

Such findings suggest the need for a different conception of how M and F are related. In our view M-F designates a set of traits (yet to be specified) that distinguish males from females in the population but vary independently within the same person. Each trait may be a bipolar continuum, such as bold-timid, stingy-generous, or truthful-deceitful. Or it may be unipolar in the sense that the continuum lies between an extreme degree of the trait and its absence; for example, very competitive-not at all competitive, very emotional-not at all emotional. In either case males and females could distribute themselves along the intervening axis in varying admixtures of timidity and boldness or intensity of aggressiveness, so that the two distributions would overlap, perhaps only a little and perhaps a lot. We should still have to decide how sharply the sexes must be divided for the trait to qualify as a component of M-F. To test this hypothesis, however, requires more refined methods than checking a list of adjectives.

Self-descriptions

As a measure of M-F, a profile of the social stereotype, male or female, is admittedly unsatisfactory. It depicts, not how the sexes behave but how they are popularly supposed to behave. Any normal person past early childhood probably knows more about himself than anyone else does. Granting that such subjects are willing to cooperate, we can expect them to provide more accurate information about themselves than about the so-called typical male or female. Let us see what more has been learned about M-F by asking children and adults of both sexes to describe their own responses.

Terman and Miles (1936) published the classical study in the field. Though they started with full awareness of the usual preconceptions, their method was strictly empirical. To construct their famous Attitude-Interest Analysis Test, they gathered a large number of paper-and-pencil minitasks, calling for associations to words and inkblots, for responses about the strength of emotional reactions and ethical attitudes, and about attraction or repulsion by sundry activities. These were tried out on many children and young adults, and only those items that clearly differentiated males from females were included in the final form.

The Terman-Miles test has been given to groups of all descriptions, and almost invariably the boys or men average closer to the masculine extreme than the girls or women. (One exception was a group of passive male homosexuals, whose mean score was more feminine than that of a group of female college athletes.) This bias does not mean that men and women are really as different as the test makes them appear, even in the areas it represents. Due to the way the items were selected they exaggerate whatever differences exist. For our purpose this property gives such scales their special value. They serve as detective devices, ferreting out differences that might otherwise escape notice. Each test thus provides its own definition of M-F. By examining the contents we may discover the nature of what is being measured.

To this end Terman and Miles made a careful study of the responses of 500 to 600 seventh-grade, high school junior, and college students to the 546 items of the test. One underlying dimension emerged along which the sexes tended to segregate. The authors gave it no name, but they described two aspects: one having to do with interests, the other with temperament. The males preferred outdoor exploits, scientific achievements, or business ventures. The females were drawn to domestic and esthetic activities and were more concerned with caring for the young and those in trouble. Temperamentally the males came through as bold, assertive, and thick-skinned; the females, as personally sympathetic, timid, and sensitive. If the authors had sought a name for their M-F dimension, they might have done worse than to call it "instrumental-expressive" or "agentic-communal".

Since the pioneering work of Terman and Miles, a baker's dozen of personality inventories has appeared including among their scales a measure of M (Guilford & Zimmerman 1949), F (California Psychological Inventory; Gough 1964), or M-F (Minnesota Multiphasic Personality Inventory, MMPI; Dahlstrom et al. 1972). Most of them used the same method of item selection as the original, even borrowing from a common pool of items. Intercorrelations usually fall between .30 and .45, suggesting that each test defines M and F somewhat differently. Later we shall follow up this suggestion, but first let us consider another major attempt to discover the most significant differences between the sexes.

Bennett and Cohen (1959) asked how men and women perceived themselves and their social environments and what were their motives and values. To find out they conducted a thoroughly systematic survey involving 1,300 subjects aged 15 to 64. (They even applied corrections to match the age curves of the U.S. census.) Their method was to have a subject rank adjectives according to how accurately they described him (or his motives or values or people in general). These scores, averaged separately for males and females and tested, of course, for dependability of differences, could be depicted in a series of paired profiles for the areas in question.

Here is a drastically reduced version of the authors' conclusions. Men and women are much alike in the way they see themselves and their fellows and in their aspirations; that is, their profiles show similar overall contours. On closer view differences appear: some peaks are higher for males, others for females, and the same is true of the valleys. In their self-concepts, for example, women are understanding, tender, sympathetic: in a word, maternal. Men are undistinguished in these ways (but definitely *not* tender). Again women describe themselves as timid, nervous, and uncertain; men feel less so. But neither sex claims to be brave, powerful, or firm.

For motives the same story recurs. Men, more than women, wish to be successful; women, more than men, crave love and security. But these are strong needs for both sexes. As to values, both men and women subscribe to being progressive, independent, natural, and youthful, but women are more emphatic in their endorsement than men. Neither sex enjoys being hard, cold, distant, or suspicious, but men are less repelled than women. As for other people, they are generally accepted as friendly, cheerful, and decent, especially by women. Could they be lying or evil? Of course not; but men are less sure.

Finally, Bennett and Cohen were impressed by a sex difference repeatedly encountered in their data: women tended to be more extreme than men in their evaluations. Masculinity was not so much claimed by men as *dis*claimed by women. Men, on the other hand, seldom eschewed feminine traits. The authors were led to an interesting conjecture: the feminine mode of thinking may characterize both sexes, but in males it is partly inhibited by exposure to an environment with undertones of the jungle.

Stereotypes and Self-ratings

We have scratched the surface of self-ratings without unearthing any radical departures from stereotypical M-F. We may ask whether the two concepts are really interchangeable. Several attempts have been made to find out. One finding has been repeatedly confirmed: M-F tests referring to men and women in general show many more significant sex differences than when they concern the self (Lunneborg 1970; Nichols 1962). Can this datum be accepted at face value, or does it simply mean that subjects are reluctant to admit certain stereotyped traits as their own? If the latter is true, there should be a larger proportion of socially approved traits in self-ratings than in the stereotypes. What is the evidence?

Sherriffs and McKee (1957) followed up their study of stereotypes, cited above, by asking other students to check the same list of adjectives to describe themselves. Comparing self-ratings with stereotypes, the authors found favorable and unfavorable traits reduced by almost the same relative amounts.

Rosenkrantz et al. (1968) devised a test of M-F consisting of over 100 bipolar rating scales (aggressive-not at all aggressive). They had college students of both sexes rate the typical adult male, the typical adult female, and the self. Other subjects checked which pole of each trait was more socially desirable. Confirming Sherriffs and McKee, students rated themselves less masculine or feminine than the typical adult. Looking at the traits, the authors expected to find a correlation between average departure from the stereotype and social desirability. But of six correlatons only one was significant ($p < .02$).

Spence et al. (1975), using bipolar items from Rosenkrantz's test, had students rate the ideal as well as the typical male and female. The authors distinguished three groups of traits: male-valued, if the ideals of both sexes deviated toward the masculine pole; female-valued, if both favored the feminine; sex-specific, if the ideal of each sex was displaced toward its own pole. Again we find that male and female undergraduates, rating themselves on the same bipolar scales, showed some, but not all, of the stereotyped sex differences. Testing the possibility of a bias toward socially approved models, Spence et al. correlated ratings of self with stereotype in all three classes of trait. Out of eighteen correlations five were significant ($p < .05$). Relatively independent, was the authors' verdict.

Here we have three studies using different methods, all showing self-described M and F to be less extreme than the stereotypes and all discounting social desirability as the cause. We find these data somewhat reassuring; it is good to know that self-concepts and sexual stereotypes stand measurably apart. This is, of course, far from saying that a child's gender identity is independent of social norms, as chapter 6 will abundantly verify.

Components of Masculinity and Femininity

So far we have explored the concept of M-F as expressed in two forms: (1) the generalized picture or stereotype of men and women in Western culture; and (2) the individual pictures given by the self-reports of males and females, mostly high school and college students. We have seen some of the difficulties of measurement in this field; yet certain tentative conclusions have emerged. There are indications—in the content of the tests, in the fairly low correlations among them—that M-F includes a variety of traits shared by men and women to different degrees. But we are still unable to describe clearly and confidently, much less to understand, the essential differences in personality between the sexes.

Eventually we face the basic issue of origins. Meanwhile there are a number of questions still outstanding. What are the fundamental traits expressed in the many specific responses distinguishing males from females? How many such traits must be recognized in order to account for the differences? Do the same traits characterize both sexes, differing only in amounts, or are some peculiar to females and others to males? If some traits are shared, do they differ in relative importance to one sex as compared with the other?

As suggested in chapter 3, factor analysis is a statistical procedure for finding answers to such questions. Suppose a group of high school students has taken a battery of tests or checked a large number of self-report items on a personality inventory. Factor analysis starts with the intercorrelation between the tests or items and unearths a much smaller number of components, or factors, along with the relative amount each test owes to each factor (its factor loading). Techniques are available, such as rotation of axes, to simplify the factor structure and make the components easier to identify (Comrey 1973).

Factor analysis, then, should tell us some of the things we want to know about M-F. Remember, however, that the method itself is not aimed at measuring group differences in mean scores but at specifying the capacities or traits that underlie whatever differences may be found. We are therefore most interested in studies that provide separate analyses of male and female responses. From them we can learn, not just how the sexes differ within single dimensions, such as ambition or sensitivity, but if and how they differ in the *pattern* of traits.

Factor Analysis of Stereotypes. Masculine and feminine stereotypes provide material as suitable for factor analysis as the self-concepts of real men and women. In fact, a brief report of one such study (Broverman et al. 1972) suggests that the stereotypes may be too obvious to require statistical aid. A male group and a female group rated an "adult man" and an "adult woman" on forty-one items already shown to be highly discriminating. The four sets of ratings were separately analyzed, and in all four the two leading factors to emerge were clearly identical. One had heavy loadings in the male-valued items (independent, decisive, logical, confident) and was labeled "competency." The other factor loaded the female-valued items (sympathetic, tender, literary, artistic) and was named "warmth and expressiveness." As expected, adult man received high ratings in the competenency cluster, low in warmth-expressiveness; for adult woman the reverse was true. Unfortunately the authors did not say whether the order of importance of the two factors (in terms of total contribution to all items) was the same in both sexes or, as might be supposed, the opposite.

A study by Reece (1964) gave strikingly similar results, and more information. Reece made up his own test, a series of bipolar rating scales to measure six hypothetical factors he expected or hoped to find. Undergraduates of both sexes rated four concepts: typical M, typical F, ideal M, and ideal F.

We cannot pause to follow Reece through his four separate analyses. Enough to say, he recovered all six predicted factors from the typical ratings and most but not all from the ideal ones; the order varied from one concept to another. The two major factors, however, turned out to be the same for all four concepts. One, loading heavily on scales like powerful-helpless and strong-weak, was identified as "potency." The other, represented by harsh-tender, cruel-kind, unfeeling-sensitive, callous-considerate, implied "social behavior." But the two factors carried by no means equal weight. For typical M, potency was much the more important possession; for typical F, social behavior took precedence.

Turning to the concepts of ideal M and F, we find the disproportion between factors I and II sharply reduced. In other words, it is almost as important for the ideal male to be considerate toward others as to be rugged; and the ideal female is less likely than the typical one to be gentle to the point of subservience.

Factor Analysis of Self-ratings. Earlier we promised to consider what factors might be common to the various personality inventories that have included M-F scales. Terman and Miles (1936) interpreted the sex differences they found in terms of a single dimension with two aspects; one comprising the special interests typical of each sex, the other defined by divergent temperaments.

Ford and Tyler (1952) put this "double-aspect theory" to the test of factor analysis. They gave most of the Terman-Miles inventory to about 300 boys and girls in junior high school and factor-analyzed the results. In each sex the first factor to emerge had the highest loadings in the subtests for emotional response. The authors labeled this factor "toughness" in the boys, "sensitivity" in the girls. Factor II had to do with interests, as shown in preferences among occupations, books, and activities. A third factor appeared in the girls' scores but not the boys'; the authors were not sure of its nature but guessed it might arise from awareness of expected social role. Ford and Tyler concluded that M-F, as measured by the Terman-Miles test, had at least two independent dimensions, possibly more.

When Lunneborg (1972) tackled the same problem twenty years later, she had many more instruments at her disposal, as we have seen. Besides, the earlier results were probably out of date. From eight M-F scales she compiled 450 true-false items, which she gave to over 500 college students to answer for themselves. Only 177 of the items distinguished males from females at the .01 level (that is, the difference would have occurred by chance less than 1 time in 100).

Separate factor analyses of all 450 items yielded nine factors for the women and ten for the men. Lunneborg set up two conditions that a factor had to meet in order to qualify as a genuine component of M-F. First, its loaded items had to discriminate consistently between males and females. Second, it had to be found in both sexes. By these criteria she was able to identify four factors: power (factor I for males, III for females), neuroticism (I for females, II for males), scientific interests (IV for females, not numbered for males), and religiosity (numbers not given). From the directions of sex difference, power and scientific interest were called masculine; neuroticism and religiosity, feminine.

Lunneborg's definition seems to us too narrow. It amounts to a strictly bipolar position. We agree that to be masculine or feminine a factor must differentiate the sexes, but not that it has to be present in both. (To be present means to have enough range of variation within one sex to show up as a factor.)

In her doctoral dissertation Muriel Abbott (1969) took the position that M is not necessarily the opposite of F but may denote the presence of masculine rather than feminine characteristics. Her method differed from Lunneborg's in several respects. Her subjects were high school students, about 200 of each sex. (Terman and Miles had found the clearest differences among high school juniors.) First she reduced her pool of over 500 true-false items to 150 that clearly distinguished girls from boys. By a process of cluster analysis she assigned these items to appropriate subgroups, thirteen masculine and thirteen feminine, then factor-analyzed the clusters separately for boys and girls. For the males three factors contributed 60 percent of the "common factor variance"; for the females four factors accounted for 70 percent. According to their factor labels, the boys turned out to be (I) tough, self-assertive, venturous; (II) impersonal, self-sufficient; (III) enterprising, realistic. By the same token the girls were (I) self-concerned, timid; (II) insecure, dependent; (III) considerate of others; (IV) interested in the esthetic, social, and domestic.

Abbott made no attempt to identify any of these factors as common to both sexes. She did, however, point out some of the bipolar gradients linking male and female behaviors independently of factor boundaries: for example, the self-assertiveness of male factor I with the "noncompeting sensitivity to others" of female factor III; the timid conventionality of female factor I with the untidy enterprise of male factor III; the impersonality of male factor II with the personal involvement of female factor IV. True, as the author noted, there was no feminine submissiveness to balance the aggressive self-assertion of male factor I. Abbott recognized the difference between an opposite trait and its absence. But absence of an opposite did not necessarily throw a trait out of the picture. Masculinity and femininity emerge from Abbott's analysis as two small groups of factors, each factor unique to its own sex but related to those of the opposite sex in ways yet to be explored.

Homosexuality

For all its shortcomings, the evidence for a sex difference in temperament is persuasive; men and women do seem to differ in one or more clusters of traits, conforming to notions of masculinity and femininity generally held in our society. Pivotal to these concepts is the belief in heterosexuality: normal males prefer females as sex objects, and vice versa. It has long been supposed that homosexuals are inverted in other respects as well; that is, male homosexuals are somewhat feminized, and lesbians behave like men.

Measuring devices now make it possible to examine this doctrine. A good deal of effort has gone into the task, much of it concerned with improving the scales and deciding whether homosexuality should be considered a pathological condition (still unsettled). Solid evidence is hard to gather in this field, and we can report only a few indications of the shape of disclosures to come.

As part of their classical study, Terman and Miles (1936) gave their test to over 100 male homosexuals and a much smaller number of lesbians. These scores could then be compared with groups from widely varied segments of the population. The results were impressive. Terman and Miles distinguished between active and passive types according to the preferred role in sexual relations. Of thirty-six male groups tested for M-F, a group of forty-four active homosexuals ranked fifth from the top in masculinity. A group of seventy-seven of the passive type stood at the foot of the ladder in thirty-sixth place; as noted earlier, they scored below the most masculine of the female groups, women college athletes. (In emotional reactions the passive male homosexuals (PMH) equaled the average for men in general, convincing the examiners that their feminine response to other sections of the test were not faked.) From the test items separating them most sharply from high school juniors, Terman and Miles drew a composite picture of the PMH: fastidious; domestic; timid; enjoying literature, art, music, and drama; rejecting activities calling for aggressiveness, leadership, and energy.

Of women taking the M-F test, eighteen lesbians were surpassed in masculinity only by the female athletes just mentioned. Classified by type, the eleven actives equaled the athletes (thus surpassing the PMH); the seven passives reached the same level as 300 female college students.

Later investigators have not just lost sight of the active-passive dichotomy; they reject it as oversimplifying and misleading (Hooker 1965). Many homosexuals, they point out, shift roles from time to time or show no preference. Were the earlier observations inaccurate, or has the social scene changed? In either case, how masculine or feminine are homosexuals today?

Two studies compared homosexuals with heterosexuals in response to Cattell's Sixteen Personality Factors Questionnaire (Cattell & Stice 1957). In one the homosexuals proved to be more dominant, more self-sufficient, and more reserved than their controls, as well as less tense and less careful about practical details. In the second study the homosexuals were more tense, tender-minded, affected by feelings, suspicious, emotional, and prone to guilt; but they were also more unconventional and self-sufficient. As the reader may have guessed, the first was a group of lesbians (Hopkins 1969), the second a group of male homosexuals (Evans 1970). Lesbians gave similar results when tested with the MMPI (Ohlson & Wilson 1974); along with alertness, low anxiety, and self-confidence went social introversion, described as a "cynical isolation."

Two studies using Gough and Heilbrun's Adjective Check List (1965) give us another opportunity to compare male and female homosexuals. The males, relative to heterosexuals, checked themselves as lower in need to achieve, confidence, and endurance, but more dependent, submissive, and neurotic (Evans 1971). The females were *less* dependent and submissive than heterosexuals; on the other hand, they were lower in endurance and personal adjustment (Hassell & Smith 1975).

On the whole these few data point to an inversion of personal traits in both sexes, but the inversion is incomplete, giving an impression of inconsistency. In males we see sensitivity offset by unconventionality; in females, independence coupled with poor social adjustment. Such inconsistencies are perhaps to be expected as long as the homosexual's environment remains hostile. (The determinants of homosexuality are discussed in chapter 7.)

References

Abbott, M.M. 1969. "An Analysis of the Components of Masculinity and and Femininity." Doctoral dissertion, Columbia University, 1969. *Dissertation Abstracts International* 29:3464B. University Microfilms, no. 69, 3048.

Bakan, D. 1966. *The Duality of Human Existence.* Chicago: Rand McNally.

Bennett, E.M., and Cohen, L.R. 1959. "Men and Women: Personality Patterns and Contrasts." *Genetic Psychology Monographs* 59:101-155.

Broverman, I.K.; Vogen, S.R.; Broverman, D.M.; Clarkson, F.E.; and Rosenkrantz, P.S. 1972. "Sex-Role Stereotypes: A Current Appraisal." *Journal of Social Issues* 28(2):59-78.

Carlson, R. 1971. "Sex Differences in Ego Functioning." *Journal of Consulting and Clinical Psychology* 37:267-277.

Cattell, R.B., and Stice, G.H. 1957. *Handbook for the Sixteen Personality Factors Questionnaire.* Champaign, Ill.: Institute for Personality and Ability Testing.

Comrey, A.L. 1973 *A First Course in Factor Analysis.* New York: Academic Press.

Constantinople, A. 1973. "Masculinity-Femininity: An Exception to a Famous Dictum." *Psychological Bulletin* 80:389-407.

Dahlstrom, W.G.; Welsh, G.S.; and Dahlstrom, L.E. 1972. *An MMPI Handbook* .Rev. ed., vols. 1 and 2. Minneapolis: University of Minnesota Press.

Evans, R.B. 1970. "Sixteen PF Scores of Homosexual Men." *Journal of Consulting Psychology* 34:212-215.

Evans, R.B. 1971. "Adjective Check List Scores of Homosexual Men." *Journal of Personality Assessment* 35:344-349.

Ford, C.F., Jr., and Tyler, L.E. 1952. "A Factor-Analysis of Terman and Mile's M-F Test." *Journal of Applied Psychology* 36:751-753.

Gough, H.G. 1964. *California Personality Inventory Manual.* Palo Alto, Calif.: Consulting Psychologists Press.

Gough, H.G., and Heilbrun, A.B. 1965. *The Adjective Check List manual.* Palo Alto, Calif.: Consulting Psychologists Press.

Guilford, J.P., and Zimmerman, W.S. 1949. *The Guilford-Zimmerman Temperament Survey: Manual of Instructions and Interpretations,* Beverly Hills, Calif.: Sheridan Supply.

Gutmann, D. 1965. "Women and the Conception of Ego Strength." *Merrill Palmer Quarterly* 11:229-240.

Hassell, J., and Smith, E.W. 1975. "Female Homosexuals' Concepts of Self, Men, and Women." *Journal of Personality Assessment* 39:154-159.

Hooker, E. 1965. "Male Homosexuals and Their 'Worlds.'" In J. Marmor, ed. *Sexual Inversion.* New York: Basic Books.

Hopkins, J.H. 1969. "The Lesbian Personality." *British Journal of Psychiatry* 115:1433-1436.

Jenkin, N., and Vroegh, K. 1969. "Contemporary Concepts of Masculinity and Femininity." *Psychological Reports* 25:679-697.

Lunneborg, P.W. 1970. "Stereotypic Aspects in Masculinity-Femininity Measurement." *Journal of Consulting and Clinical Psychology* 34:113-118.

_____ . 1972. "Dimensionality of MF." *Journal of Clinical Psychology* 28:313-317.

Nichols, R.C. 1962. "Subtle, Obvious, and Stereotype Measures of Masculinity-Femininity." *Educational and Psychological Measurement* 22:449-461.

Ohlson, E.L., and Wilson, M. 1974. "Differentiating Female Homosexuals from Female Heterosexuals by Use of the MMPI." *Journal of Sexual Research* 10:308-315.

Parsons, T., and Bales, R.F. 1955. *Family Socialization and Interaction Process*. Glencoe: Free Press.

Reece, M.M. 1964. "Masculinity and Femininity: A Factor-Analytic Study." *Psychological Reports* 14:123-139.

Rosenkrantz, P.; Vogel, S.; Bee, H.; Broverman, I.; and Broverman, D.M. 1968. "Sex Role Stereotypes and Self-concepts in College Students." *Journal of Consulting and Clinical Psychology* 32:287-295.

Sherriffs, A.C., and Jarrett, R.F. 1953. "Sex Differences in Attitudes about Sex Differences." *Journal of Psychology* 35:161-168.

Sherriffs, A.C., and McKee, J.P. 1957. "Qualitative Aspects of Beliefs about Men and Women." *Journal of Personality* 25:451-464.

Spence, J.T.; Helmreich, R.; and Stapp, J. 1975. "Ratings of Self and Peers on Sex Role Attributes and Their Relation to Self-esteem and Conceptions of Masculinity and Femininity." *Journal of Personality and Social Psychology* 32:29-39.

Terman, L.M., and Miles, C.C. 1936. *Sex and Personality*. New York: McGraw-Hill.

6

Social Factors in Gender Development

How do little boys and little girls develop into men and women? In answer we shall trace the development of gender (masculinity or femininity) in the growing child. Two concerns prompt this undertaking. First, before attempting an objective appraisal of sex differences in personality we need to become fully aware of the strongly biased atmosphere in which American boys and girls are reared. We must therefore take a closer look at the powerful forces in the social milieu pressing them into distinct molds; we should then be in a better position to judge how much difference, if any, remains to be accounted for. Second, it is urgent to bear in mind that the child responds to inner as well as outer signals; even the young colt led to water does not necessarily drink.

Sex and Gender

The genital anatomy that identifies the newborn as male or female also specifies its potential gender as masculine or feminine, respectively. Thus unless special precautions are taken, the stage is already set for babies of opposite sex to be treated differently in subtle ways. In our complex society, however, gender identity is not the one-to-one correlate of sex that it is in more primitive ones where function is the direct counterpart of structure. In the contemporary scene many variables have been introduced between the structure of sex and the function of gender. Some of the presumably biological differences between males and females have been selected by society for inclusion in masculine and feminine role patterning, while others have not been culturally sex-linked. An example of the latter is skill at spatial visualization, in which boys excel but which is not part of the role prescription for masculinity; to be masculine a boy need not display this ability, nor is the girl who does considered unfeminine. Certain other characteristics that seem to emerge spontaneously are exploited in the differentiation of the sexes. A case in point is aggressiveness and the associated competitive-resistive qualities favoring males that Western culture strongly reinforces in boys. These two instances of commonly accepted sex differences may suffice to accentuate the biological separateness of the sexes, a separateness that may or may not be keyed into the social role system. In either case, the genetic potentials set limits within which environmental factors may operate effectively.

From the moment the new baby is placed in a pink or blue blanket, society lays its imprint upon it and begins to shape its gender. The first vague awareness of the world around it is mediated through colors, tones, and pressures long before words are used to symbolize meanings. The full impact of social shaping, however, is not realized until cognitive development makes it possible for the infant to understand and to make appropriate discriminations. Meanwhile, emerging genetic characteristics form the basis of a readiness to learn the sex-differential stereotypes.

Sex-role orientation may appear as early as the end of the first year. By age 2 children are able to recognize and apply such labels as boy, girl, he, and she (Thompson 1975). Between age 2 and 3, gender identity becomes so firmly set as to be virtually irreversible. By the time the child is ready for school he will have achieved constancy in his concept of gender (Thompson & Bentler 1973), which he will express in his preferences for and adoption of an appropriate masculine or feminine role.

Developmental Changes in Play

Toy Preferences. The toys and games of young children are early signs of their gender leanings. Within the first year, the very way the baby handles toys was found to differ for the two sexes: boys vigorously attacking; girls merely examining them (Goldberg & Lewis 1969). In the case of infants a little older than a year, marked sex differences in toy preferences have been noted, but before age 3 the choices are determined by such intrinsic qualities as the novelty or complexity of the toy rather than stereotyping (Corter & Jamieson 1977). After 3 sex-typed differences become the rule, reflecting the child's understanding and acceptance of the prevailing concepts of gender (Jacklin & Mischel 1973).

In discussing the course of development from early undifferentiated choices to the later more clearly masculine- or feminine-typed preferences, Maccoby and Jacklin (1974) point out the impossibility of identifying particular innate versus learned linkages because of the continual interaction between these two sources of behavior. Society may choose to label as masculine or feminine the toys that respectively attract boys and girls even when they bear no necessary relationship to the gender roles. Examples are blocks in the case of boys and artwork in that of girls. Specific sex typing at the nursery school level is reflected in the girls' interest in dolls and play kitchens, in sewing and stringing beads, or in dressing up in heels and hats. Boys, by contrast, are more often engaged in rough-and-tumble outdoor games or in playing with guns, trucks, tractors, fire engines, and carpenters' tools. Evidence for the continuing stereotyping of sex roles, in spite of the influence of women's liberation, appears in the use of the housekeeping corner in the playroom, by a group of 3-to-5-year-olds (Barry & Barry 1976). The boys gradually rejected this feminine environment while the girls came to accept it as more appropriate as they grew older.

Sex differences have been found in preferences for toys and for pictures of toys in children from 5 years of age on (DeLucia 1972). Strong feelings may be expressed about the fitness of the toys and inappropriate ones rejected (Hartup et al. 1963). This tendency came out in a situation where preschool children were offered a toy "for keeps." Having made a spontaneous choice suitable for their gender, they could not be persuaded by the teacher to exchange it for an opposite-sex-typed toy. For example, the suggestion that a boy swap an airplane for a necklace not only was resisted by the child, but the teacher making the suggestion was considered sick, overworked, or suffering from mental disturbance (Ross & Ross 1972). That the sex appropriateness of a toy also determines its attractiveness was recently demonstrated with a group of first- and second-grade children. A neutral Mr. Munchie was given boy appeal or girl appeal, according to a prearranged label: for the "boy condition" Mr. Munchie was described as a toy for boys like basketball; for the "girl condition," he was a toy like jacks. The toy's attractiveness was scaled by the children, and found to depend on its apparent appropriateness, the boys preferring the masculine and the girls the feminine Mr. Munchie (Montemayor 1974).

Spontaneous Play Constuctions. Basic gender orientation is reflected not only in the preference reactions of children to alternatives presented to them, but more significantly in their spontaneous play constructions. Erikson (1951) approached the problem by analyzing play projections of 11-, 12-, and 13-year old subjects in the Berkeley Guidance Study, a study recently replicated with positive results (Wambach 1975). The children were given the task of building toy movie scenes on a table, later photographed for evaluation. The child's way of using space proved to be the dominant property of these constructions and the dimension in which sex differences loomed large, with the girls emphasizing inner and the boys outer space. The typical girl's theme is a house interior in which people and animals are generally static and peaceful, but whose tranquility is sometimes broken by unannounced intruders. Boys constructed exteriors of houses with walls and protrusions or high towers. In these settings people and animals are outside in active motion or caught up in sudden stoppage of motion as in traffic tie-ups. Erikson interpreted his results in terms of differences between the sexes in experiencing the "ground plan of the body," which predisposes them toward certain types of play that come naturally.

Further support for Erikson has come from Cramer's (1975) studies of play interests of boys and girls from preschool age to puberty. These children were asked to make up stories to certain ambiguous pictures as well as to construct movie scenes from play materials. Sex differences were found than seemed to parallel the sex anatomy. These differences became greater in the older subjects who were approaching puberty. Examples were increased concern with entrances, intrusions, and inner commotion in the girls' productions, and with towers, erection, and downfall in the boys'. While these results do lend interesting confirmation of Erikson's report, neither the original nor the later work shows to what extent the children's constructions are spontaneous expressions of their bodily experiences. Could they not reflect to some degree conformity to certain aspects of the gender shaping to which they had already been subjected? Certainly there is room here for both biological and social programming.

Theories of Gender Development

Once a gender label has been assigned and recognized, appropriate attitudes and behaviors are expected to follow, with salient linkages between masculinity and aggressiveness, and between femininity and nurturance. The question as to why brothers and sisters reared by the same parents learn to behave differently has received different answers from the leading schools of psychology.

Psychoanalytic. The classical Freudian theory provided a most comprehensive account of the genesis of gender roles. Although an exhaustive critique of this approach would be out of place here, we may point out its chief relevant aspects. It assumes a predetermined relationship between biological genital differences and psychological characteristics of males and females. According to Freud, the major differences between the sexes evolve during an Oedipal stage of development when the son's filial love for his mother places him at risk of castration by his father-rival. In self-defense, he renounces his mother as lover and takes an aggressive stance toward the world by identifying with his aggressor-father. Meanwhile, the girl, under no pressure to establish her separateness from her mother, is allowed to identify with her and continue her dependent love for her (Bronfenbrenner 1960). Envying the boy his penis for both its intrinsic physical possibilities as well as for the greater prestige it carries in patriarchal Western culture, the girl may emulate certain masculine-type behaviors such as the rough play of the tomboy or the achievement striving of the professional woman. The Oedipal conflict at the core of Freudian theory has enjoyed a charismatic popularity worthy of the great myth on which it is based, but its generalizations have failed to allow for the crucial part played by cultural variation, a point beyond the scope of the present discussion (Rosenberg & Sutton-Smith 1972).

Erikson's reformulation of the psychoanalytic approach assumes, as we have seen, that the nature of male and female genitals leads to distinctly different ways of orienting toward the world and consequently to basic differences in masculinity-femininity (M-F).

Social Learning. According to social learning theory, sex differences in personality are for the most part a function of learning. In other words, M-F reflects environmental norms and values which children internalize through direct cultural transmission. By observing and imitating both parents, the boy or girl learns, at first vicariously, a wide diversity of potential behaviors that are not necessarily sex-typed (Heilbrun 1973). From this matrix, items for performance in specific situations may be selected. The child is rewarded for copying various prosocial actions of either parent or other adult model, but unacceptable actions, including sex-inappropriate behaviors, are not reinforced.

Sex typing, however, is not merely the product of training practices aimed at eliciting masculine or feminine behavior by direct reinforcement of specific sex-appropriate acts as claimed by strict behaviorism (Mischel 1970). As Maccoby and Jacklin (1974) point out, direct shaping fails to account for many details of sex-typed behavior, since children often adopt sex-typed patterns of play and exhibit interests for which they have never been rewarded and avoid sex-inappropriate activities for which they have never been punished.

Cognitive-Developmental. Neither the biological nor the social learning theories were adequate to explain the age changes in M-F concepts because they failed to take into account the qualitative changes in the child's thinking about sex roles as he grows up. The cognitive-developmental approach (Kohlberg 1966; Kohlberg & Ullian 1974) offers an alternative to the psychoanalytic and the social learning theories that attempts to remedy their deficiencies. According to this position, masculine-feminine identities are not merely functions of constant biological propensities or of societal conditions, but rather represent developmentally changing ways of viewing and interpreting differences between the sexes. It is only after the individual has developed clear concepts of his bodily architecture and tendencies that he can begin to learn the gender patterns expected of him. This learning involves imitating the observable actions of like-sexed people around him, and also empathizing with their inner attitudes and feelings. Having attained this prerequisite cognitive development of his own M-F, the child is at last in a position to follow appropriate models.

Empirical findings support this contention. In interviews through doll play at a nursery school, children showed an increasing preference for watching a model of the same sex (Slaby & Frey 1976). Similarly, preschool boys and girls have been found to prefer storybook girls and boys performing such stereotyped roles as ballerina and mailcarrier, respectively (Jennings 1975).

The child's first concepts of gender role are oversimplified, cartoonlike exaggerations that are gradually modified by experience with real-life models. By age 6 or 7, the child equates the "is" of his sex identity with social values: if you are a boy, it is good to be a boy; if you can't be a girl, you don't want to be one. Males are seen as more powerful, aggressive, authoritarian, and smarter than females. Kohlberg and Ullian (1974) describe the boy at this stage as a full-fledged male chauvinist. As he grows older, however, he becomes more flexible in his attitudes. Interviews with boys from age 6 through the college freshman year showed that the stereotypes of sex roles operating with compelling force at 6 had gradually become perceived as voluntary choices. Other evidence bearing on the problem of developmental changes in sex roles comes from a comparative study of 8- and 12-year-olds (Falkenberg et al. 1977). The children were asked whether a girl or a boy would behave as described in each of a series of narratives. The results showed that the subjects at both age levels understood the subjective as well as the more objectively observable aspects of sex roles. Age changes did appear, however, in attitudes toward sex role differences: older children were more skeptical and critical of the traditional roles, while the younger ones took them for granted.

Age changes in role perception have led Ullian (1976) to expand the cognitive-developmental theory. Through interviews with subjects of both sexes from 6 to 18 years of age, she was able to distinguish several levels of concept formation representing successive ways of describing sex differences in appropriate behavior for males and females. At the earliest level, biological and occupational roles are assumed to stem from such innate physical differences as size, strength, hair length, and voice characteristics. Thus a 6-year-old says, with charming disregard of syntax, "men are born to be stronger because they do more work than girls."

The middle levels represent a societal orientation with increasing awareness of a social system which distinguishes between males and females in terms of social roles. At this stage, children automatically attribute to members of each sex the abilities and qualities necessary to fulfill these roles. The 10-year-old child, for example, accommodating his concept of M-F to the constraints of future social roles, maintains that the boy does not take care of the home because he has a big responsibility to look for a job.

At the final level, individual psychological orientation supercedes both the biological and the societal. Principles of equality and freedom take the place of conformity to traditional standards and roles. In his attempt to go beyond the customary sex-role stereotype, the young adult tries to construct a set of attributes that have validity for both males and females. Asked to define the ideal woman, a college student responded: "Personally, the ideal woman to me can be beautiful, and soft, but the ideal man may also be soft in the same way, because he is soft-spoken, not domineering over anyone, but still with ambition so he can get things done" (Ullian, p.43).

Pleck's (1975) phasic theory of gender-role development also contains built-in changes paralleling the individual's increasing maturity. From the phase of confused, amorphous sex-role concepts, the child moves on to learn the "rules" of role differentiation, that is, the traditional social sex stereotypes. At this level he expects rigid conformity to the norms and will brook no deviation. Finally he outgrows the rigid stereotypes and, transcending their limitations, reaches a stage of psychological androgyny which permits the expression of human qualities without reference to their masculinity or femininity.

Modeling

Parental Examples. As awareness of gender develops, the child looks at the surrounding world for potential models. The home, of course, provides the first live one in the parents (Emmerich 1961). From preschool age to preadolescence, both boys and girls are likely to choose the same-sexed parent as their behavioral model as well as their favorite parent (Kagan et al. 1961). More important than the sex as such, however, are certain other attributes. Both girls and boys will imitate the dominant parent whether father or mother (Hetherington 1965). Warmth is another facilitator of identification according to Mussen and Rutherford (1963). In a group of first graders they reported that highly masculine boys as well as highly feminine girls as measured on an M-F scale, perceived the like-sexed parent as significantly warmer and more nurturant than did those with respectively lower scores on the scale. There is recent evidence that masculinity in a son is related not to the father's masculinity but to a combination of dominance, nurturance, and participation in the son's care (Lynn 1976).

Actually, the process of identification for either boy or girl normally involves modeling after the mother in some respects and the father in others. The contribution of both parents has been confirmed by many studies. In recalling childhood experiences, one group of male and female college students indicated their mother's acceptance as the most important socializing factor (Burger 1975), while another, made up entirely of women, attributed their autonomy to their father's treating them as worthy persons whose talents did not refute their femininity (Lozoff 1973). Girls modeling after a masculine father are likely to possess the dual aspects of feminine expressiveness and masculine instrumentalism. A permissive home atmosphere apparently encourages the active, adventurous behavior expected of the masculine role while authoritarianism creates pressure toward more passive, submissive conformism traditionally associated with femininity (Sears et al. 1965). Recent work confirmed the role flexibility of the accepting home. Among well-fathered children, Biller (1972) found spontaneous sex-role blending in which the boys as well as the girls were nurturant and sensitive, and the girls as well as the boys, assertive and independent.

The Absentee Father. Although parents usually provide the most substantial sex-role models, when they are not available other sources must be tapped. In the absence of masculine models, a boy's sex-role orientation is likely to suffer (Drake & McDougall 1977). Unless adequate substitutes can be found, boys deprived of fathers tend to show more dependent and less aggressive behavior than those from two-parent homes. Their essentially unmasculine self-concepts are often concealed behind a defensive posture of rigid and exaggerated adherence to sex-role standards (Biller 1974). Girls with absentee fathers also have more problems related to their sexuality and become overly dependent on their mothers. They apparently need their fathers to complement their mothers in encouraging feminine behavior.

The Peer Group. Even before their preferential imitation of the father or other adult males, boys show sex-typed preferences for the activities and behavior of their peers. Although adult models are usually more effective, peer culture exerts an important influence on sex-role developments (Lynn 1969). By providing external verification of their masculinity, age mates can be especially valuable to boys in their difficult task of achieving gender identity (Steinmann & Fox 1974).

Siblings also serve as role models either supplementing or substituting for parents. An early study showed that girls with brothers more than two years their senior were seen by their teachers as tomboyish, while boys with older sisters were judged "sissyish" (Koch 1955). Close affiliation between children of opposite sex apparently facilitates understanding of the complementary gender role, though the one that is adopted is usually that of one's own sex because the likeness is better liked (Garai 1966).

Teachers and Books. The growing child's ideas of gender are conveyed to him not only through parent and peer models from his daily life, but also by entertainers, athletes, and other public figures. Teachers exert an especially strong influence in molding the role behavior demanded by the stereotype of dependent girl and achieving boy (Levitin & Chananie 1972; Ricks & Pyke 1973). This traditionalism and a general emphasis on feminine values in the schools may be due to the predominance of female teachers in the early grades (Fagot & Patterson 1969).

Curriculum structure and textbooks support the prevailing sex-role images and values (Saario et al. 1973). Stereotyping is nowhere more evident than in children's readers. Analysis of stories in the first three grades featured boys in a wide variety of occupations while girls were almost exclusively limited to being housewives. The classical survey of third-grade readers by Child, Potter, and Levine in 1946, which showed females as kind and sociable in a passive, lazy way while males were engaged in active achievement as bearers of knowledge and wisdom, received confirmation a generation later (Jacklin & Mischel 1973). In this second survey of children's readers from kindergarten through the third grade, the old stereotypes were reinforced with no sign of egalitarian attitudes. In still another comparison of essentially the same two periods in children's literature, Hillman (1974) also reported surprisingly little change. In 120 books analyzed from the 1930s to the mid-1970s, the males were still cast in aggressive-competitive roles, the females in affiliative-dependent ones.

The stability of the stereotypes suggests the need for additional role models in both literature and life. The effectiveness of egalitarian models in storybooks has recently been demonstrated for children as young as 4 or 5 (Flerx et al. 1976). Until the 1970s, however, there were no children's books about women doctors, nor were happy career women depicted in cinema, TV, or theater. Little girls were still shown helping mother in the kitchen or fetching things for father, who was engaged in the more exciting activities of constructing and exploring the world. The aspiring girl was still considered deviant and in need of help. Moreover, marital and career success were depicted as mutually exclusive (Manes & Melnyk 1974).

Television. As in the case of children's books, sex-role models on TV have also been analyzed (Sternglanz & Serbin 1974). The most popular programs during 1971-1972 were chosen, including Popeye, Superman, Pebbles, Josie and the Pussycat, and others. Sex differences in visibility of male and female social roles stand out. For females, it appeared inappropriate to make plans and carry them out, or to be aggressive: they were expected to be deferent and passive. Girls were punished if they abandoned the sedate female style by even moving rapidly. The only way for a girl to be successful was through the use of magic. Four-fifths of the females in title roles were depicted as bewitched. Examples were the series *Bewitched* and *Teenage Witch*. Males, on the other hand, were allowed to be aggressive, constructive, and even nurturant, but without deferring to others.

So far the cultural male models have focused on the strong, silent cowboy and the superficial playboy, who keep their cool and remain emotionally uninvolved. Instead of reinforcing the traditional, however, television could become a powerful change agent for increasing socially desirable nonstereotyped behavior in both males and females (McArthur & Eisen 1976). Such TV shows as *Bachelor Father* and *My Three Sons* presented new models in which the father, though still the provider, had become more sensitive and communicative (Bernard 1975). The collapse of sharp sex typing may mean hope for the rise of a new multidimensional man who will transcend the tough macho type by including feminine virtues of tenderness, compassion, and caring (Fogarty et al. 1971).

Artifacts and Activities. Besides the influences, real or symbolic, to which the child is subjected at home and school, there are various artifacts of sex roles which may affect his behavior. Clothing such as caps and belts, hosiery and lingerie, and such household items as flashlights, tools, dustpans, and irons have been "correctly" sex-typed by preschoolers (Vener & Snyder 1966). Appropriate dolls also extend the young child's sex-role experiences. The contrast between Dressy Bessie's apron and kitchen utensils, and Dapper Dan's cowboy suits clearly conveys the social message. The creator of Barbie has promised her a doctor's outfit "when there are enough women doctors." This is a frank admission that the role of this doll, at least, is to reflect the existing social situation rather than to introduce role changes. From this material it is obvious that the toys and artifacts, like the media, reinforce the status quo and have not been utilized for their innovative possibilities.

Children's Projected Adult Roles

Sex typing of roles was clear in the responses of a group of 3-to-6-year-olds to interviews and picture choices about their projected adult roles. For these children, many of whom were heavy TV viewers, the world was already dichotomized into male and female occupations, with masculine cowboy and feminine nurse as paradigms. When asked to assume the opposite-sex role, the boys chose nurse; the girls, doctor. Perhaps the most revealing outcome of this study was one little boy's remark, "If I were a girl, I'd have to grow up to be nothing!" (Beuf 1974).

From the second grade on, the sex typing of occupational choices is firmly entrenched (Scheresky 1976). In one sample no overlap between the sexes was found except for one boy who selected the feminine goal of teacher instead of the more usual policeman. The importance of cultural shaping for these vocational attitudes was revealed in a study comparing several age levels. Groups of kindergarteners, eighth graders, college undergraduates, and adults from age 30 to 75 were questioned about the sex appropriateness of a list of occupations. The results pointed to the greater conservatism of the kindergarten children in comparison with all the others. The youngest group presumably reflected the traditionalism of their homes. With increasing exposure to public discussion of the issue as they progressed through school, the older subjects adopted increasingly liberal attitudes (Shepard & Hess 1975).

Another approach to the impact of social shaping on individual attitudes is the comparative study of subcultural effects. In this area Rabban's (1950) pioneer work still stands as a model. He compared the effects of social class on gender-role identity of children from age 3 to 8. Using toy preferences, he found that boys and girls from industrial working-class homes became aware of gender-role patterns earlier than did their counterparts from the suburban middle classes, as if in preparation for their earlier encounter with the realities of a less sheltered life. More subcultural studies are needed to firmly establish the relationship between early social training and specific sex-role attitudes and behaviors.

This review of M-F development in our society points up the consistency of gender-role stereotypes wherever sampled, and their persistence over time. In the course of child development, we noted the emergence of sex differences in orientation. Whether they originate in biological predisposition or not, males and females have been regularly dichotomized by the various socializing agencies that exert pressure on the growing child. Trends toward social equality between the sexes, however, with their de-emphasis on gender differenes have called into question the traditional concepts of M-F. The critical issue is in what ways biology sets limits to the homogenizing or rather androgynizing of the social roles of men and women.

References

Barry, R.J., and Barry, A. 1976. "Stereotyping of Sex Roles in Preschool Kindergarten Children." *Psychological Reports* 38 (3, pt. 1.):948-950.

Bernard, J. 1975. *Women, Wives, Mothers: Values and Options*. Chicago: Aldine.

Beuf, A. 1974. "Doctor, Lawyer, Household Drudge." *Journal of Communication* 24:142-145.

Biller, H.B. 1972. *Sex-Role Learning: Some Comments and Complexities from a Multidimensional Perspective*. Washington, D.C.: Symposium on Sex-Role Learning in Childhood and Adolescence.

———. *Paternal Deprivation: Family, School, Sexuality, and Society*. Lexington, Mass.: D.C. Heath.

Bronfenbrenner, U. 1960. "Freudian Theories of Identification and Their Derivatives." *Child Development* 31:15-40.

Burger, G.K. 1975. "Recalled Parental Behavior, Sex Roles and Socialization. *Journal of Clinical Psychology* 31:292-298.

Child, I.L.; Potter, E.H.; and Levine, E.M. 1946. "Children's Textbooks and Personality Development: An Exploration in the Social Psychology of Education." *Psychological Monographs* 60 (3), (whole no. 279).

Corter, C., and Jamieson, N. 1977. "Infants' Toy Preferences and Mothers' Predictions. *Developmental Psychology* 13:413-414.

Cramer, P. 1975. "The Development of Play and Fantasy in Boys and Girls: Empirical Studies." *Psychoanalysis and Contemporary Science* 4:529-567.

De Lucia, L. 1972. "Stimulus Preference and Discrimination Learning." In J.F. Rosenblith, W. Allensmith, and J.P. Williams, eds. *The Causes of Behavior*. Boston: Allyn & Bacon.

Drake, C.T., and McDougall, D. 1977. "Effects of the Absence of a Father and Other Male Models on the Development of Boys' Sex Roles." *Developmental Psychology* 13:537-538.

Emmerich, W. 1961. "Family Role Concepts of Children Ages Six to Ten." *Child Development* 32:609-624.

Erikson, E.H. 1951. "Sex Differences in the Play Configurations of Preadolescents." *American Journal of Orthopsychiatry* 21:667-692.

Fagot, B .I., and Patterson, G.R. 1969. "An in vivo Analysis of Reinforcing Contingencies for Sex-Role Behaviors in the Preschool Child." *Developmental Psychology* 1:563-568.

Falkenberg, S.; Rahm, T.; and Waern, Y. 1977. "Sex Role Concepts in Eight- and Twelve-Year Olds." *Scandinavian Journal of Psychology* 18:31-37.

Flerx, V.C.; Fidler, D.S.; and Rogers, R.W. 1976. "Sex Role Stereotypes: Developmental Aspects and Early Intervention." *Child Development* 47:998-1007.

Fogarty, M.P.; Rapoport, T.; and Rapoport, R.N. 1971. *Sex, Career, and Family Including an International Review of Women's Roles*. London: Allen & Unwin.

Garai, J.E. 1966. "Formation of the Concept of 'Self' and Development of Sex Identification." In A.H. Kidd and J.L. Rivoire, eds. *Perceptual Development in Children*. New York: International Universities Press, pp. 344-388.

Goldberg, S., and Lewis, M. 1969. "Play Behavior in the Year-Old Infant: Early Sex Differences." *Child Development* 40:21-31.

Hartup, W.W.; Moore, S.G.; and Sager, G. 1963. "Avoidance of Inappropriate Sex Typing by Young Children." *Journal of Consulting Psychology* 27:467-473.

Heilbrun, A.B., Jr. 1973. "Parent Identification and Filial Sex-Role Behavior: The Importance of Biological Context." In J.W. Cole and R. Dienstbier, eds. *Nebraska Symposium on Motivation*, vol. 21, Lincoln: University of Nebraska Press, pp. 125-174.

Hetherington, E.M. 1965. "A Developmental Study of the Effects of the Sex of the Dominant Parent on Sex Role Preference, Identification and Imitation in Children." *Journal of Personality and Social Psychology* 2:188-194.

Hillman, J.S. 1974. "An Analysis of Male and Female Roles in Two Periods of Children's Literature." *Journal of Educational Research* 68:84-88.

Jacklin, C.N., and Mischel, H.N. 1973. "As the Twig is Bent: Sex Role Stereotyping in Early Readers." *School Psychology Digest* 2:30-38.

Jennings, S.A. 1975. "Effects of Sex Typing in Children's Stories on Preference and Recall." *Child Development* 46:220-223.

Kagan, J.; Hosken, B.; and Watson, S. 1961. "The Child's Symbolic Conceptualization of the Parents." *Child Development* 32:625-636.

Koch, H. 1955. "Some Personality Correlates of Sex, Sibling Position, and Sex of Sibling among Five- and Six-Year-Old Children." *Genetic Psychology Monographs* 52 (pt. 1):3-50.

Kohlberg, L. 1966. "A Cognitive-Developmental Analysis of Children's Sex-Role Concepts and Attitudes." In E.E. Maccoby, ed. *The Development of Sex Differences: Stanford Studies in Psychology V*. Stanford, Calif.: Stanford University Press, pp. 82-173.

Kohlberg, L. and Ullian, D. 1974. "Stages in the Development of Psychosexual Concepts and Attitudes." In R.C. Friedman, R.M. Richart, and R.L. Vande Wiele, eds. *Sex Differences in Behavior*. New York: Wiley.

Levitin, T.E., and Chananie, J.D. 1972. "Responses of Female Primary School Teachers to Sex-typed Behaviors in Male and Female Children." *Child Development* 43:1309-1316.

Lozoff, M. 1973. "Fathers and Autonomy in Women." *Annals of the New York Academy of Sciences* 208:91-97.

Lynn, D.B. 1969. *Parental and Sex-Role Identification: A Theoretical Formulation*. Berkeley, Calif.: McCutchan Publishing Corp.

———. 1976. "Fathers and Sex-Role Development." *Family Coordinator* 25:403-409.

Maccoby, E.E., and Jacklin, C.N. 1974. *The Psychology of Sex Differences*. Stanford, Calif.: Stanford University Press.

Manes, A.L., and Melnyk, P. 1974. "Televised Models of Female Achievement." *Journal of Applied Social Psychology* 4:365-374.

McArthur, L.Z., and Eisen, S.V. 1976. "Television and Sex-Role Stereotyping." *Journal of Applied Social Psychology* 6:329-351.

Mischel, W. 1970. "Sex-typing and Socialization." In P.H. Mussen, ed. *Carmichael's Manual of Child Psychology*, vol. 2. New York: Wiley, pp. 28-37.

Money, J. 1973. "Gender Role, Gender Identity, Core Gender Identity: Usage and Definition of Terms." *Journal of the American Academy of Psychoanalysis* 1:397-402.

Montemayor, R. 1974. "Children's Performance in a Game and Their Attraction to It as a Function of Sex-typed Labels." *Child Development* 45:152-156.

Mussen, P.H., and Rutherford, E. 1963. "Parent-Child Relations and Parental Personality in Relation to Young Children's Sex-Role Preferences." *Child Development* 34:589-607.

Pleck, J.H. 1975. "Masculinity-Femininity: Current and Alternative Paradigms." *Sex Roles* 1:161-178.

Rabban, M. 1950. "Sex-Role Identification in Young Children in Two Diverse Social Groups." *Genetic Psychology Monographs* 42:81-158.

Ricks, F.A., and Pyke, S.W. 1973. "Teacher Perceptions and Attitudes That Foster or Maintain Sex Role Differences." *Interchange* 4:26-33.

Rosenberg, B.G., and Sutton-Smith, B. 1972. *Sex and Identity*. New York: Holt, Rinehart & Winston.

Ross, D.M., and Ross, S.A. 1972. "Resistance by Preschool Boys to Sex-Inappropriate Behavior." *Journal of Educational Psychology* 13:342-346.

Saario, T.N.; Jacklin, C.N.; and Tittle, C.K. 1973. "Sex Role Stereotyping in the Public Schools." *Harvard Educational Review* 43:386-416.

Scheresky, R. 1976. "The Gender Factor in Six-to-Ten-Year-Old Children's Views of Occupational Roles." *Psychological Reports* 38:1207-1210.

Sears, R.R.; Rau, L.; and Alpert, R. 1965. *Identification and Child Rearing*. Stanford, Calif.: Stanford University Press.

Shepard, W.O., and Hess, D.T. 1975. "Attitudes in Four Age Groups toward Sex Role Division in Adult Occupations and Activities." *Journal of Vocational Behavior* 6:27-39.

Slaby, R., and Frey, K.S. 1976. "Development of Gender Constancy and Selective Attention to Same-Sex Models." *Child Development* 46: 849-856.

Steinmann, A., and Fox, D.J. 1974. *The Male Dilemma: How to Survive the Sexual Revolution*. New York: Aronson.

Sternglanz, S.H., and Serbin, L.A. 1974. "Sex Role Stereotyping in Children's Television Programs." *Developmental Psychology* 10:710-715.

Thompson, S.K. 1975. "Gender Labels and Early Sex Role Development." *Child Development* 46:339-347.

Thompson, S.K., and Bentler, P.M. 1973. "A Developmental Study of Gender Constancy and Parent Preference." *Archives of Sexual Behavior* 2:379-385.

Ullian, D.Z. 1976. "The Development of Conceptions of Masculinity and Femininity." In B. Lloyd and J. Archer, eds. *Exploring Sex Differences*. New York: Academic Press, pp. 25-47.

Vener, A.M., and Snyder, C.A. 1966. "The Preschool Child's Awareness and Anticipation of Adult Sex Roles." *Sociometry* 29:159-168.

Wambach, R.L. 1975. "Sex Differences in Play Configurations of Preadolescent Children: A Comparative Study." *Dissertation Abstracts International* 35(7-A):4266.

7 Genetic and Hormonal Deviations

The birth of a baby is customarily heralded by the familiar, "It's a boy!" (a girl!); concordance between sex anatomy and gender is assumed. The rare cases of sex-gender discrepancy raise critical issues regarding sex differences (Stoller 1968, 1975). As we pointed out in chapter 6, the conviction of belonging to one sex rather than the other appears early and is deeply imprinted on the child. Although the emerging gender identity is a blend of prenatal and postnatal components, specific native versus acquired elements cannot be sorted out but must be viewed as interacting agents in shaping the developing individual. If the two aspects are not congruent, the confusions of identity found in various forms of deviant sexuality are likely to occur (Gershman 1970). In a biological male with a feminine gender or in a biological female with a masculine one, the expected pattern of sex identity, gender behavior, and object choice breaks down. Such cases may be expected to offer clues to the interaction of learned and unlearned factors in masculinity (M) and femininity (F). We shall look for them in homosexuals, transsexuals, certain hermaphrodites, and discordant twin pairs.

Homosexuals

Becoming a Gay Man. The homosexual life-style is so widespread in our culture as to constitute a special subculture, the "gay" world, in contrast to normative "straight" society. Among gays there is so much diversity that Bell (1973) suggested the plural, homosexualities, instead of the often misleading umbrella term, homosexuality, which implies a uniformity that is not the case. The only common denominator underlying all forms is preference for love objects of the same sex. Among gay men, some who choose male sexual partners may nonetheless manifest typical or even stereotypical masculine behavior. Others, in addition to taking on homosexual partners, also adopt an opposite-sex gender role. These so-called sexual inverts are effeminate in appearance, and though accepting themselves as unquestionably male (Townes et al. 1976), adopt the behavior and orientation of females. At the extreme of femininity are the individuals who wish to renounce their biological sex altogether and to validate their self-concept by sex-change surgery. Such homosexuals have made the transition to transsexualism.

Freudian Oedipal theory provided the point of departure for understanding sexual deviation in males. Although, the first love object for both boys and girls is the mother, the boy's task is to free himself from a tendency to identify with her and to shift to his father. When the parental models are unsatisfactory, the child may fear both closeness to his mother and aggression from his father, a situation that facilitates abnormal development of sexuality. An unacceptable father model prevents the boy from relinquishing his initial identification with his mother and turns him toward effeminate homosexuality in a lifelong search for male love objects. In cases where the father is not altogether objectionable but expresses insufficient love to make a fully satisfactory model, the boy may become a masculine-appearing homosexual through partial identification with his aggressor-father.

The classical and controversial study of family origins of homosexuality was that of Irving Bieber and his associates (1962). Their subjects were male homosexuals undergoing psychoanalysis. Reports of their parental relationships during the rearing period, as evaluated by their analysts, were compared with those of a control group of heterosexual analysands. According to the authors, the homosexuals were differentiated from the controls by the greater prevalence among them of a particular parental pattern. This consisted of a close-binding intimate (CBI) mother who behaved seductively toward her son and dominated her husband, while the father tended to have a detached, often hostile attitude that evoked hate, fear, and lack of respect in the son. In such cases both parents prevented the boy from expressing the assertive behavior necessary for a heterosexual orientation. Although the homosexual subjects showed a wide diversity of personality patterns, they shared a central fear of experience with the opposite sex.

Bieber's research has been criticized on various grounds: for using respondents who were undergoing psychiatric treatment; for failure to establish complete separation between the main and comparison groups on the independent variable of homosexuality; for the questionable validity of the reports by the patients, compounded by the subjectivity of the analysts' evaluations; and for overgeneralization of the hypothesized parental syndrome. Nevertheless, in spite of the continuing controversy (Bieber 1976; Friedman 1976; Socarides 1976), an impressive array of supporting evidence has been gathered.

A replication of Bieber's study (Braaten & Darling 1965) was made on a group of student patients with homosexual problems, matched with a corresponding group of controls at the Cornell University Students' Medical Clinic. In general, the results support those of the original investigation. Again the CBI mother and detached father predominate the scene in the gay subjects' childhood. Although this pattern presumably contributes to the development of their homosexuality, it does not occur exclusively in the background of homosexuals, nor is it the only parental combination to be found in their records. In view of these findings the authors caution against attributing to it a specific etiological role in the populations of male homosexual subjects under consideration.

Another investigation following the Bieber model and using the same questionnaire was based on subjects who had never been in therapy (Evans 1969). As in the original study, the relationships with parents recalled by the homosexuals were poorer than those reported by the controls and clearly conformed to Bieber's "triangular" hypothesis. It was not clear, however, whether the parental pattern was the cause of the son's deviant sexual development or the result of his personality characteristics.

A summary of the main relevant studies points up consistently and unequivocally the poor relationships with parents in the childhood backgrounds of male homosexuals. This is true whether the subjects were drawn from clinical or criminal populations (Nash & Hayes 1965; Schofield 1965), from men serving in the armed forces (O'Connor 1964), or from those functioning adequately in the community (Stephan 1973; Thompson et al. 1973). In all these comparisons, involving a variety of subjects and forms of interrogation, the crucial differential between homosexual and control is the gay respondent's faulted relationship with his parents, especially his father.

Indirect support for these trends comes from research following Bieber's design but with the addition of female homosexuals (Gundlach & Riess 1968). A comprehensive questionnaire containing items about family relationships as well as other areas of living was administered to nonpatient members of homophilic organizations. Intercomparisons among four carefully matched groups—female homosexuals, female heterosexuals, male homosexuals, and male heterosexuals—were made. Of these, the male homosexuals were found to differ significantly from all the others. The differences were in their experiences of greater overprotectiveness and seductiveness on the part of their mothers, coupled with a less favored position with their fathers. These findings are strikingly similar to the trends already noted, revealing once again the occurrence of disturbed child-parent relationships in the families of homosexual boys. If further confirmation is needed, it may be found in a recent interview study of gay men who reported predominantly unhappy experiences in early childhood (Ibrahim 1976).

Learning the Lesbian Life-style. In women homosexuality, or lesbianism, contrasts with male forms in its low profile and better integration with mainstream culture. The traditionally strong social sanctions against sexual behavior outside marriage, especially in the case of girls, have sometimes backfired by inadvertently encouraging overcloseness between females. In families that taboo boy-girl relationships as bad, a girl who would risk social ostracism by intimacy with boys may enjoy emotional ties to other girls without fear of punishment. Behind an asexual facade associated with conventional feminine appearance, sexual deviance may gradually develop from a crushy, romantic attachment to an overt sexual relationship. She may not recognize her problem at first, but when she does become aware of her homoerotic leanings she is in danger of a severe identity crisis which may be resolved by adopting a bisexual orientation (Blumstein & Schwartz 1976). During the high school years, girls with lesbian tendencies may engage in some dating and sex play with boys in spite of their essential alienation from heterosexuality, but they eventually come to see themselves as women who are different in that they prefer other women to men as lovers (Gagnon and Simon 1973).

It should be emphasized here, as in the case of male homosexuality, that the choice of a gay life-style does not necessarily signify greater emotional maladjustment. Comparing matched groups of lesbians and heterosexuals, Oberstone and Siskoneck (1976) found no significant differences in test profiles, work records, or pathological tendencies toward drinking, drugs, or suicide.

The homes of homosexual women apparently provide them with less security than is found in the family backgrounds of heterosexual controls inasmuch as the parents are often less loving both toward their girls and toward each other (Siegelman 1974). Mothers of lesbians are apt to be overbearing and overcontrolling, dominating everyone but especially the girl whose rebellion leads her to adopt the lesbian life-style (Saghir & Robins 1973). The fathers often fail their daughters too by not reinforcing their feminine overtures, thereby contributing to their deviation (Wolff 1971). Under the circumstances, the mother's love remains the core of the girl's striving, and the source of her tomboyish, competitive stance.

Where the mother is weak and the father strong, the father may become the model for the girl, who sometimes goes to the extreme of transsexualism and, adopting his behavior and clothing, may seek normal women as lovers. Or if a weak mother is also long-suffering, she may evoke a protective attitude in her daughter, who will take over the role of succoring husband unfulfilled by the reluctant incumbent (Stoller 1975).

Another family pattern conducive to lesbianism reverses the CBI mother combined with a detached, hostile (DH) father; here the father is the CBI parent and the mother, indifferent. The father who is often puritanical, discourages his daughter's development as a female, punishing her attempts at normal sex play with boys (Kaye et al. 1967). Since the indifferent mother does nothing to counteract this negative conditioning, the little girl becomes fearful of sex and finds later experiences with men unpleasant. The homosexuality that frequently results becomes a way out of a dilemma, an attempted adaptation to the crippling inhibition to normal growth (Thompson et al. 1973).

Unlearned Factors in Male and Female. From the material we have examined, it is abundantly clear that early experiences in a child's development play a definitive part in his gender orientation. However that may be, it does not rule out the effects of unlearned prenatal priming on the young organism of either sex. A genetic interpretation of homosexuality was originally bolstered by Kallmann's (1952*a*, 1952*b*) twin studies showing higher concordance for homosexuality in identical than in fraternal pairs. Chromosomes by themselves cannot directly affect behavior, but through their activation of the fetal gonads they might indirectly affect sexual differentiation (Pare 1965). Even the hormones, however, cannot be held immediately responsible for behavior. Although some correlations between male homosexuality and decreased plasma testosterone have been reported (Kolodny et al. 1971; Starká et al. 1975), the evidence in favor of an endocrine basis for this condition is very weak (Meyer-Bahlburg 1977; Schiavi & White 1976). It is the individual's psychological experiences and social expectancies that determine the direction of his sexual impulses and choice of sex objects, while unlearned factors define the limits within which they may operate (Perloff 1965). In cases where genetic, hormonal, or anatomical deviations interfere with normal growth, a new baby, under suitable circumstances, may become predisposed to a homosexual orientation as less demanding than heterosexual adjustment (Ellis 1963). For further light on this problem let us turn to transsexualism, the most extreme form of gender disturbance, in which the individual's very core-gender identity is in question.

Transsexuals

The Male-to-Female Syndrome. The prevailing view runs something like this: male transexuals are distinguished by an intolerable anxiety over separation from their mothers and are motivated by an unconscious wish to merge with her. Their fusion fantasy contaminates their male core-gender identity, making it ambiguous if not female (Person & Ovesey 1974*a*). They often think of themselves as "women trapped in men's bodies." Like typical homosexuals, they choose men as lovers, but since they do not reciprocate as male lovers they are soon rejected. They prefer straight men as lovers toward whom they can relate as women. Their feminized identity makes the idea of sex relations with women seem unnatural to them. As one put it, "When I used to dress like a boy I felt like a lesbian" (Warnes & Hill 1974).

Ever since George-to-Christine Jorgensen's famous successful sex conversion, great interest has been directed toward identifying a specific male-to-female transsexual syndrome. Robert Stoller (1969) was among the first to bring order out of chaos by formulating what he perceived as a specific rearing pattern in "true transsexuals," who in his opinion had developed a sense of female identity within the first year and a half. His syndrome includes the following features:

1. A chronically depressed, bisexual, ex-tomboy mother
2. A distant, passive father who is often absent from the home
3. An empty, angry, but continuing marriage between the parents
4. An especially beautiful infant boy
5. A symbiotic mother-son relationship involving the mother's prolonged holding the baby against her body, thereby giving the son a "blissful" sense of closeness with her which interferes with the normal process of individuation

This syndrome has been beautifully confirmed in the case of "the three sisters," who were three male transsexuals in one family (Sabalis et al. 1974). Here a CBI mother who had been tomboyish in her own girlhood was coupled with a father described as a "romantic stranger." In this family scene there was also a grandmother who reinforced the femininity of the "sisters," all of whom cross-dressed, played and felt like girls, and were regarded as sissies. Later they passed for women and dated men, at the same time repudiating homosexuality.

All cases of primary transsexualism, however, do not conform to Stoller's syndrome, but do have in common an abhorrence of their male bodies and an extraordinary eagerness to part with their troublesome sex organs. The bizarreness of their gender identity would suggest delusional thinking were it not for their clear recognition that they belong to the male sex while adopting a feminine gender. The female identity is presumably experienced more as a wish or as woman-envy than as a conviction. In any case, the emotional disturbance goes beyond the M-F dimension, invading the total personality. These people are socially withdrawn, unassertive, and asexual personalities who experience an empty kind of depression coupled with their extreme separation anxiety. A continuing fantasy of fusion with the mother is sometimes acted out through sex-change surgery (Ovesey & Person 1973), a procedure whose therapeutic value is currently in question.

A transsexual's development does not always clearly prefigure the ultimate outcome but may sometimes be a trial-and-error process of trying to find a satisfying social role. In a series of a dozen cases, the majority reported awareness of feeling like girls by age 5, followed by a period of ambivalence and confusion concerning their true gender. The confusion persisted into adolescence when they sought relief in homosexuality, which failed to solve their problem. Cross-dressing as "drag queens" led them to permanent transvestism, with open admission of their female identity and evenutal application for sex-change surgery (Levine et al. 1975).

The transsexual's gender confusion no less than that of his sex puts him in an ambiguous social situation where he is apt to be rejected by straight and gay worlds alike. Thus it becomes a social problem, increasing the victim's extreme separation anxiety, extending it from his mother to all society. A special minority subculture comparable with that of homosexuals seems to be emerging which may be a source of comfort to these lost ones (Lothstein 1979). Raising conscious awareness of this poorly understood condition through public education should eventually supply the support needed to ameliorate it.

Feminine Boys. Centers for gender problems recently established in many medical facilities have promoted the study of "feminine boys," who from early childhood behave more like girls than boys (Rosen et al. 1977). Although such boys do not all become transsexuals or homosexuals, adults with atypical gender identities are largely drawn from this matrix. Like Wålinder's transsexuals who reported cross-gender interests in childhood, feminine boys have been distinguished from normals in their play behavior by choosing more sedentary, less athletic games (Bates & Bentler 1973). They prefer not only the quieter activities of girls but girls' toys to play with and girls themselves as playmates (Green 1974a, 1976).

In the homes of feminine boys there is often the picture noted among other sexual deviates of the distant father whose anxious concern over his own masculinity precludes tolerance for aberration in his son, coupled with the CBI mother who plays the dominant role in the family. In spite of their presumably unfavorable effects on the child's development, these feminizing influences are apparently neither necessary nor sufficient to account for the boys' femininity since all boys reared in such homes do not become transsexuals, nor are all adult transsexuals reared in such homes. There is even some negative evidence regarding the assumed destructiveness of parental relationships. In Zuger's (1970b) series of twenty-six persistently feminine boys compared with a control group of eighty-four normal ones, no differences in parental attitudes could be found. According to the author, these findings weaken the case for environmental priority.

In evaluating conflicting results in this complicated field of sex-gender discrepancy, one must not lose sight of the efficacy of intervention in altering behavior by intensive, early reinforcement of masculine behavior. In such cases the therapeutic goal is not to force a gender reorientation but merely to expand their behavior repertory to include a balance between feminine and masculine skills. In our society, for example, a boy with athletic training has a better chance of avoiding failure and social isolation and exercising a wider range of options in his life (Rekers et al. 1977).

Female-to-Male Transsexuals. Benjamin and Ihlenfeld (1973) report that a greater proportion of males than females seek surgical sex change. At first glance this finding may seem surprising in view of the higher prestige accorded males in Western culture. Deeper analysis, however, suggests that the greater social desirability of masculinity makes it more acceptable in females than is femininity in males. Just as a tomboy is more acceptable than a sissy and indeed often converts to more conventional feminine behavior in adolescence (Green 1979), a girl with masculine tendencies seldom finds it necessary to resort to the extreme of sex-change surgery. She may still function comfortably as a female, sometimes enjoying even better status than her more traditional peers. It is in cases where a girl has acquired a homosexual orientation with a masculine gender-role identity that the transsexual syndrome is likely to occur. In fact, according to Person and Ovesey (1974*b*), transsexualism in females is always secondary to a predominant homosexuality, rather than the equivalent of primary male transsexualism.

In the rare cases where female-to-male transsexualism is attempted, both psychological and surgical difficulties are powerful barriers against it. The surgery invoves removal of the entire reproductive tract, supplemented by the plastic formation of an artificial penis of questionable efficiency, and continuing male hormone therapy (Pauly 1969, 1974). Whatever the predisposing pressures, the transsexual women who have been studied are generally characterized by a history of tomboyism from childhood and a distaste for their breasts, associated with a lack of desire for pregnancy or motherhood (Money & Breman 1969).

Prenatal Priming or Postnatal Press? In transsexuals, as in homosexuality, the causes must be sought in the interaction among various contributing elements. While there is some evidence that prenatal priming through hormonal deviations may supplement postnatal experiences if they are in the same direction (Money & Primrose 1969), neither factor alone is sufficient to account for any single case. A female identity in an apparent male may result from chromosomal errors, androgen deficiency at the critical phase in neural development, or early experiences superimposed on a predisposed organism (Green 1974*b*).

More impressive, however, are certain anomalous cases in whom an urgent inner drive seems to run counter to the external press toward normal development. A vivid example is Stoller's (1964) case of a male child born without penis or testes, whose thrust toward maleness was nevertheless strong enough to counteract both his anatomical deficiencies and the parents' feminizing efforts.

Hermaphrodites

Discrepancies between sex and gender are pointed up by the "experiments of nature" in the anatomically ambiguous hermaphrodites who show elements of both sexes. These anomalies result from various prenatal errors in chromosomes, hormones, or genital anatomy. The confusion in the development of such an intersexed person is magnified by parental doubts about the child's sex which are inadvertently communicated to him. The result is that while developing aspects of both sexes, he feels that he belongs to neither and seems to exist outside both (Roeske & Banet 1972).

During the 1970s, extensive research has furthered our understanding of these troubled people. In this effort no one has done more than John Money and his team at Johns Hopkins University to bring out prenatal dispositions as they interact with postnatal social programs. Money (1973) made the crucial test of comparing pairs of subjects matched for sex anatomy but reared for different genders. Some of the most dramatic cases are genetic females who at birth appear to be males, and genetic males who at birth appear to be females.

Masculinized Genetic Females. In genetically female infants an overproduction of fetal androgens makes sex assignment difficult (Ehrhardt & Baker 1974). Such cases are represented by the adrenogenital syndrome (AGS), in which both external genitalia and behavior are masculinized. Compared with their unaffected sisters and mothers, girls with AGS are tomboys, preferring boys to girls as playmates and boys' play activities to those of girls. (Incidentally, in boys with this disorder there is an exaggeration of all aspects of masculinity.)

As an example of his paired comparisons, Money described a pair of genetic females with AGS, both of whom were born with masculinized external genitals. One was reared as a girl after surgical removal of the inappropriate penis and the construction of a vaginal opening. Although displaying the expected tomboyism, this girl accepted her feminine gender. The other member of the pair at birth looked like a male with undescended testes. He was reared as a boy until the age of 12 when he was diagnosed as AGS. By this time his masculinity was displayed by such behavior as writing love letters to his girlfriend. The doctors decided not to interfere with his masculine gender identity but rather to reinforce it by removing the ovaries and uterus that had developed, and by administering male hormones. In this pair hormonal effects obscured the genetic status and the sex assignment became the decisive factor. This matched pair is shown in Figure 7-1.

Such studies indicate the extraordinary impact of the postnatal components of gender differentiation on the prenatal elements interacting with them. Supporting evidence comes from a Soviet report of twenty-four anatomically intersexed patients (Lev-Ran 1974). In those of the same age and clinical features who were assigned different sexes, the gender identity followed the neonatal assignment and the resultant socializing experiences.

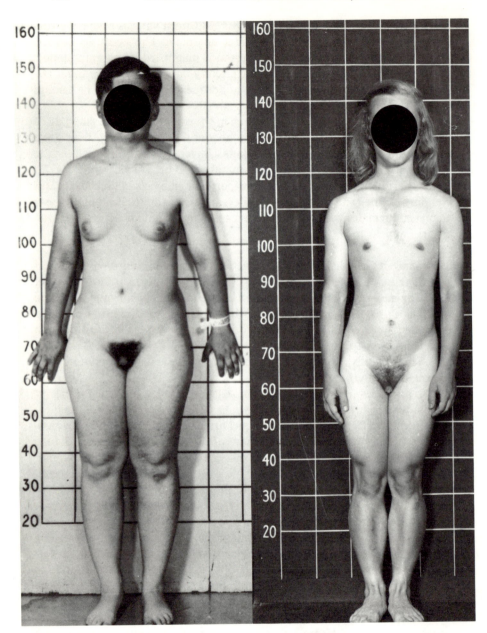

Figure 7-1. Late treated, matched pair of patients concordant for diagnosis of hermaphroditism in a genetic female with the adrenogenital

Figure 7-1. *(continued).*

syndrome, but discordant for sex of rearing, hormonal status at the age of puberty, and gender identity differentiation. Hormonal status was eventually corrected to agree with identity and surgical feminization of the genitalia was effected for the girl. The boy's penis needed no genital surgery ever. Ages as photographed are 12 years, 3 months (girl) and 13 years, 0 months (boy).

Feminized Genetic Males. The counterpart of the prenatally masculinized genetic female is the feminized genetic male. This condition may be induced directly by administering female hormones to pregnant mothers. Comparison of groups of prepubertal and postpubertal boys who had been exposed in this way to estrogens with matched controls whose mothers had not been injected, showed a reduction in assertiveness, athletic ability, and general masculinity (Yalom et al. 1973). We are left to assume that the prenatal condition primed the organism for lowered masculinity which the postnatal rearing failed to counteract (see end of chapter 9).

More extreme degress of feminization may be found in cases of intersexualism resulting from failure of the body cells to utilize the normal male hormone secreted by the fetal testis. A baby born with such a testicular feminization syndrome appears female but will be found to lack a uterus. Since there is no sexual ambiguity, the individual is assigned as a female and reared accordingly. She grows up as a girl, albeit a sterile one, who is likely to marry eventually and adopt children. On such cases, the male chromosomal pattern obviously has no direct masculinizing effect, so that the behavior must be a function of the combined neurohumoral and social factors (Money & Ogunro 1974).

The point is well brought out in one of Money's matched pairs of this testicular feminization syndrome, which parallels the pair of genetic females with AGS already noted. In one member of such a feminized pair, the infant was assigned as a female and later experienced a normal feminizing puberty except for the lack of menstrual periods. There was no evidence of psychosexual conflict concerning core-gender role. The other member of the pair, however, did not fare so well. A slightly large clitoris in addition to a small undescended testis led to this "female's" reassignment as a boy at 4½ months. When at 13 the "boy" began to grow breasts, he had them surgically removed so as not to threaten his masculine identity and the corresponding role which he accepted. As an adult, however, he found to his chagrin that others did not accept him as a complete man because of an extraordinarily youthful appearance caused by his androgen failure.

Identical Twins, Same Sex but Opposite Gender

No matched pair of hermaphrodites diagnosed as same sex but reared differentially can equal the intrinsic control as well as the intrinsic appeal of Money's pair of biologically identical male twins socialized for different genders (Money 1973; Money & Ehrhardt 1972). The accidental ablation of one infant's penis during circumcision necessitated sex reassignment at 17 months and rearing as a girl. At this time the name and clothing were changed from masculine to feminine, followed by genital reconstruction and estrogen-replacement therapy. By the age of 9 when the case was formally reported, the gender differentiation was complete, except for tomboyish traits in the "girl" whose high level of activity and abundant energy were regarded by the mother as greater than normal for girls. It was also significant that she dominated her twin brother, though in a "motherhen" way of fussing over him.

There was no question of the children's acceptance of their respective gender roles after the biological functions of the two sexes had been explained by their wise and cooperative mother. The girl's literal penis envy was expressed at age 5 on one occasion when her twin bragged about his while sharing a bath with her. The sister reacted by angrily slapping him on the offending member, and was comforted by her mother's pointing out some of the advantages of being female. As the twins grew, their divergent interests corresponded to their gender differences: the boy focused on cars, garages, gas pumps, and various tools; the girl, on dolls, doll accessories, hair ribbons, bracelets, and pretty dresses. It would be difficult to find a clearer demonstration of the importance of postnatal training, which fortunately in this case allowed the prenatal priming to be comfortably integrated with it as tomboyism and an acceptable form of dominance behavior.

Prior to this extraordinary twin pair, the evidence for identical twins with different gender identities failed to give unequivocal support to environmental interpretations. As indicated earlier, Kallmann's reports of higher frequency of concordance for homosexuality in one-egg than in two-egg twins seemed to strengthen the genetic argument. Later series (Heston & Shields 1968) also showed higher concordance between identical than fraternal twins, but since the concordance was incomplete even for the identicals, interaction between genetic and environmental factors had to be assumed to explain the occurrence of homosexuality. In certain intensively studied cases, critical early experiences have apparently induced the shift toward cross-gender development in one member of the twinship. Factors contributing importantly to the "selection" of the homosexual twin are often mediated through the mother's attitude or the particular part played by the father in the family scene (Mesnikoff et al. 1963). Physical differences between the male twins, from slight variations in size and weight to severe illness involving hospitalization of one, in some cases led the mother to take a more protective attitude toward her less robust son, who as a consequence became overdependent on her and adopted a feminine orientation (Green & Stoller 1971). A case in point is that of the identical twins, Paul and Michael (Davison et al. 1971). The healthier Michael grew up with the typical boyish interests in engines, cars, and football, and eventually became a mechanic. Paul, who suffered severe gastrointestinal infection shortly after birth, identified with his mother who nursed him through his illness and continued to take special care of him afterward. Unlike his brother, he preferred the company of girls, was considered a sissy, and as a vocation chose the nurturing role of chef.

Even fantasies on the part of the parents may have influenced the child's gender, as in a case where a mother's frustrated wish for a daughter was acted out in feminizing training on the strength of a nurse's casual remark that the baby was "pretty enough to be a girl" (Parker 1964).

In certain recently reported twinships, one member appeared to be transsexual, manifesting girlish interests from early childhood. Stoller's (1976) Mohave Indian identical male twins illustrate the point. Although both were strong and healthy, one accepted the typical all-boy role of riding and sports, while the other chose the feminine way, playing with a younger sister's dolls and cross-dressing. These activities continued into adolescence. Never shamed for his femininity by his tribesmen, he was simply accepted as a boy who felt like a girl. In this case, though no information is given to indicate differential treatment of the twins within the family that could account for their different gender orientations, subtle cues undetected by outside observers may have caused the divergence.

Another instance is Zuger's (1976) 20-year-old male twin pair who were also discordant for gender from early childhood and who carried over their divergence into homosexual and heterosexual patterns in later life. In the homosexual twin, who was more sickly as a child than his brother, the feminine tendencies were noticed by his mother when he was 3 or 4 years old, as indicated by his cross-dressing, girlish play activities, gestures, and the expressed desire to be a girl. In Zuger's opinion, the familial factors were not significant in the development of the sexual deviance. We are left to speculate, however, on the possible influence of the father's frequent absences from home as well as the inevitable reinforcement of the boy's femininity by the music and dancing program set up for him in contrast to the athletic training of his twin. On a still deeper level, one would wish to know how symbiotic the relationship between the deviant twin and his mother had been during infancy before the feminine behavior pattern emerged.

The studies we have reviewed on identical twins discordant for gender identity show that external events can influence the course of the individual's orientation. It is still a moot question as to how effective such events would be in the absence of underlying predispositions.

Another approach to this problem is through analysis of circulating sex hormones. Friedman et al. (1976) determined blood levels of sex steroids in a pair of male identical twins of divergent gender whose psychological test results confirmed their gender differentiation. There was no indication, however, that the sexual orientation was related to the blood levels of testosterone or estradiol. As in the case of unpredictability of hormonal therapy in homosexuality noted above, analysis of the total biosocial context is needed for a complete understanding of the role of the various contributing components.

In general, the evidence cited in this chapter supports Money's interactional position regarding the origin of gender identity. This he cogently advances in his reply to Zuger's (1970a) argument favoring the predominance of prenatal determinants as compared with social learning. Money contends that although the prenatal components do influence personality characteristics as in the tomboyism and decreased maternalism found in AGS, they do not dictate the final story of gender identity but are incorporated by the postnatal experiences to produce gender identity as the end product. In light of this flexibility, Money advocates easing up on sex stereotypes and allowing more leeway for individual variations in both sexes to find their most comfortable expression.

References

Bates, J.E., and Bentler, P.M. 1973. "Play Activities of Normal and Effeminate Boys." *Developmental Psychology* 9:20-27.

Bell, A.P. 1973. "Homosexualities: Their Range and Character." In J.K. Cole and R. Dienstbier, eds. *Nebraska Symposium on Motivation*, vol. 21. Lincoln: University of Nebraska Press, pp. 1-26.

Benjamin, H., and Ihlenfeld, C.L. 1973. "Transsexualism." *American Journal of Nursing* 73:457-461.

Bieber, I. 1976. "Psychodynamics and Sexual Object Choice: I. A Reply to Dr. Richard C. Friedman's Paper." *Contemporary Psychoanalysis* 12:366-369.

Bieber, I.; Dain, H.J.; Dince, P.R.; Drellich, M.G.; Grand, H.G.; Gundlach, R.H.; Kremer, M.W.; Rifkin, A.H.; Wilbur, C.B.; and Bieber, T.B. 1962. *Homosexuality: A Psychoanalytic Study*. New York: Basic Books.

Blumstein, P.W., and Schwartz, P. 1976. "Bisexuality in Women." *Archives of Sexual Behavior* 5:171-181.

Braaten, L.J., and Darling, C.D. 1965. "Overt and Covert Homosexual Problems among Male College Students." *Genetic Psychology Monographs* 71:269-310.

Davison, K.; Brierly, H.; and Smith, C. 1971. "A Male Monozygotic Twinship Discordant for Homosexuality: A Repertory Grid Study." *British Journal of Psychiatry* 118:675-682.

Ehrhardt, A.A., and Baker, S.W. 1974. "Fetal Androgens, Human Central Nervous System Differentiation, and Behavior Sex Differences." In R.C. Friedman, R.M. Richart, and R.L. Vande Wiele, eds. *Sex Differences in Behavior*. New York: Wiley.

Ellis, A. 1963. "Constitutional Factors in Homosexuality: A Reexamination of the Evidence." In H.G. Beigel, ed. *Advances in Sex Research*. New York: Harper & Row, pp. 161-186.

Evans, R.B. 1969. "Childhood Parental Relationships of Homosexual Men." *Journal of Consulting and Clinical Psychology* 33:129-135.

Friedman, R.C. 1976*a*. "Psychodynamics and Sexual Object Choice." *Contemporary Psychoanalysis* 12:94-108.

———. 1976*b*. "Psychodynamics and Sexual Object Choice: III. A Rereply to Dr. I. Bieber and C.W. Socarides." *Contemporary Psychoanalysis* 12:379-385.

Friedman, R.C.; Wollesen, F.; and Tendler, R. 1976. "Psychological Development and Blood Levels of Sex Steroids in Male Identical Twins of Divergent Sexual Orientation." *Journal of Nervous and Mental Disease* 163:282-288.

Gagnon, J.H., and Simon, W. 1973. *Sexual Conduct: The Social Sources of Human Sexuality*. Chicago: Aldine.

Gershman, H. 1970. "The Role of Core Gender Identity in the Genesis of Perversions." *American Journal of Psychoanalysis* 30:58-67.

Green, R. 1974*a*. *Sexual Identity Conflict in Children and Adults*. New York: Basic Books.

———. 1974*b*. "The Behaviorally Feminine Male Child: Pretranssexual? Pretransvestic? Prehomosexual? Preheterosexual?" In R.C. Friedman, R.M. Richart, and R.L. Vande Wiele, eds. *Sex Differences in Behavior*. New York: Wiley.

———. 1976. "One Hundred Ten Feminine and Masculine Boys: Behavioral Contrasts and Demographic Similarities." *Archives of Sexual Behavior* 5:425-446.

———. 1979. "Childhood Cross-gender Behavior and Subsequent Sexual Preferences." *American Journal of Psychiatry* 136:106-108.

Green, R., and Stoller, R.J. 1971. "Two Monozygotic (Identical) Twin Pairs Discordant for Gender Identity." *Archives of Sexual Behavior* 1:321-327.

Gundlach, R.H., and Riess, B.F. 1968. "Self and Sexual Identity in the Female: A Study of Female Homosexuals." In B.F. Riess, ed. *New Directions in Mental Health*. New York: Grune & Stratton, pp. 205-231.

Heston, L.L., and Shields, J. 1968. "Homosexuality in Twins: A Family Study and a Registry Study." *Archives of General Psychiatry* 18:149-160.

Ibrahim, A. 1976. "The Home Situation and the Homosexual." *Journal of Sex Research* 12:263-282.

Kallmann, F.J. 1952*a*. "Comparative Twin Study on the Genetic Aspects of Male Homosexuality." *Journal of Nervous and Mental Disease* 115:283-297.

_____. 1952*b*. "Twin and Sibship Study of Overt Male Homosexuality." *American Journal of Human Genetics* 4:136-146.

Kaye, H.E.; Berl, S.; Clare, J.; Eleston, M.R.; Gershwin, B.S.; Gershwin, P.; Kogan, L.S.; Torda, C.; and Wilbur, C.B. 1967. "Homosexuality in Women." *Archives of General Psychiatry* 17:626-634.

Kolodny, R.C.; Masters, W.H.; Hendryx, J.; and Toro, G. 1971. "Plasma Testosterone and Semen Analysis in Male Homosexuals. *New England Journal of Medicine* 285:1170-1174.

Levine, E.M.; Shaiova, C.H.; and Mihailovic, M. 1975. "Male to Female: The Role Transformation of Transsexuals." *Archives of Sexual Behavior* 4:173-185.

Lev-Ran, A. 1974. "Gender Role Differentiation in Hermaphrodites." *Archives of Sexual Behavior* 3:391-424.

Lothstein, L.M. 1979. "Psychodynamics and Sociodynamics of Gender-Dysphoric States." *American Journal of Psychotherapy* 33:214-238.

Mesnikoff, A.M.; Rainer, J.D.; Kolb, L.C.; and Carr, A.C. 1963. "Intrafamilial Determinants of Divergent Sexual Behavior in Twins." *American Journal of Psychiatry* 119:732-738.

Meyer-Bahlburg, H.F.L. 1977. "Sex Hormones and Male Homosexuality in Comparative Perspective." *Archives of Sexual Behavior* 6:297-325.

Money, J. 1973. "Prenatal Hormones and Postnatal Socialization in Gender Identity Differentiation." In J.K. Cole and R. Dienstbier, eds. *Nebraska Symposium on Motivation*, vol. 21. Lincoln: University of Nebraska Press, pp. 221-295.

Money, J., and Breman, J. 1969. "Sexual Dimorphism in the Psychology of Female Transsexuals." In R. Green and J. Money, eds. *Transsexualism and Sex Reassignment*. Baltimore: Johns Hopkins University Press, pp. 137-152.

Money, J., and Ehrhardt, A. 1972. *Man and Woman, Boy and Girl*. Baltimore: Johns Hopkins University Press.

Money, J., and Ogunro, C. 1974. "Behavioral Sexology: Ten Cases of Genetic Male Intersexuality with Impaired Prenatal and Pubertal Androgenization." *Archives of Sexual Behavior* 3:181-205.

Money, J., and Primrose, C. 1969. "Sexual Dimorphism and Dissociation in the Psychology of Male Transsexuals." In R. Green and J. Money, eds. *Transsexualism and Sex Reassignment*. Baltimore: Johns Hopkins University Press, pp. 115-131.

Nash, H., and Hayes, T. 1965. "The Parental Relationships of Male Homosexuals: Some Theoretical Issues and a Pilot Study." *Australian Journal of Psychology* 17:35-43.

Oberstone, A.K., and Siskoneck, H. 1976. "Psychological Adjustment and Life Style of Single Lesbian and Single Heterosexual Women." *Psychology of Women Quarterly* 1:172-188.

O'Connor, P.J. 1964. "Aetiological Factors in Homosexuality as Seen in RAF Psychiatric Practice." *British Journal of Psychiatry* 110:381-391.

Ovesey, L., and Person, E.S. 1973. "Gender Identity and Sexual Psychopathology in Men: A Psychodynamic Analysis of Homosexuality, Transsexualism, and Transvestism." *Journal of American Academy of Psychoanalysis* 1:53-72.

Pare, C.M.B. 1965. "Etiology of Homosexuality: Genetic and Chromosomal Aspects." In J. Marmor, ed. *Sexual Inversion*. New York: Basic Books, pp. 70-80.

Parker, N. 1964. "Homosexuality in Twins: A Report on Three Discordant Pairs." *British Journal of Psychiatry* 110:489-495.

Pauly, I.B. 1969. "Adult Manifestations of Female Transsexualism. In R. Green and J. Money, eds. *Transsexualism and Sex Reassignment*. Baltimore: Johns Hopkins University Press, pp. 59-87.

_____ . 1974. "Female Transsexualism." *Archives of Sexual Behavior* 3: 509-526.

Perloff, W.H. 1965. "Hormones and Homosexuality." In J. Marmor, ed. *Sexual Inversion*. New York: Basic Books, pp. 44-69.

Person, E.S., and Ovesey, L. 1974*a*. "The Transsexual Syndrome in Males: I. Primary Transsexualism" *American Journal of Psychotherapy* 28:4-20.

_____ . 1974*b*. "The Transsexual Syndrome in Males: II. Secondary Transsexualism." *American Journal of Psychotherapy* 28:174-193.

Rekers, G.A.; Bentler, P.M.; Rosen, A.C.; and Lovaas, O.I. 1977. "Child Gender Disturbances: A Clinical Rationale for Intervention." *Psychotherapy: Theory, Research and Practice* 14:2-11.

Roeske, N.A., and Banet, A.G. 1972. "Gender Identity: The Problem of a True Hermaphrodite." *Journal of American Academy of Child Psychiatry* 11:132-156.

Rosen, A.C.; Rekers, G.A.; and Friar, L.R. 1977. "Theoretical and Diagnostic Issues in Child Gender Disturbances." *Journal of Sex Research* 13:89-103.

Sabalis, F.A.; Appenzeller, S.N.; and Moseley, W.B. 1974. "The Three Sisters: Transsexual Male Siblings." *American Journal of Psychiatry* 131:907-909.

Saghir, M.T., and Robins, E. 1973. *Male and Female Homosexuality: A Comprehensive Investigation*. Baltimore: Williams & Wilkins.

Schiavi, R.C., and White, D. 1976. "Androgens and Male Sexual Function: A Review of Human Studies." *Journal of Sex and Marital Therapy* 2:214-225.

Schofield, M.G. 1965. *Sociological Aspects of Homosexuality: A Comparative Study of Three Types of Homosexuality.* Boston: Little, Brown.

Siegelman, M. 1974. "Parental Background of Homosexual and Heterosexual Women." *British Journal of Psychiatry* 124:14-21.

Socarides, C.W. 1976. "Psychodynamics and Sexual Object Choice: II. A Reply to Dr. Richard C. Friedman's Paper." *Contemporary Psychoanalysis* 12:370-378.

Starká, L.; Sipová, I.; and Hynie, J. 1975. "Plasma Testosterone in Male Transsexuals and Homosexuals." *Journal of Sex Research* 11:134-138.

Stephan, W.G. 1973. "Parental Relationships and Early Social Experiences of Activist Male Homosexuals and Male Heterosexuals." *Journal of Abnormal Psychology* 82:506-513.

Stoller, R.J. 1964. "A Contribution to the Study of Gender Identity." *International Journal of Psychoanalysis* 45 (pt. 2-3):220-226.

———. 1968. *Sex and Gender.* New York: Science House.

———. 1969. "Parental Influence in Male Transsexualism." In R. Green and J. Money, eds. *Transsexualism and Sex Reassignment.* Baltimore: Johns Hopkins University Press.

———. 1975. *Sex and Gender.* Vol. 2: *The Transsexual Experiment.* New York: Aronson.

———. 1976. "Two Feminized Male American Indians." *Archives of Sexual Behavior* 5:529-538.

Thompson, N.L.; Schwartz, D.M.; McCandless, B.R.; and Edwards, D.A. 1973. "Parent-Child Relationships and Sexual Identity in Male and Female Homosexuals and Heterosexuals." *Journal of Consulting and Clinical Psychology* 41:120-127.

Townes, B.D.; Ferguson, W.D.; and Gillan, S. 1976. "Differences in Psychological Sex, Adjustment, and Familial Influences among Homosexual and Nonhomosexual Populations." *Journal of Homosexuality* 1:261-272.

Wålinder, J. 1967. *Transsexualism: A Study of Forty-Three Cases.* Göteborg: Scandinavian University Books.

Warnes, H., and Hill, G. 1974. "Gender Identity and the Wish to be a Woman." *Psychosomatics* 15:25-29.

Wolff, C. 1971. *Love between Women.* New York: Harper & Row.

Yalom, I.; Green, R.; and Fisk, N. 1973. "Prenatal Exposure to Female Hormones." *Archives of General Psychiatry* 28:554-561.

Zuger, B. 1970a. "Gender Role Determination: A Critical Review of the Evidence from Hermaphroditism." *Psychosomatic Medicine* 32:449-467.

———. 1970b. "The Role of Familial Factors in Persistent Effeminate Behavior in Boys." *American Journal of Psychiatry* 126:1167-1170.

———. 1976. "Monozygotic Twins Discordant for Homosexuality: Report of a Pair and Significance of the Phenomenon." *Comprehensive Psychiatry* 17:661-669.

8 Activity Level

In the last few chapters we have explored the dynamic differences at the core of masculinity (M) and femininity (F) and tried to get a general view of their development. In the chapters that follow we shall take up these basic motivators one at a time and look for the biological and social factors in their origins.

It makes sense to start with a trait that may underlie all the others, and might conceivably survive even if all the others were demolished. We refer to a possible sex difference in output of energy, or level of activity. Here is a concept that lies midway between such physical characteristics as basal metabolism, lung capacity, and muscle-fat ratio and such directed needs as dominance and affiliation. In the former measurements boys exceed girls throughout most of the period of growth (Falkner 1966). Indeed with this in mind we might find it surprising if males did not turn out to be more inclined to strenuous physical activity than females. But let us look at the evidence.

Course of Development

From our point of view we should not be surprised to find males more active than females early in life, even in infancy. A study of newly born babies is of some interest here (Knop 1946). If an infant lying on its back is pulled gently upward by the wrists, it will either submit passively or resist more or less vigorously. Knop tested almost 700 babies of both sexes within twenty-four hours of delivery and again eight days later. Estimating resistance on a scale of four steps, he found that the males pulled back significantly harder than the females ($p < .05$). Otherwise girl and boy babies seem to be about equal in limb movement and locomotion during the first year. Thereafter, when a difference in general activity does appear, it favors the boys (Maccoby & Jacklin 1974).

Under what conditions does this difference show itself? These have been only partly explored, but one of the most important factors seems to be social. When playing alone, preschool boys and girls are equally active (Routh et al. 1974); but in groups (and boys form groups more readily than girls) the boys step up their activity while the girls do not (Halverson & Waldrop 1973).

Second, a sex difference is more likely to show if children are free to choose among various types of play. According to one study (Harper & Sanders 1975), when free to choose, 4-year-old boys played outdoors more than girls; while Sally and Sue made things at the craft tables or in the kitchen, Jimmy and Joey were outdoors pushing a sand tractor, climbing the jungle gym, or puttering around the equipment shed. Incidentally, stereotyping influences, if any, were inconspicuous: the supervisors were female and treated both sexes alike; while interviewed parents thought dresses and jeans equally suitable for a girl to wear when playing outdoors.

Aberrations

Extreme degrees of a trait are often more revealing than normal levels. This is true of hyperactivity, a syndrome that has received increasing attention in the last few decades. Once attributed to brain damage (minimal brain dysfunction), it is now generally considered a behavior problem of childhood, though it may appear in early infancy and last throughout life (Ross & Ross 1976). (Some mothers of hyperactive children reported that even before birth they kicked harder than the others.) Experts insist that it is not simply the upper extreme of normal activity. Highly distractible, reckless, defiant, often destructive, the hyperkinetic child appears to be driven by an inner tension beyond his control.

Hyperactivity is of interest to us because it occurs in boys so much more often than in girls. A rough count of subjects in thirteen studies reported by Ross and Ross (1976) gives a sex ratio of over 5:1. There is also evidence that hyperactivity persists longer in boys. Huessy et al. (1973) examined 500 schoolchildren successively in the second, fourth, and fifth grades. Of 101 children diagnosed hyperkinetic in the second or fourth grade, 74 were boys and 27, girls. Reexamined in fifth grade, 70 percent of the boys and 26 percent of the girls were still hyperkinetic, a highly significant difference in rate of recovery.

A basic question is whether hyperactivity is merely the upper end of the normal distribution, or whether it should be recognized as a clinical disorder. The issue has sparked a number of investigations. The answer is not yet clear, but more information has emerged about differences in activity between boys and girls.

In an early study Macfarlane et al. (1954) used interviews with mothers to unearth the behavior problems of 126 normal children from 21 months to 14 years of age. Sex differences in the type of problem reported stood out sharply. When boys made trouble it was by being overactive and too competitive, demanding too much attention, and by temper tantrums as well as lies and thefts. Problem girls on the other hand tended to suck their thumbs and to be reserved, timid, and oversensitive. The authors defined overactivity as the two highest steps of a five-step rating scale. Not surprisingly, more boys than girls were overactive (though not always significantly) at every age. Few correlations with other traits appeared, but those that did were interesting: overactive males were likely to be negativistic as infants and destructive in nursery school; their female counterparts were relatively fearless but subject to swings of mood.

Other investigators, focusing on activity rather than problems of conduct, agreed that boys were more energetic than girls and brought out further correlates. Goggin (1975) found that in preschool boys high activity went with strong social involvement: attempts to get help and approval from adults and to dominate peers. No such relationships were true of preschool girls. But Battle and Lacey (1972), analyzing records from the Fels Longitudinal Study, give us a view of later developments. For their male subjects activity was linked with resistance to adults throughout the first ten years. In females the same linkage appeared but not until they went to elementary school.

In summary, these studies of normal children suggest that the syndrome of hyperactivity exaggerates differences already present between girls and boys in general.

Origins

Social. Here as elsewhere psychologists are prone to look for causes in social pressures at an early age. Where physical activity is concerned, parents are supposed to encourage boys and discourage girls. One bit of evidence cited above (Harper & Sanders 1975) testified that this is not always so.

Social influence, however, may take different forms. Battle and Lacey, finding that mothers of hyperactive sons were critical and rejecting from the start, suggested that their attitude might have been responsible for the boys' defiance. A similar rejection of tomboys by teachers, they ventured, might have produced the delayed resistance noted in the more active girls.

Critics of the early-experience hypothesis ask why parents should respond differentially to their sons and daughters. Sooner or later we face the old question: which came first, the hen or the egg? In this case it might be reworded as follows: given the interaction between adult and child, what does each contribute to the outcome?

To tackle this issue Inoff and Halverson (1977) secured observations and ratings of children's behavior during free play in a nursery school. Forty of these children, twenty of each sex, were selected for special attention. Interactions of each child with a female caretaker were divided into those initiated by the caretaker and those initiated by the child. The question that chiefly concerns us is: what kind of child, as judged by his behavior, initiated the most interactions with the caretaker? To answer it, the investigators correlated the frequencies of such interactions with the children's ratings and with factors derived from the observations of their behavior.

The results showed that the boys making most contact with the caretaker were impatient, excitable, outgoing, and involved with their peers. The girls that did likewise were nonaggressive, fearful, and inactive. Assuming that the children came to the caretaker to relieve stress, the authors conclude that stress came from activities of high intensity for boys and low intensity for girls.

We are still not told how this difference in the source of discomfort came about; our search is simply pushed back further into infancy. There we find a well-known study by Goldberg and Lewis (1969). Sixty-four 13-month-old infants, thirty-two male and thirty-two female, were observed for fifteen minutes of free play with their mothers present. The girls took much longer than the boys to leave the mother and returned sooner and more often; they spent more time "talking" to the mother. The boys played more vigorously and farther away.

Are we safe at last in assuming that these results stem from an inborn temperamental difference? It happens that the same infants had been previously observed with their mothers at 6 months of age (Kagan & Lewis 1965). At that time it had been noted that the mothers of girl babies touched and spoke to them more than the mothers of boys. So the factor of learning could not be ruled out.

But another well-known study took account of even earlier interactions. Moss (1967) observed thirty mothers with their first-born babies three times at weekly intervals during the first month. In contrast with Kagan and Lewis' observations at 6 months, these mothers held and attended male infants more than female. A likely explanation appeared in the further finding that the male infants fussed more than the females, who in turn slept more than the males. (When either of these differences was eliminated statistically by adjusting for covariance, the difference in maternal contact became insignificant.)

Though fussing is a far cry from overactivity, these findings invite speculation. Perhaps, if girls *do* learn in infancy to be more passive than boys, it is because mothers learn that it is more rewarding to fondle a docile baby than a fretful one.

Biological. Aside from the higher metabolic rate and more imposing musculature of the male, do we have any reason to believe he is innately more active than the female? There is some evidence that the hyperactive syndrome runs in families. Morrison and Stewart (1973*a*, 1973*b*) found that hyperactive children (forty-eight boys and two girls) had more parents, aunts, and uncles who were hyperactive when children than did a control group. As an argument for biology, this finding would not carry much weight. But another finding in the same study was more arresting: there were significantly more hyperactive relatives among the extended families of hyperactive children reared by their own families than in the foster families of adopted ones.

Of course, if hyperactivity is considered an expression of pathology, the sex difference in it may be set aside as irrelevant to the main issue. But if a linkage with the normal condition can be established, this difference is not so easy to ignore. Waldrop and her associates have done that or something close to it. In a series of studies of normal children they found an association between hyperactive tendencies and minor physical anomalies, commonly present in cases of Down's syndrome (mongolism); for example, abnormal size of head, eyes wide apart, third toe longer than second. For boys this relationship appeared both in nursery school and elementary school; it was also confirmed in boys referred to a Hyperactivity Clinic (Quinn & Rapoport 1974). For girls it was less consistent, appearing in one sample only. In three others there was either no relation or the girls with physical anomalies tended to be inhibited and fearful (Waldrop & Halverson 1971; Waldrop et al. 1976). Though favoring a congenital interpretation, the authors were impartial enough to point out that a social one could be made: hyperactivity *might* be rewarded in boys and punished in girls. But that seems unlikely.

As noted in chapter 3, studies of twins provide the best available evidence for or against the inheritance of differences. We were able to find only two such studies dealing with activity. In one (Scarr 1966), twenty-eight pairs of dizygotic (DZ) and twenty-four pairs of monozygotic (MZ) female twins between 6 and 10 years old were given toys to choose and slides to view; the scope of their activities was gauged by interview. Times of choosing and viewing yielded a moderate ratio of heritability (.40); but as to preference for active over sedentary pastimes the ratio was zero (that is, the correlations within MZ and DZ pairs were equal).

In the second study, Willerman (1973) asked the mothers of over ninety pairs of twins to answer questionnaires from which to determine the twins' levels of activity and whether they were MZ or DZ. The correlations within MZ pairs were significantly larger than within DZ ($p < .001$), and the heritability ratios derived from them were .82 for males and .58 for females, indicating, in the author's words, a "substantial heritable component."

In retrospect, it seems fairly safe to say that boys prefer more strenuous activity than girls. As to the roles of heredity and environment in producing this result, the evidence, inconclusive as it is, makes it unsafe to rule out either factor.

References

Battle, E.S., and Lacey, B. 1972. "A Context of Hyperactivity in Children, Over Time." *Child Development* 43:757-773.

Falkner, F., 1966. *Human Development*. Philadelphia: Saunders.

Goggin, J.E. 1975. "Sex Differences in the Activity Level of Preschool Children as a Possible Precursor of Hyperactivity." *Journal of Genetic Psychology* 127:75-81.

Goldberg, S., and Lewis, M. 1969. "Play Behavior in the Year-Old Infant: Early Sex Differences." *Child Development* 40:21-31.

Halverson, C.F., and Waldrop, M.F. 1973. "The Relations of Mechanically Recorded Activity Level to Varieties of Preschool Play Behavior." *Child Development* 44:678-681.

Harper, L.W., and Sanders, K.M. 1975. "Preschool Children's Use of Space: Sex Differences in Outdoor Play." *Developmental Psychology* 11(1):119.

Huessy, H.R.; Marshall, C.D.; and Gendron, R.A. 1973. "Five Hundred Children Followed from Grade 2 through Grade 5 for the Prevalence of Behavior Disorder." *Acta Paedopsychiatrica* 39:301-309.

Inoff, G.E., and Halverson, C.F. 1977. "Behavioral Disposition of Child and Caretaker-Child Interaction." *Developmental Psychology* 13:274-281.

Kagan, J., and Lewis, M. 1965. "Studies of Attention in the Human Infant." *Merrill-Palmer Quarterly* 11:95-137.

Knop, C.A. 1946. "The Dynamics of Newly Born Babies." *Journal of Pediatrics* 29:721-728.

Maccoby, E.E., and Jacklin, C.N. 1974. *The Psychology of Sex Differences*. Stanford, Calif.: Stanford University Press.

Macfarlane, J.W.; Allen, L.; and Honzik, M.P. 1954. *A Developmental Study of the Behavior Problems of Normal Children between 21 Months and 14 Years*. Berkeley: University of California Press.

Morrison, J.R., and Stewart, M.A. 1973a. "A Family Study of the Hyperactive Child Syndrome." *Biological Psychiatry* 3:189.

_____. 1973b."The Psychiatric Status of the Legal Families of Adopted Hyperactive Children." *Archives of General Psychiatry* 28:888.

Moss, H.A. 1967. "Sex, Age, and State as Determinants of Mother-Infant Interaction." *Merrill-Palmer Quarterly* 13:19-36.

Quinn, P.O., and Rapoport, J.L. 1974. "Minor Physical Anomalies and Neurological Status in Hyperactive Boys." *Pediatrics* 53:742-747.

Ross, D.M., and Ross, S.A. 1976. *Hyperactivity: Research, Theory, and Action*. New York: Wiley.

Routh, D.K.; Schroeder, C.S.; and O'Tuama, L.A. 1974. "Development of Activity Level in Children." *Developmental Psychology* 10:163-168.

Scarr, S. 1966. "Genetic Factors in Activity Motivation." *Child Development* 37:663-673.

Waldrop, M.F.; Bell, R.Q.; and Goering, J.D. 1976. "Minor Physical Anomalies and Inhibited Behavior in Elementary School Girls." *Journal of Child Psychology and Psychiatry and Allied Disciplines* 17:113-122.

Waldrop, M.F., and Halverson,C.F., 1971. "Minor Physical Anomalies and Hyperactive Behavior in Young Children." In J. Hellmuth, ed. *Exceptional Infant: Studies in Abnormalities*, vol. 2. New York: Brunner Mazel.

Willerman, L. 1973. "Activity Level and Hyperactivity in Twins." *Child Development* 44:288-293.

9　Aggressiveness and Dominance

Few would dispute the statement that human males are more aggressive than human females. Even aggressive women's liberators might be willing to accept it. Statistics on crime are impressive (Moyer 1974): many more crimes of violence (robbery and murder) have been committed by males than females in all nations throughout history. Recently female juvenile delinquents seem to be catching up (*Time* 1977). But in 1975 only 11 percent of juveniles arrested for violent crimes were girls.

Critics will be quick to point out that such statistics are decidedly a product of the different social pressures, restrictions, and incentives operating on girls and boys. More reliance is rightly placed on studies carefully planned to control such conditions as far as possible. Studies of this type, and there are many, have been well summarized and critically reviewed by several authorities (Oetzel 1966; Feshbach 1970; Maccoby & Jacklin 1974; Rohner 1976). On the whole they agree, with some reservations and provisos, that throughout most of the life span and across most known cultures, males are readier to fight than females.

Dominance and aggression would seem to go together; nevertheless their joint treatment may be challenged. Dominance is often achieved by attack and maintained by threat of repetition. But the correlation is far from perfect. Fights do not always lead to pecking orders. A female chimpanzee in her "swelling" may dominate a usually assertive male. In our own species a mild parent may still dominate an aggressive son.

At the human level the relation between truculence and dominance is most apparent in the free play of children. In other situations dominance may be acquired by accident of birth, a swollen bankroll, or other devices. Maccoby and Jacklin dealt with the two traits in separate contexts and arrived at distinct conclusions. They held that a sex difference in aggressiveness has biological roots, while a sex difference in dominance is extremely doubtful. Our own hypothesis is that male aggressiveness, especially toward other males, and male dominance, especially toward females, have through the ages made for successful reproduction and survival, implying a sex difference in both respects. Our discussion of dominance, however, will be limited to childhood, where the evidence is less equivocal than in later years.

Most observers agree that small boys take to scuffling and rough-and-tumble play more than girls. There is some question, however, about how early dominance and subordination are established (Gellert 1961; Freedman 1972; Knudson 1973). With this reservation in mind we may take McGrew's (1972) study of 3- and 4-year-olds in two British nursery schools as an example. The boys in these groups did considerably more than their share of fighting and play fighting. When girls fought, it was usually with a boy. The girls did not fight enough to produce a dominance hierarchy, but the boys made quite a definite one, clearly related to activity and sociability as well as to success in battle. It is worth a passing note that the dominant boys were older and heavier than their subordinates and had been longer at nursery school. In their first day at a new school boys appeared more fearful and inhibited than girls.

Even if, as our preliminary survey suggests, males are more aggressive and possibly more dominant than females, the big problem is still ahead: how to explain it. For unknown reasons some find it easier to believe that heredity is primarily to blame; others are more comfortable with the idea that the difference is largely acquired. Proponents of either side would be more convincing if they could point to specific ways in which aggressiveness is learned or unlearned on the one hand, or inherited on the other. The rest of the chapter may be considered a step toward meeting this requirement.

Social Factors

Usually the approach through learning looks for possible sources of positive or negative reinforcement (reward or punishment). For example, what about adult intervention? Smith and Green (1975) watched aggressive incidents in fifteen English nursery groups. Of 239 squabbles all but 32 involved males. Adults intervened in less than half of the incidents, most of these involving both sexes. What interested the investigators was that when adults interfered the aggressor had his way only 26 percent of the time; without interference his rate of success was 63 percent. It seems unlikely, as the authors pointed out, that the boys' greater pugnacity was due to differential reward by adults.

Is peer acceptance a factor? To find out, McGuire (1973) followed up his observations of free play in preschool children—showing the boys to be more aggressive—with sociometric interviews. Each child rated the others, identified by their pictures, for popularity. The outcome was remarkable. Moderately aggressive boys proved popular, while the least and most aggressive boys received low ratings. Highly aggressive girls, on the other hand, were given high marks in popularity.

These results are not easy to explain. One thing is clear: they give little support to the idea that peer approval spurs male aggressiveness. The converse seems more likely, that aggressiveness has some effect on peer acceptance. McGuire (1973), adapting a suggestion by Maccoby (1966), speculated that the curve relating social acceptance to aggressiveness resembles an inverted U; that is, as aggression increases, acceptance rises to a peak and then declines. From the further assumption that male aggression varies along the entire scale but female aggression is confined to the lower portion, McGuire's results might be deduced.

Aggressiveness in males and females may differ not only in its external social consequences but in its inner dynamic context. For example, females are generally thought to be more empathic than males; that is, more sensitive to others' emotional states. Such awareness might cool their rage before it flared into action.

Experimental evidence has failed to substantiate the belief in woman's stronger empathy (Maccoby & Jacklin 1974). But in a study of the relation between empathy and aggression, the Feshbachs (1969) turned up an interesting sex difference. They measured both traits in two groups of children, 4 to 5 and 6 to 7 years old. Oddly enough, a relation appeared in the boys' data but not in the girls'. In the younger group boys scoring high in empathy were rated *more* aggressive than those scoring low; in the older group this relation was reversed. Here again Maccoby's suggestion of an inverted-U relation, this time between aggression and empathy, might prove useful in explaining a sex difference.

Other investigators have studied the influence of various moods on social behavior. Harris and Siebel's (1975) experiment is of special interest to us because they tested both aggression and altruism in third-grade girls and boys. Altruism was measured by how many balloons a child was willing to share with less fortunate children. Aggressiveness was measured by the number of assaults made on available toys. Mood was varied by asking the children to think angry, sad, or happy thoughts or, in the control group, to count to thirty. For all subjects combined, true to our social norms the girls shared more balloons than the boys, while the boys abused toys more than the girls. As for altruism, self-induced moods had no effect on balloon sharing by either sex.

Results on aggression were more interesting. The two control groups, male and female, scored alike. But in the mood-inducing groups the boys showed increased aggression; the girls showed a loss. How could this happen? Perhaps, as the authors suggested, any emotion enhances the strongest of competing responses. In a boy one such response to the toys was aggressive. In a girl a stronger response was the anxiety induced by the aggressive impulse itself.

In one of Bandura's well-known experiments on the modeling of social behavior (Bandura et al. 1963), 3-to-6-year-old boys were more likely than girls to imitate aggressive models, whether real or in movies. A similar experiment by Hapkiewicz and Stone (1974) throws further light on sex differences in aggressive and sharing behavior. Boys and girls aged 6 to 10, in same-sexed pairs, saw one of three movies: (1) *The Three Stooges*, full of aggression by real actors; (2) an aggressive cartoon starring Mighty Mouse and cats; (3) an innocuous film about music. The test was a second movie (from Walt Disney's *Fantasia*) visible though a peephole with room for only one child at a time. Aggression was scored in terms of pushing, grabbing, and verbal attack; sharing, in terms of taking turns at the peephole.

The results were quite clear-cut. In aggressiveness the boys surpassed the girls by a wide margin (chance probability < .005). In sharing, the girls were ahead by a similar amount (p < .0002). Both differences were larger following the real-life movie than either of the others. The authors concluded fittingly: the real-life film activated the prevailing response tendency of the viewer; in the male this was aggression, in the female, cooperation.

So far we have said nothing about the most obvious factor: social stereotypes. Boys are brought up to believe that it is manly to fight other males who threaten whatever they hold dear. But no gentleman, even in anger, is supposed to lay hands on a woman. Girls on the other hand are taught that physical conflict is unladylike and should be left to men. Or at least it is commonly assumed, though without hard evidence that we know of, that these are the ways children are indoctrinated.

It is not easy to produce real aggression in the laboratory. The most successful method has been to give the subject a task involving the delivery of a disagreeable stimulus, typically an electric shock, to another person. (This is what the subject is led to believe. Actually there is no shock and the other person is either an accomplice or nonexistent.)

In one experiment by Buss (1966), for example, the subject's task was to teach the accomplice a simple concept, using shock as a punishment for errors. Strength of shock was left up to the subject, thus providing a measure of aggression. College students, twenty of each sex, took part in the experiment, and for each group half the accomplices were male and half female. Buss found that males gave stronger shocks than females and that both sexes shocked male more severely than female "victims," though in a previous experiment the females had not discriminated between the sexes.

If these results reflected social stereotypes, it would be interesting to know how early they were acquired. To find out, Poorman et al. (1976) did a similar experiment comparing 4- and 5-year-olds with 12- and 13-year-olds and using noise as a punishment instead of shock. They found no sex difference in overall aggressiveness. The only striking effect they *did* find involved the males: preschool boys inflicted louder noises on female than male "targets" (p < .05), while preadolescent boys tended to give more decibels of punishment to other males than to females (p < .10). This shift may be readily accounted for. The question remains, why should the males be the only ones affected? Is this generally true?

In a variant of Buss's method aimed to get the subjects more personally involved, the subject is pitted against an opponent (imagined) in a test of reaction time (Taylor 1967). The slower contestant in each trial receives a shock of an intensity set for that trial by his opponent. Here the subject's setting, the measure of his aggressiveness, depends in part on how his fictitious rival has treated *him*. (Actually the experimenter controls who gets the shock and how much.)

In one experiment Taylor and Epstein (1967) used college students of both sexes as subjects and opponents and scheduled steadily increasing shocks. Both male and female subjects replied in kind, but the ones who pushed the shock levels highest were the women whose opponent was a man. This experiment and others like it (Shortell & Biller 1970) suggest that the females of our species are not the gentle sufferers of popular mythology. Yet on the whole the studies sampled here have testified to the force of masculine and feminine stereotypes. Can we trust the laboratory for an untouched portrait?

Field Experiments. One may still object that most laboratory studies of human behavior are to some degree artificial. A subject who is trying to please an experimenter may be unable to act naturally, even if that is just what the experimenter wants him to do. Studies of aggressiveness are no exception. So a few hardy souls have ventured to assess aggressiveness in men and women going about their daily lives, unaware that they are actually taking part in an experiment.

Driving behavior in traffic offers inducements to students of human aggression. At a light-controlled intersection, for example, all movement in a lane depends on the first car. To induce frustration Doob and Gross (1968) kept the first car stationary for the duration of the green light; they measured aggressiveness by whether and how soon the driver behind honked his horn. Incidentally to their main question (whether an old Rambler would evoke more honks than a Crysler Imperial), they noted that male drivers honked significantly sooner than females. Deaux (1971) repeated the experiment and found an insignificant difference. But she did find another difference opposite in direction to one we met with earlier in the laboratory: frustrated drivers, male or female, honked more if the offending driver was a woman than if it was a man.

For a chance to observe aggressiveness in a face-to-face encounter, the United Kingdom offers the roundabout: a circular driveway giving access to diverging routes. The customary rule is that traffic in the roundabout has the right-of-way over an entering vehicle. Leff and Gunn (1973) were concerned with other, personal factors that might influence the outcome of meetings at these points. During several hours of observation they recorded the sex of each driver and which one took precedence. Female drivers in the roundabouts were too few for statistics. But for encounters with a male driver in the roundabout the results were as follows: 31 percent of entering males broke the rule and preceded the other car as compared with 19 percent of females. This difference was significant at the .01 level. It is a pity that we do not know what proportions of males and females would have taken priority over a female in the roundabout. Then we could tell how much of the sex difference belongs in the domain of aggression or dominance and how much in conforming with laws.

Field experiments on aggressiveness are not limited to car driving. Among the most imaginative and daring of the exploits in this category are those of Mary Harris of the University of New Mexico. At her behest intrepid students and research assistants, of both sexes, bumped into strangers in crowded shopping centers (Harris 1973) and cut in front of persons waiting in lines at cafeterias or box offices (Harris 1974) in order to record the animosity of those affected.

In most of these situations women responded as aggressively as men. In fact, in one experiment on behavior in queues, more women than men expressed objection, verbally or otherwise, to an attempt to displace them. More consistent, on the whole, has been a sex difference in the ability to arouse aggression: in most of Harris' situations male assistants provoked more aggression than female assistants, regardless of whether the subject was male or female. But again we are reminded that in the case of the stalled cars (Deaux 1971) female drivers were honked at more than males.

To judge from the few data available, which sex is the more aggressive—whether on the dispensing or receiving end—depends heavily on social context. Figuratively we might say that the freeway is masculine territory, the shopping center feminine. That is too glib. But it serves to point up the enormous power of sex roles in determining social behavior.

Biological Factors

But are sex roles everything? It might be wise at this point to broaden the scope of our search to include other animals. Since *Homo sapiens* alone boasts a culture, a sex difference found to be prevalent in other species would strengthen the argument for a biological origin. Such is the case with aggressiveness, at least among vertebrates.

Students of rodent behavior agree that, except for hamsters, males are generally more aggressive and dominant than females. Barnett (1963) found that in colonies of wild Norway rats only the males defended territories. (Females would fight, however, to protect a nest and pups.) Among albino rats females sometimes fight, but their battles are less decisive than those of males (Seward 1945). As for mice, Lagerspetz (1964) limited her studies of aggression to males when she found that her females simply would not fight. At the primate level we are reminded of the Harlows' description of infant monkeys at play: the small males wrestling and roughhousing, the females chasing and fleeing (Harlow & Harlow 1965). In general, whether we look to mammals, birds, reptiles, or even fishes, we find the male doing more than his share of the fighting. Where an order of dominance occurs, in lizards or llamas, the "boss" is likely to be male (Cloudsley-Thompson 1965).

Absence of a culture, however, does not guarantee that a differential trait is inborn. The aggressiveness underlying male dominance, for example, could result from victories won by stronger jaws or tougher horns. Proof is still needed that the buck, as distinct from the doe, is born rather than raised to be a fighter. Evidence is available on several species, but we shall depend mainly on data from the most prolific sources—mice, rats, and monkeys—with passing reference to other forms. Species with smaller brains serve our purpose because their behavior more directly reflects bodily needs and biological imperatives. Large-brained primates offer the advantage of closer similarity to humans, but the disadvantage of a thicker overlay of learning.

Genetic Evidence

Animals. Since the pioneering experiments of Schjelderup-Ebbe (1935), the dominance hierarchy, or peck order, was a well-known feature of the barnyard. It promised a convenient tool for measuring individual differences in readiness and ability to fight. If so, it might be used to show whether such differences were inherited or acquired.

Potter (1949) took a first step by putting different breeds of fowl together in mixed flocks and showing that White Leghorns pecked Brown Red Games significantly more often than chance would predict. Potter's experiment holds special interest for us in that his flocks were composed of hens only. The next step was to see if, by selective breeding, two strains could be produced, one aggressive, the other submissive. This, too, has been successfully done (Craig et al. 1965).

Further evidence comes from dogs. Pawlowski and Scott (1956) studied the development of dominant-subordinate relationships in four breeds by testing pairs of puppies within each breed with a bone to compete for. By the end of the first year clear-cut differences had appeared among the breeds. Scored for proportion of firm dominant-subordinate relations, wirehaired fox terriers were highest, followed by basenjis, cocker spaniels, and beagles in that order, though not all differences were significant.

Noteworthy are the results on male-female pairs: in two breeds, basenjis and fox terriers, male dominance was complete; in the other two, cockers and beagles, males and females were equally likely to dominate.

Oddly, less information is available on rats, but one piece comes as a bonus. Two strains had been selectively bred for timidity and fearlessness in an open field. Hall and Klein (1942) paired males of the eighth and ninth generations with one another to test for aggressiveness. Not surprisingly, the timid rats proved clearly less pugnacious than the fearless ones.

Turning to mice, we find that intensive inbreeding has produced a large number of genetically pure strains. When males of such strains are tested for truculence, the average scores of different strains cover a wide range (Southwick & Clark 1968). But different investigators ranking the same strains do not agree closely. This probably does not mean that readiness to fight is largely learned, but that its triggering depends on many environmental conditions, such as housing and method of testing (Thiessen 1976).

However, there are other indications that strain differences are not entirely inbred. Southwick (1968), for example, tested the effect of cross-fostering on interstrain differences in aggressiveness. Newborn litters of mice were exchanged between mothers of a passive and an aggressive strain, who nursed them until weaned. In later tests of fighting, cross-fostered males of the passive strain proved much more combative than uncrossed control groups, while those of the aggressive strain were as pugnacious as their own controls. Here was good evidence for an environmental factor. Whether it was a matter of the mother's solicitude or the chemistry of her milk Southwick was unwilling to guess.

Lagerspetz (1964) pioneered in the selective breeding of mice for aggressiveness. As we have already seen, she found females too pacific for her purpose, so she tested and selected only male offspring in each generation, choosing from their sisters the mothers of the next. It took only one generation to establish the nonaggressive strain; in the other line militancy was still increasing in the seventh generation. Are we to infer that Lagerspectz' females were devoid of fighting potential? We can be fairly sure that an attack on a nestful of young would have met with fierce resistance. Perhaps male and female mice differ, not in pugnacity, but in the conditions necessary to arouse it. But such a conclusion would be premature.

Ebert and Hyde (1976) reported an experiment in selective breeding for aggression based on female mice. For their parental stock they used wild mice, and in each generation the females only were selected by pitting them against tame females. Within four generations the high and low lines had diverged significantly from their controls. What happened to the males? The answer came from the fifth generation, when the authors tested both males and females against opponents of the same sex. While the females continued to show significant differences among high, low, and control lines, the males gave either insignificant or inconsistent results. Evidently the genetic determiners of male and female aggressiveness are not the same.

A possible clue to the difference may be found in another experiment (Selmanoff et al. 1975). The investigators crossed two inbred strains of mice differing in aggressiveness and staged duels between males of both the parental and hybrid strains. As we should expect, the hybrid scores fell between the parental ones; more remarkably, the reciprocal hybrids differed from each other. Those with fathers from the more aggressive strain were more prone to fight than those sired by the less warlike. Twenty generations later the experiment was repeated with the same result, making the combined interhybrid differences highly significant (p < .001).

This evidence of sex linkage pointed directly at the Y chromosome of the male sperm cell as somehow holding the key to male pugnacity. But the authors warn us not to overrate its scope, since similar experiments with other strains of mice have failed to confirm it. They conclude that the Y chromosome is only one of various genetic factors controlling violence in the mouse.

Humans. If the strands linking chromosomes to temperament in animals are hard to unravel, at the human level they appear hopelessly tangled. A breakthrough seemed imminent not long ago when a supposedly rare chromosomal pattern, 47, XYY, was found in a surprising number of cases among the more unruly male inmates of a mental hospital (Jacobs et al. 1965). (In this pattern an extra Y chromosome brings the usual chromosome count of 46 to 47.) Since the cases discovered were also unusually tall, somewhat retarded, and prone to anger, the XYY syndrome included these characteristics.

But a label, like a stereotype, can be misleading, and the double-Y chromosome as a source of male aggressiveness is still a hypothesis in search of proof. The extensive efforts to settle the matter have been ably reviewed by Owen (1972), Jarvik et al. (1973), and Meyer-Bahlburg (1974). How is the search going?

A primary question is whether XYY's are really more common among convicts than in the population at large. Probably the best way to get an unbiased estimate of the population rate is to count the number in a large sample of consecutive newborn males. Surveys of this nature, cited by the above reviewers, agree that the incidence of the XYY genotype is just under two cases per thousand males.

What is the percentage in mental hospitals and jails? Many of the studies in Owen's tables cannot be used because the samples examined were limited to males above 5 ft. 11 in. or 6 ft. tall. Pooling the results of five remaining surveys we come up with a rate of six to seven per thousand, or between three and four times the number of males in general, a highly significant discrepancy (p < .001). This finding is certainly provocative, but it takes more than that to put the hypothesis on solid ground. We should first have to make sure that the discrepancy was due to an effect of the extra Y chromosome on aggressive behavior. There are other possibilities.

First, as Meyer-Bahlburg suggested, the same effect might be caused by other chromosomal aberrations, not just an extra Y. Patients with Klinefelter's syndrome, for example, are masculine in body type, but they have two X chromosomes and a single Y (47, XXY). If two Y chromosomes were expected to heighten aggressiveness, two X's should lower it.

In their review of the XYY problem Jarvik et al. included comparable data on XXY. According to the surveys cited, the expected frequencies of both syndromes in newborn males were about the same, between one and two per thousand. In mental hosptials and jails both rates increased: Klinefelter's syndrome to eight per thousand, XYY to eleven per thousand. Tentative as they are, these figures cast doubt on the militant role of the Y chromosome.

Second, we have no assurance that the elevated rate of XYY's in jails and hospitals was due to their aggressiveness. True, the case studies are full of references to temper outbursts or fits of violent rage, but adequate controls are lacking and standardized tests of personality give the hypothesis little support (Owen 1972). When criminal records are compared, those of XYY's contain no more crimes of violence than those of XY's; if anything, crimes against persons by XYY's were fewer.

A stronger case could be made for the extra Y if we knew how its effect might be exerted on the developing organism. The likeliest mediator, of course, is the male sex hormone. We shall consider the relation of testosterone to aggression and dominance in the next section. Here we may ask whether it bears any relation to the double-Y pattern of chromosomes. In his cogent discussion Meyer-Bahlburg included a review of thirty-four studies dealing with the pituitary-gonadal hormones in XYY males. He reported "no gross abnormalities of androgen or gonadotrophin production in the XYY syndrome" (p. 446). Acknowledging, however, that many of the studies lacked experimental rigor, Meyer-Bahlburg left open the possibility of subtle endocrine disorder.

Hormonal Evidence

Testosterone, the most potent of the androgens, is about twenty times as plentiful in human males as in females (Rose et al. 1974). Could this biochemical product, under appropriate circumstances, somehow impel a social animal to dominate his fellows? If the idea is sound, we should be able to establish a connection, however remote, between the presence of testosterone in its blood and the belligerence of its behavior.

Animals. Here again the mouse, symbol of timidity, has contributed a lion's share of evidence. It has shown the expected relationship in several ways, though not in all. A straightforward correlation between individual serum levels of testosterone and scores for aggressiveness proved insignificant (Selmanoff et al. 1977). But it has been observed that males start to fight at about 30 days, the age when testosterone levels increase sharply (Barkley & Goldman 1977).

A more incisive and generally preferred method is to deprive the blood of most of its testosterone by castration (or by using females) and replace it by injection or implanting pellets. Beeman's (1947) trail-breaking experiments demonstrated that in at least two strains of mice castration led to a loss of aggression when tested after 24 days or more, and that the loss could be repaired by implanting testosterone pellets under the skin. Other investigators have confirmed and extended her work (Luttge 1972; Leshner & Moyer 1975). But injections of testosterone sometimes fail to restore aggressiveness (Bevan et al. 1958) or dominance (Lee & Naranjo 1974), and the critical factors are not fully understood.

In all this experimental activity the female of the species has not been neglected. Inevitably the question came up: would androgens also make female mice readier to fight? An early experimental answer was no (Tollman & King 1956), but more recent efforts have changed it to a provisional yes, without stating the provisions. Juvenile females injected with testosterone for several weeks did more and more fighting (Svare & Gandelman 1975); mature spayed females, after prolonged daily testosterone injections, fought with one another and attacked passive males (Svare et al. 1974). It would appear that female mice have malelike mechanisms for aggressive behavior but a higher threshold to the facilitative action of the male hormone.

What could produce such a difference in sensitivity? A plausible answer had already been offered by a team of investigators (Phoenix et al. 1959) who injected pregnant guinea pigs with androgen: the female offspring were born with masculinized genitals and later showed plenty of mounting but no lordosis (receiving). Similar results were produced in rats (Gerall & Ward 1966).

To explain these findings Young et al. (1964) proposed a hypothesis that runs essentially as follows: sexual differentiation does not depend entirely on whether the chromosomes are XX or XY. Early in development there is a second critical period in which the maleness or femaleness of body and brain is determined by the presence or absence of androgens in the circulation. (In guinea pigs this "sensitive" period occurs before birth; in rats and mice, with their shorter gestation, just after.) From there it takes only a short step to assume that androgen in a newborn rodent, for a limited time only, has the special function of sensitizing aggressive mechanisms for later arousal. It follows that males are more aggressive than females largely because only males have testes.

Here, too, mice of both sexes have been kept busy supplying information. For at least one inbred strain such a critical period has been found to fall within the first 6 days after birth. Castration of male pups on day 0 or 2 led to a sharp reduction in androgen-induced adult fights and battle scars (Peters et al. 1972). Females of the same strain were given a single injection of androgen between 0 and 48 hours after birth. As adults, spayed and injected with testosterone, they were grouped for three days before being scored for wounds received in battle. Groups injected on the day of birth contained the highest percentages of wounded Amazons; at 48 hours only the heaviest dose was effective (Whitsett et al. 1972). (For confirming evidence of the defeminizing effect of neonatal testosterone in a noninbred strain see Edwards [1971].)

Before leaving the mouse we might do well to ask if estrogens have any influence on aggression, whether to dampen it or enkindle it to a lesser degree than androgens. Results are not yet conclusive. The few encountered suggest that estrogen injected in either male or female adults *probably* depresses aggression (Edwards & Burge 1971; Luttge 1972; Suchkowski et al. 1971). Injected neonatally in females, estrogen may exert a moderate priming effect on later aggression; in males its effect, if any, seems to be depressive (Bronson & Desjardins 1968; Edwards & Herndon 1970).

Turning from mouse to monkey, we find it harder to uncover evidence for an endocrine source of aggression. This should not be surprising: with its highly developed brain the primate responds to a much more complicated situation than the rodent. But that merely obscures the effect of a single factor, such as the chemical effect of a sexual hormone.

Considering all the primates, we have probably learned most from the rhesus monkey. Signs of a connection between androgen and aggression can be found in the records of the colony on Cayo Santiago, off the coast of Puerto Rico. They show not only a much higher death rate for mature males than females, but more wounds and deaths among males in the mating season than in the rest of the year. Combined with the growth of testes observed at the same time, these data suggest that increased androgen lowers the threshold to fighting (Wilson & Boelkins 1970). Free-ranging castrated males in the same area added more evidence: with some noteworthy exceptions—two prepubertal castrates defeated two intact males twice their weight—their aggressiveness declined along with their sexual behavior (Wilson & Vessey 1968).

The study just cited is not the only equivocal report on combativeness after castration. Phoenix et al. (1973) found castrated males no easier to handle than before surgery; moreover, the castrates remained dominant over their female partners.

Insignificant correlations between plasma testosterone and social dominance have been reported for rhesus (Gordon et al. 1976) and a related species, the Japanese macaque (Eaton & Resko 1974). But one positive report is worth stopping to consider because its authors have thrown a fresh light on the problem. A team at the Yerkes Primate Center (Rose et al. 1971) segregated thirty-four rhesus males, to avoid complications due to sex, and observed their interactions. Blood testosterone correlated .47 with aggressiveness and .53 with social rank, not close relationships but significant. The authors took the unorthodox position that dominance might be the cause, rather than the result, of testosterone level. In a test of this hypothesis four rhesus males, each dominant over a group of thirteen females, were put individually in an all-male group and badly beaten; their plasma testosterone fell an average of 80 percent in a week. Return of two of them to their harems restored the hormone to its former level (Rose et al. 1972). A follow-up study of the same four males in different social groups provided further examples of dramatic shifts of status with corresponding shifts of androgen level (Rose et al. 1975). The authors suggested that a "feedback loop" might be involved: social defeat would lower the testosterone level, which in turn would diminish the impulse to fight; success in battle might push such a cycle in the opposite direction.

If the case for androgens seems less convincing in rhesus than rodent, it may be partly because so far we have considered only their activating function. Nothing has been said about the possibility of an early "organizing" or sensitizing function, as predicted for guinea pigs and mice. But this omission can be quickly remedied.

Phoenix and Goy wondered if a comparable process took place at the primate level. Harlow's laboratory had already uncovered remarkable sex differences in the social behavior of young rhesus monkeys (Rosenblum 1961). Male infants and juveniles threatened, started play, engaged in rough-and-tumble and chasing play much more often than their female playmates. The next step, taken by Phoenix and Goy, was to treat pregnant rhesus monkeys with androgen, then test the female offspring in small groups of peers. Predictions were strikingly confirmed: in all the sex-differentiating aspects of play the small "hermaphrodites," their genitals unquestionably malelike, were between the normal males and females (Phoenix 1974). Since males castrated at birth played with the reckless abandon of intact males, the experimenters concluded that the patterns of social play had been sex-typed before birth by the levels of androgen in the fetal circulation. Blood samples of male and female fetuses have confirmed this conclusion (Resko et al. 1973). We do not yet know whether the effect is confined to "play fighting" or includes serious conflict at a later stage.

Steps have been taken, however, to determine a critical period for establishing dominance (Joslyn 1973). Rhesus female infants were injected with testosterone from the seventh to the fifteenth month and tested with male age mates before, during, and after treatment. Starting at the bottom of the social order, they displaced males in rank, suppressed their play and mounting, and equaled them in competition for water. The results suggest a critical period for dominance in the first year, but only further experiments will tell whether at that time the hormone is playing an activating or an organizing role.

Humans. Ironically, just where we most want the information, it is hardest to get. At the human level, where cultural influences become nearly inescapable, the experimenter has least freedom in his choice of method. Surgery, for example, is practically ruled out except for prevention or cure of pathology.

As Moyer (1974) reminds us in his excellent review, humans have for centuries resorted to castration to make farm animals more tractable. It has also been used, in some times and places, as a method of "rehabilitating" sex criminals. To judge from the few published reports, the operation is generally effective in weakening the sex drive and preventing recurrence of sexual offenses. But as to its success in reducing violence, there is less agreement.

In his study of 224 Norwegian cases Bremer (1959) found the treatment of no value as a general pacifier. At one Kansas state training school, however, results were so encouraging that the staff tried an experiment. They gave castrated boys daily injections of testosterone over several weeks. When some subjects started to relapse into vandalism the androgen was discontinued, whereupon their conduct soon recovered stability (Hawke 1950).

Injection of estrogens to pacify violent males has been called "chemical castration." Moyer documented the successful use of several estrogenic substances for this purpose. (One of them, stilbestrol, has become much better known as The Pill.)

The trouble with both forms of castration, in these settings, is that we cannot separate a direct effect on aggressiveness from an indirect effect by way of the sexual drive. In fact, thwarting of an unruly libido is often the most likely cause of a sex offender's destructiveness. For less contaminated evidence we shall have to look elsewhere.

Direct attempts to correlate aggressive behavior with androgen in the blood have proven as frustrating at the human as at the animal level. Every positive correlation can be matched by one close to zero, though negative r's occur rarely, if at all. The reader can find a succinct and cogent review of this literature by Rada et al. (1976). Here a closer look at one of the studies reviewed, plus brief mention of two others not included, will provide a glimpse of the inquiry in its present state.

Persky et al. (1971) measured testosterone in eighteen young men and gave them a battery of paper-and-pencil tests of personality, including the Buss-Durkee Hostility Inventory (BDHI; Buss & Durkee 1957). This is a questionnaire designed to measure a cluster of traits such as verbal and physical assault, irritability, and resentment. The author found a significant correlation between rate of producing testosterone and total score on the BDHI ($r = .66, p < .01$). A further analysis of the scores yielded a factor, identified as aggressive feelings, that correlated even more significantly with the hormone ($r = .69, p < .001$). In a second group, of older men, the only significant correlation was a negative one between testosterone production rate and age.

Since testosterone levels fluctuate from day to day, the risk of sampling error is high. In a similar experiment (Doering et al. 1974) twenty young men gave blood samples every other day for two months along with self-ratings of hostility, anxiety, and depression; they also kept daily diaries of anger, sexual activity, and stress. Comparing day-to-day fluctuations in plasma testosterone with those in mood, the authors found no sign of interdependence. When they averaged each subject's daily scores over the two-month period and correlated them across subjects, the results were no more enlightening. Levels of testosterone correlated positively with depression, negatively with sexual activity, and not at all with anger.

Both of the preceding studies were done with few subjects. Monti et al. (1977) took blood samples from 101 men in their 20s and had them fill out several personality tests, including the BDHI, and self-reports on sex. Again the ties of testosterone with aggressiveness proved threadbare. The only significant correlations were with anxiety, suspicion, and frequency of masturbation.

What about the effects of sexual hormones on early development of aggressive mechanisms, prenatal in guinea pigs and monkeys, postnatal in rats and mice? Is anything similar to be found in humans? In chapter 7 we cited some clinical evidence that is appropriate to mention here. The adrenogenital syndrome (AGS) concerns genetic females exposed to androgens before birth; typically such cases were found to grow up as tomboys in their choice of playmates, toys, clothes, and goals. In testicular feminization (androgen-insensitivity) genetic males, unable to utilize testosterone and usually reared as a girl, show no preference for a masculine style of life.

In the context of aggression another hormonal disturbance of pregnancy catches our attention. We may ask what happens if a normal male fetus is exposed to supplementary female hormones? A chance to answer that question is provided by the sons of mothers with diabetes who receive regular injections of estrogen and progesterone to maintain pregnancy.

Yalom et al. (1973) had an experimental group of twenty 16-year-old boys with the prenatal history just described. The ideal control group would consist of boys with diabetic mothers *not* treated with estrogen-progesterone. Yalom et al. could find only eight such cases, so they added a second control group of fourteen boys with healthy mothers. Data were based on interviews with mother and son, behavioral observtions, and personality tests. Here we are concerned with rank orderings and self-reports on aggression.

In liking to fight, frequency of fighting, and self-estimated toughness the experimental subjects were lowest, the "diabetic" controls highest, and the normal controls in the middle. In total scores on nineteen items concerned with aggressiveness the estrogenized subjects were significantly lower than either control group. These results have met with some skepticism on the grounds of inadequate control for the mothers' diabetes (Ehrhardt 1977). It is true that the diabetic control group (with untreated diabetic mothers) was too small. On the other hand, it should be noted that the boys in this group were consistently *more* aggressive than those with healthy mothers, which suggests that a more rigorous control of this factor would have enhanced, rather than diminished, the apparent effect of the hormones.

The crucial experiment, proving beyond doubt that androgens have a positive influence on human aggressiveness (or estrogens a negative one) remains to be done. It may never be. This is not necessarily a pessimistic but a realistic view. The weight of present evidence, animal and human, experimental and clinical, points toward a view of prenatal hormone effects as "setting a bias on the neural substratum" that regulates behavior (Reinisch 1974). Owing to the variety of external and experiential factors, such a bias may reveal itself, not in some ideal circumstance where other factors are precisely balanced, but in a preponderance of positive results among many of doubtful significance. Eventually the preponderance may become statistically convincing. Meanwhile the reader may decide for himself whether the bias is indeed in the data or "in the eye of the beholder."

References

Bandura, A.; Ross, D.; and Ross, S.A. 1963. "Imitation of Film-mediated Aggressive Models." *Journal of Abnormal and Social Psychology* 66:3-11.

Barkley, M.S., and Goldman, B.D. 1977. "A Quantitative Study of Serum Testosterone, Sex Accessory Organ Growth, and the Development of Intermale Aggression in the Mouse." *Hormones and Behavior* 8:208-218.

Barnett, S.A. 1963. *A Study in Behaviour*. London: Methuen.

Beeman, E.A. 1947. "The Relation of the Interval between Castration and First Encounter to the Aggressive Behavior of Mice." *Anatomical Record* 99:570-571.

Bevan, J.M.; Bevan, W.; and Williams, B.F. 1958. "Spontaneous Aggression in Young Castrated C3H Male Mice Treated with Three Dose Levels of Testosterone." *Physiological Zoology* 31:284-288.

Bremer, J. 1959. *Asexualization*. New York: Macmillan.

Bronson, F.H., and Desjardins, C. 1968. "Aggression in Adult Mice: Modification by Neonatal Injections of Gonadal Hormones." *Science* 161:705-706.

Buss, A.H. 1966. "Instrumentality of Aggression, Feedback, and Frustration as Determinants of Physical Aggression." *Journal of Personality and Social Psychology* 3:153-162.

Buss, A.H., and Durkee, A. 1957. "An Inventory for Assessing Different Kinds of Hostility." *Journal of Consulting Psychology* 21:343-349.

Cloudsley-Thompson, J.L. 1965. *Animal Conflict and Adaptation*. Chester Springs, Pa.: Dufour.

Craig, J.V.; Ortman, L.L.; and Guhl, A.M. 1965. "Genetic Selection for Social Dominance Ability in Chickens." *Animal Behaviour* 13:114-131.

Deaux, K. 1971. "Honking at the Intersection: A Replication and Extension." *Journal of Social Psychology* 84:159-160.

Doering, C.H.; Brodie, H.K.H.; Kraemer, H.; Becker, H.; and Hamburg, D.A. 1974. "Plasma Testosterone Levels and Psychologic Measures in Men over a Two-Month Period." In R.C. Friedman, R.M. Richart, and R.L. Vande Wiele, eds. *Sex Differences in Behavior*. New York: Wiley.

Doob, A., and Gross, A. 1968. "Status of Frustrator as an Inhibitor of Hornhonking Responses." *Journal of Social Psychology* 76:213-218.

Eaton, G.G., and Resko, J.A. 1974. "Plasma Testosterone and Male Dominance in a Japanese Macaque (*Macaca fuscata*) Troop Compared with Repeated Measures of Testosterone in Laboratory Males." *Hormones and Behavior* 5:251-259.

Ebert, P.D., and Hyde, J.S. 1976. "Selection for Agonistic Behavior in Wild Female *Mus musculus*." *Behavior Genetics* 6:291-304.

Edwards, D.A. 1971. "Neonatal Administration of Androstenedione, Testosterone, or Tetosterone Propionate: Effects on Ovulation, Sexual Receptivity, and Aggressive Behavior in Female Mice." *Physiology and Behavior* 6:223-228.

Edwards, D.A., and Burge, K.G. 1971. "Estrogenic Arousal of Aggressive Behavior and Masculine Sexual Behavior in Male and Female Mice." *Hormones and Behavior* 2:239-245.

Edwards, D.A., and Herndon, J. 1970. "Neonatal Estrogen Stimulation and Aggressive Behavior in Female Mice." *Physiology and Behavior* 5:993-995.

Ehrhardt, A.A. 1977. "Prenatal Androgenization and Human Psychosexual Behavior." In J. Money and H. Musaph, eds. *Handbook of Sexology*. Amsterdam: Excerpta Medica.

Feshbach, N.D. and Feshbach, S. 1969. "The Relationship between Empathy and Aggression in Two Age Groups." *Developmental Psychology* 1:102-107.

Feshbach, S. 1970. "Aggression." In P.H. Mussen, ed. *Carmichael's Manual of Child Psychology*, vol. 2. New York: Wiley, pp. 159-259.

Freedman, D.G. 1972. "Genetic Variations on the Hominid Theme: Individual, Sex, and Ethnic Differences." In F.J. Mönks, H.W. Hartup, and J. DeWit, eds. *Determinants of Behavioral Development*. New York: Academic Press, pp. 121-141.

Gellert, E. 1961. "Power Relationships of Young Children." *Journal of Abnormal and Social Psychology* 62:8-15.

Gerall, A.A., and Ward, I.L. 1966. "Effects of Prenatal Exogenous Androgen on the Sexual Behavior of the Female Albino Rat." *Journal of Comparative and Physiological Psychology* 62:370-375.

Gordon, T.P.; Rose, R.M.; and Bernstein, I.S. 1976. "Seasonal Rhythm in Plasma Testosterone Levels in the Rhesus Monkey (*Macaca mulatta*): A Three-Year Study." *Hormones and Behavior* 7:229-243.

Hall, C.S., and Klein, S.J. 1942. "Individual Differences in Aggressiveness in Rats." *Journal of Comparative Psychology* 33:371-383.

Hapkiewicz, W.G., and Stone, R.D. 1974. "The Effect of Realistic versus Imaginary Aggressive Models on Children's Interpersonal Play." *Child Study Journal* 4:47-58.

Harlow, H.F., and Harlow, M.K. 1965. "The Affectional Systems." In A.M. Schrier, H.F. Harlow, and F. Stollnitz, eds. *Behavior of Nonhuman Primates*, vol. 2. New York: Academic Press.

Harris, M.B. 1973. "Field Studies of Modeled Aggression." *Journal of Social Psychology* 89:131-139.

_____ . 1974. "Mediators between Frustration and Aggression in a Field Experiment." *Journal of Experimental Social Psychology* 10:561-571.

Harris, M.B., and Siebel, C.E. 1975. "Affect, Aggression, and Altruism." *Developmental Psychology* 11:623-627.

Hawke, C.C. 1950. "Castration and Sex Crimes." *American Journal of Mental Deficiency* 55:220-226.

Jacobs, P.A.; Brunton, M.; Melville, M.M.; Britain, R.P.; and McClemont, W.F. 1965. "Aggressive Behaviour, Mental Subnormality, and the XYY Male." *Nature* 208:1351-1352.

Jarvik, L.F.; Klodin, V.; and Matsuyama, S.S. 1973. "Human Aggression and the Extra Y Chromosome: Fact or Fantasy?" *American Psychologist* 28:674-682.

Joslyn, W.D. 1973. "Androgen-induced Social Dominance in Infant Female Rhesus Monkeys." *Journal of Child Psychology and Psychiatry and Allied Disciplines* 14:137-145.

Knudson, M.E. 1973. "Sex Differences in Dominance Behavior of Young Human Primates." *Dissertation Abstracts International* 34:2430B.

Lagerspetz, K. 1964. *Studies on the Aggressive Behavior of Mice.* Helsinki: Suomalainen Tiedeakatemia.

Lee, C.T., and Naranjo, J.N. 1974. "The Effects of Castration and Androgen on the Social Dominance of BALB/cJ Male Mice." *Physiological Psychology* 2:93-98.

Leff, J., and Gunn, J. 1973. "The Interaction of Male and Female Car Drivers at Roundabouts." *Accident Analysis and Prevention* 5:253-259.

Leshner, A.I., and Moyer, J.A. 1975. "Androgens and Agnostic Behavior in Mice: Relevance to Aggression and Irrelevance to Avoidance of Attack." *Physiology and Behavior* 15:695-699.

Luttge, W.G. 1972. "Activation and Inhibition of Isolation-induced Intermale Fighting Behavior in Castrated Male CD-1 Mice Treated with Steroidal Hormones." *Hormones and Behavior* 3:71-81.

Maccoby, E.E. 1966. "Sex Differences in Intellectual Functioning." In E.E. Maccoby, ed. *The Development of Sex Differences.* Stanford, Calif.: Stanford University Press.

Maccoby, E.E., and Jacklin, C.N. 1974. *The Psychology of Sex Differences.* Stanford, Calif.: Stanford University Press.

McGrew, W.C. 1972. *An Ethological Study of Children's Behavior.* New York: Academic Press.

McGuire, J.M. 1973. "Aggression and Sociometric Status with Preschool Children." *Sociometry* 36:542-549.

Meyer-Bahlburg, H.F.L. 1974. "Aggression, Androgens, and the XYY Syndrome." In R.C. Friedman, R.M. Richart, and R.L. Vande Wiele, eds. *Sex Differences in Behavior.* New York: Wiley.

Monti, P.M.; Brown, W.A.; and Corriveau, D.P. 1977. "Testosterone and Components of Aggressive and Sexual Behavior in Man." *American Journal of Psychiatry* 134:692-694.

Moyer, K.E. 1974. "Sex Differences in Aggression." In R.C. Friedman, R.M. Richart, and R.L. Vande Wiele, eds. *Sex Differences in Behavior.* New York: Wiley.

Oetzel, R.M. 1966. "Annotated Bibliography." In E.E. Maccoby, ed. *The Development of Sex Differences.* Stanford, Calif.: Stanford University Press, pp. 323-351.

Owen, D.R. 1972. "The 47, XYY Male: A Review." *Psychological Bulletin* 78:209-233.

Pawlowski, A., and Scott, J.P. 1956. "Hereditary Differences in the Development of Dominance in Different Breeds of Puppies." *Journal of Comparative and Physiological Psychology* 49:353-358.

Persky, H.; Smith, K.D.; and Basu, G.K. 1971. "Relation of Psychologic Measures of Aggression and Hostility to Testosterone Production in Man." *Psychosomatic Medicine* 33:265-277.

Peters, P.J.; Bronson, F.H.; and Whitsett, J.M. 1972. "Neonatal Castration and Intermale Aggression in Mice." *Physiology and Behavior* 8:265-268.

Phoenix, C.H. 1974. "Prenatal Testosterone in the Nonhuman Primate and Its Consequences for Behavior." In R.C. Friedman, R.M. Richart, and R.L. Vande Wiele, eds. *Sex Differences in Behavior*. New York: Wiley.

Phoenix, C.H.; Goy, R.W.; Gerall, A.A.; and Young, W.C. 1959. "Organizing Action of Prenatally Administered Testosterone Propionate on the Tissues Mediating Mating Behavior in the Female Guinea Pig." *Endocrinology* 65:369-382.

Phoenix, C.H.; Slob, A.K., and Goy, R.W. 1973. "Effects of Castration and Replacement Therapy on the Sexual Behavior of Adult Male Rhesus." *Journal of Comparative and Physiological Psychology* 84:472-481.

Poorman, P.; Donnerstein, E.; and Donnerstein, M. 1976. "Aggressive Behavior as a Function of Age and Sex." *Journal of Genetic Psychology* 128(2):183-187.

Potter, J.H. 1949. "Dominance Relations between Different Breeds of Domestic Hens." *Physiological Zoology* 22:261-280.

Rada, R.T.; Kellner, R.; and Winslow, W.W. 1976. "Plasma Testosterone and Aggressive Behavior." *Psychosomatics* 17:138-142.

Reinisch, J. 1974. "Fetal Hormones, the Brain, and Human Sex Differences: A Heuristic, Integrative Review of the Recent Literature." *Archives of Sexual Behavior* 3:51-90.

Resko, J.A.; Malley, A.; Begley, D.E.; and Hess, D.L. 1973. "Radioimmunoassay of Testosterone during Fetal Development of the Rhesus Monkey." *Endocrinology* 93:156-161.

Rohner, R.P. 1976. "Sex Differences in Aggression: Phylogenetic and Encultural Perspectives." *Ethos* 4(1):57-72.

Rose, R.M.; Bernstein, I.S.; and Gordon, T.P. 1974. "Androgens and Aggressive Behavior: A Review and Recent Findings in Primates." In R.L. Holloway, ed. *Primate Aggression, Territoriality, and Xenophobia*. New York: Academic Press.

———. 1975. "Consequences of Social Conflict on Plasma Testosterone Levels in Rhesus Monkeys." *Psychological Medicine* 37:50-61.

Rose, R.M.; Gordon, T.P.; and Bernstein, I.S. 1972. "Plasma Testosterone Level in the Male Rhesus: Influences of Sexual and Social Stimuli." *Science* 178:643-645.

Rose, R.M.; Holaday, J.W.; and Bernstein, I.S. 1971. "Plasma Testosterone, Dominance Ranks, and Aggressive Behavior in Rhesus Monkeys." *Nature* 231:366-368.

Rosenblum, L.A. 1961. "The Development of Social Behavior in the Rhesus Monkey." Doctoral dissertation, University of Wisconsin.

Schjelderup-Ebbe, T. 1935. "Social Behavior of Birds." in C. Murchison, ed. *A Handbook of Social Psychology.* Worcester, Mass.: Clark University Press.

Selmanoff, M.K.; Abreu, E.; Goldman, B.D.; and Ginsburg, B.E. 1977. "Manipulation of Aggressive Behavior in Adult DBA/2/Bg and C57BL/10/Bg Male Mice Implanted with Testosterone in Silastic Tubing." *Hormones and Behavior* 8:377-390.

Selmanoff, M.K.; Jumonville, J.E.; Maxson, S.C.; and Ginsburg, B.E. 1975. "Evidence for a Y Chromosomal Contribution to an Aggressive Phenotype in Inbred Mice." *Nature* 253:529-530.

Seward, J.P. 1945. "Aggressive Behavior in the Rat: I. General Characteristics, Age and Sex Differences." *Journal of Comparative Psychology* 38:175-197.

Shortell, J.T., and Biller, H.B. 1970. "Aggression in Children as a Function of Sex of Subject and Sex of Opponent." *Developmental Psychology* 3:143-144.

Smith, P.K., and Green, M. 1975. "Aggressive Behavior in English Nurseries and Play Groups: Sex Differences and Responses of Adults." *Child Development* 46(1):211-214.

Southwick, C.H. 1968. "Effect of Maternal Environment on Aggressive Behavior of Inbred Mice." *Communications in Behavioral Biology* 1(pt. A):129-132.

Southwick, C.H., and Clark, L.H. 1968. "Interstrain Differences in Aggressive Behavior and Exploratory Activity of Inbred Mice." *Communications in Behavioral Biology* 1(pt. A):49-59.

Suchowsky, G.K.; Pegrassi, L.; and Bonsignori, A. 1971. "Steroids and Aggressive Behavior in Isolated Male and Female Mice." *Psychopharmacology* 21:32-38.

Svare, B.; Davis, P.G.; and Gandelman, R. 1974. "Fighting Behavior in Female Mice Following Chronic Androgen Treatment during Adulthood." *Physiology and Behavior* 12:399-403.

Svare, B., and Gandelman, R. 1975. "Aggressive Behavior of Juvenile Mice, Influence of Androgen and Olfactory Stimuli." *Developmental Psychobiology* 8:405-415.

Taylor, S.P. 1967. "Aggressive Behavior and Physiological Arousal as a Function of Provocation and the Tendency to Inhibit Aggression." *Journal of Personality* 35:297-314.

Taylor, S.P., and Epstein, 1967. "Aggression as a Function of the Inter-action of the Sex of the Aggressor and the Sex of the Victim." *Journal of Personality* 35:474-485.

Thiessen, D.D. 1976. *The Evolution and Chemistry of Aggression*. Springfield, Ill.: C.C. Thomas.

Time. 1977. "Youth Crime Plague." July 11, pp. 18-28.

Tollman, J., and King, J.A. 1956. "The Effects of Testosterone Propionate on Aggression in Male and Female C57BL/10 Mice." *British Journal of Animal Behaviour* 4:147-149.

Whitsett, J.M.; Bronson, F.H.; Peters, P.J.; and Hamilton, T.H. 1972. "Neonatal Organization of Aggression in Mice: Correlation of Critical Period with Uptake of Hormone." *Hormones and Behavior* 3:11-21.

Wilson, A.P., and Boelkins, R.C. 1970. "Evidence for Seasonal Variation in Aggressive Behavior by *Macaca mulatta.*" *Animal Behavior* 18:719-724.

Wilson, A.P., and Vessey, S.H. 1968. "Behavior of Free-ranging Castrated Rhesus Monkeys." *Folia Primatologia* 9:1-14.

Yalom, I.D.; Green, R.; and Fisk, N. 1973. "Prenatal Exposure to Female Hormones: Effect on Psychosexual Development in Boys." *Archives of General Psychiatry* 28:554-561.

Young, W.C.; Goy, R.W.; and Phoenix, C.H. 1964. "Hormones and Sexual Behavior." *Science* 143:212-218.

10 Fear and Anxiety

Women are commonly thought to be more subject to fear than are men. Among the mentally ill a larger proportion of females than males suffer from phobias and states of anxiety (Mayo 1976); they score higher, too, on a scale designed to measure tendencies of repress anxiety or to worry (Schwartz 1972). But the belief has a broader base: surveys of college students regularly find more and stronger fears among the coeds (Bernstein & Allen 1969; Hersen 1973).

Biologists recognize fear in animals, humans included, as an adaptive mechanism for avoiding injury. (For a provocative review of evidence for unlearned fears in humans and other animals see Marks [1969].) Is there any reason why it should be more adaptive in females than males? Applying our rather arbitrary criterion—the roles of the sexes in reproduction—we ask, is fear an asset to a female in courtship? The answer seems obvious: definitely not. Even in the stickleback fish the female has to stand her ground to seduce the approaching male. How about a mother with young newly hatched or born? In many species mothers are known to defend their young fiercely rather than abandon them to a predator.

The thesis of a sex difference in fear may require a broader base, such as the survival of the organism itself. It could be argued that since the females of many species lack the males' offensive weaponry, in a state of nature they would often do better to flee a potential enemy than to fight.

Our concern at this point, however, is with the evidence. Following Maccoby and Jacklin's admirable example, let us start with infancy and early childhood, so as to minimize the inevitable effects of social molding.

Infancy and Early Childhood

Jersild and Holmes's (1935) outstanding study of children's fears provided a foretaste of later findings. They used a variety of approaches. Parents' daily records of observed episodes of fear in their preschool children revealed slight differences between the sexes in both directions and of doubtful significance. In six of eight experimental situations, such as approaching a stranger to reach a toy or patting a large unfamiliar dog, girls showed more fear than boys and this difference was significant. Finally, as to these children's everyday behavior, nursery school teachers rated the girls only insignificantly more fearful than boys.

Though most of the studies cited by Maccoby and Jacklin found no sex differences in the early years, when a difference did turn up it was the girls who proved more timid. In the first 18 months, twice as many girls as boys cried on leaving their mothers (Kagan 1972). Bronson (1972) found girl and boy infants equally startled by novel objects and equally shy with a stranger. But he also found boys more consistent than girls in fearful responses during the first year, suggesting, to him at least, a sex-linked constitutional factor (Bronson 1969).

The last point raises an interesting possibility. A built-in aggressiveness may carry with it a reciprocal readiness for fear, and such a fear might prove to be more characteristic of males than females. A linear pecking order in monkeys, for example, depends as much on the timidity of the subordinate as on the pugnacity of the dominant. Male social hierarchies in these animals are generally more rigid than female orders.

In line with this idea Stern and Bender (1974) watched 200 preschool children approaching a stranger. The male infants tended to look away, reminding the authors of the appeasing behavior in monkeys; the females tended to act shyly (smile apprehensively, hand to face). Stern and Bender placed the female pattern in a fear system, the male in an aggressive one, not necessarily inborn.

If the reader finds this distinction too subtle to be convincing, he should be warned that such difficulties of interpretation are not uncommon. When 3-to-5-year-olds were offered a novel toy—a big clown equipped with levers, lights, and buzzers—along with four familiar ones to play with, the girls were much less willing than the boys to play with the clown (Rabinowitz et al. 1975). Were they afraid, or just less curious?

School Years

It may have been the growing interest in clinical problems that channeled the study of children's fears into the more generalized concept of anxiety. The Children's Manifest Anxiety Scale (CMAS) (Castaneda et al. 1956) consisted of statements such as "I notice my heart beats very fast sometimes," and "I worry about what other people think of me." Interspersed were a few statements to detect lying; for example, "I like everyone I know," "I tell the truth every single time." Given to fourth and sixth graders, the CMAS produced the usual result: either no significant sex difference or higher anxiety scores for girls than boys. The same was true of the Lie Scale, which incidentally proved unrelated to anxiety in either sex.

For the most thorough study of anxiety in schoolchildren we are indebted to the Yale group of Sarason and his coworkers (Sarason et al. 1960). To measure it they devised two scales—the TASC to measure test anxiety, and the GASC to measure general anxiety—supplemented by a Lie Scale (LSC) and a Defensiveness Scale (DSC) to help interpret the results. These tests proved more consistent than the CMAS in bringing out higher levels of anxiety in girls than boys. The important question is how the authors explained their finding. They held that a more lenient social climate permitted girls to admit their fears and worries but restrained boys from admitting theirs. In support of this position Hill and Sarason (1966) reported that boys, scoring below girls in anxiety, scored above them on the LSC and DSC; that is, in lying about their worries and in defensiveness. The investigators left open the question whether or not the sexes differ in basic anxiety.

Young Adulthood

To pursue this matter further, we turn briefly to work with normal adults, most of it, to be more precise, dealing with college students. A favorite measuring instrument at the college level has been the Fear Survey Schedule (FSS; Geer 1965), a list of objects or situations to be rated for the intensity of fear each arouses in the subject. Women are commonly found to list more fears than men, a finding usually referred to the male's unwillingness to admit how frightened he really is. But only a few investigators have tried to test the truth of this hypothesis.

Wilson (1967) did so by having undergraduates, 120 of each sex, make a list of their irrational fears; altogether the men listed 107, the women 191. He then asked male and female judges to rank the most frequently reported fears for silliness. It turned out that the sillier the fear, the more exclusively it was mentioned by women rather than men ($r = +.69$), a result that supports, as far as it goes, the idea of masculine suppression.

In the course of developing his test, Geer (1965) secured some relevant data. He gave his subjects, male and female, a scale for defensiveness (Ford 1964) and found the two scales inversely correlated, slightly but significantly, and to about the same degree for both sexes. This result suggests, contrary to Wilson's, that reluctance to admit fears is *not* the reason why men report fewer than women, at least not under all circumstances.

As noted by Marks (1969), another of Geer's findings argues the same point. To validate his scale he had selected men and women reporting much, some, or no fear of dogs and tested their willingness to approach a small shepherd bitch. All the men, but only the nonfearing women, touched the dog, suggesting that the men had exaggerated their fear, not concealed it.

Speltz (1976) attacked the problem experimentally, varying the degree of self-exposure demanded of his subjects. He gave college students the Geer FSS under different conditions: some remained anonymous; others were asked to note only their sex; still others had to give name, student ID number, and telephone number. As usual, females acknowledged more fears than males, regardless of anonymity.

One other experiment is of interest here because it introduced a bodily expression of emotion as a source of evidence. Katkin and Hoffman (1976) reasoned that if men in our society are under stronger pressure than women to conceal fear, a man will admit as much fear as a woman only if his is stronger. For their experiment they gave the Geer survey to college students and then chose equal numbers of males and females to form two groups, one scoring at the highest level of fear of spiders, the other at the lowest. In the experiment itself each subject was shown slides of tarantulas while changes in skin conductance provided a measure of emotional disturbance. On the Geer scale more women than men reported extreme fear of spiders, but in the matched groups there was no sex difference in skin conductance, and thus no support for the hypothesis of male defensiveness.

Returning to the main question (are females more fearful than males?), we cannot overlook an impressive series of experiments, most of which came from Kenneth Spence's laboratory at the University of Iowa. These experiments serve the double purpose of suggesting an answer to our question and lending some validity to self-reports of anxiety. The story begins with Janet Taylor's (1953) revision of her Manifest Anxiety Scale (TMAS, the same one that Castaneda et al. [1956] adapted for use with children). She tested nearly 2,000 undergraduates and found the females more anxious than the males, though the difference was not significant.

Meanwhile a series of experiments was in progress on conditioning the eyelid reflex by pairing a visual stimulus with a puff of air to the eye. Two early experiments (Spence & Taylor 1951; Spence & Farber 1953) compared conditioning in two groups of subjects, half men and half women, from the highest and lowest quartiles on the TMAS. In both experiments the high-anxiety (HA) group proved significantly faster in conditioning than the low-anxiety (LA) group. Within each group the women surpassed the men, but here the combined results of both experiments fell just short of significance.

Summarizing the entire series, Spence and Spence (1966) reported HA subjects superior to LA subjects in conditioning in twenty-three of twenty-seven experiments. Females did better than males in eighteen experiments out of nineteen; this ratio was highly significant ($p < .001$), yet the sex differences within experiments were quite small. How do these results bear on our problem? Spence interpreted them as confirming the Hull-Spence theory that performance in conditioning depends on strength of drive. In this case he attributed female superiority to the slightly stronger fear aroused by the experimental situation.

So far this conclusion seems to stand or fall with the theory it helps to support. Happily, the Spences were able to buttress it with two pieces of independent evidence. First, masking the conditioning by making it incidental to an experiment in probability learning eliminated the effects of both sex and fear. Second, the two effects could be strengthened or weakened by making the experimental situation more or less fearsome.

Field Experiments

The experimental evidence, as far as it goes, favors the tentative conclusion that women are more prone to develop fears than men. Some readers, however, may wonder if work done outside the laboratory would point in the same direction. Reports of a few pertinent studies have appeared. Here, as elsewhere, driving in traffic seems to offer the best chance to observe human behavior "in the raw."

How long, for example, will a driver wait at an intersection with no stoplight before making a left turn? Jackson and Gray (1976) found no significant difference in waiting time between male and female drivers. But a male driver with other males waited longer than a female driver with other females, and longer than a male driving alone.

In another study Ebbesen and Haney (1973) clocked 464 drivers at a T-shaped intersection to see how long they would wait before making a left turn into the freely flowing traffic on the cross-bar. Female drivers waited significantly longer than males ($p < .01$). Was it too risky? Statistics show that male drivers are involved in over twice as many fatal accidents as females per billion miles driven.

A closer look at male and female driving performance is clearly indicated. Hagen (1975) used a driving simulator to combine the advantages of laboratory and field research. (In a simulator the driver sits in a stationary car facing a roadway projected on a screen. By manipulating the usual hand and foot controls, he can produce the illusion of driving along the roadway, while his movements and their effects are recorded for later analysis.) Hagen compared eighty-nine male and seventy-four female licensed drivers between the ages of 16 and 51. He found that males drove faster than females, used the accelerator more and with greater variation, and kept closer to the center line. The basic difference between the sexes, he believed, was in the average speed maintained.

Was this difference due to unequal experience? We do not know, but further data from Hagen's study make it unlikely. For one thing, the difference in performance was much greater between males and females below the age of 25 than above it. For another, the difference between men and women who had taken driver education was no less than between those who had not. Hagen suggested that training programs be directed toward making young men drive with less daring and young women drive with more confidence.

Drivers are not the only victims of traffic accidents; pedestrians, too, proceed at risk. A study focused on this behavior was made some years ago (Cohen et al. 1955). The scene was a busy crossing in Manchester, England, with no traffic light, crosswalk, or police control. Risk taking was measured, in effect, by the estimated time a pedestrian would allow himself before he was willing to cross. Over a thousand observations were recorded on nearly 500 unsuspecting persons. Males took greater risks than females at all ages; the differences were largest below 16 and over 60 and were significant except for the group between 30 and 45.

Anxiety and the Menstrual Cycle

The case for an innate sex difference in predilection toward anxiety might be stronger if anxiety could be pinned to some physiological process or pattern involving heart rate, blood pressure, skin conductance, or the like. If such a pattern could be more easily aroused in females than males, a biological basis would seem likely. Unfortunately, efforts in this direction have so far failed. After an intensive review of the field, Martin (1961) felt obliged to conclude that no pattern of physiological responses had been revealed that would distinguish anxiety from other emotions. To our knowledge nothing has happened since to change that conclusion. We cannot even take comfort from these negative results by drawing the opposite conclusion. That is, an unlearned sex difference *may* exist even without an identifying visceral response.

One other path is open: instead of looking for a bodily fear pattern by which to compare males and females, why not start with a known biological sex difference and see if it involves fear? An obvious candidate for this purpose is the menstrual cycle, whereby a female ovum is periodically readied for fertilization. Cyclic changes in the female reproductive system result from fluctuating levels of ovarian hormones, chiefly estrogen and progesterone, under the influence of the pituitary gland and a primitive part of the brain, the hypothalamus. (Details may be found in a standard textbook of physiology.)

Since our interest is in psychological correlates, it is enough to distinguish three phases with the corresponding amounts of essential hormones in the blood. These phases are menstrual (both estrogen and progesterone are at low levels), intermenstrual (the estrogen curve shows two peaks, one before and one after ovulation, which occurs at about the midpoint of the cycle), and premenstrual (both estrogen and progesterone fall to low levels). (See figure 10-1.)

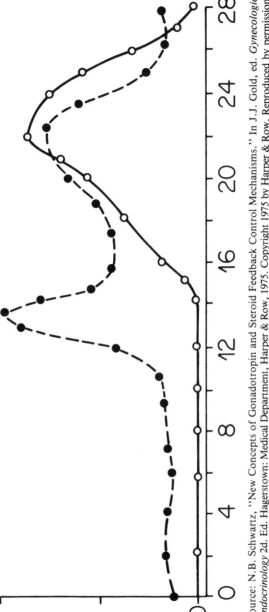

Source: N.B. Schwartz, "New Concepts of Gonadotropin and Steroid Feedback Control Mechanisms." In J.J. Gold, ed. *Gynecologic Endocrinology* 2d. Ed. Hagerstown: Medical Department, Harper & Row, 1975. Copyright 1975 by Harper & Row. Reproduced by permission.

Figure 10-1. Relative plasma concentrations of estrogen (- - -) and progesterone (———) during the menstrual cycle.

The menstrual cycle itself, present in the female but not in the male, suggests that a long-term comparison of mood shifts and emotional variations in men and women should be fruitful. To our knowledge no large-scale study of this type has been done (Wilcoxon et al. 1976). Psychological interest has been largely spurred by psychoanalytic theory (Benedek & Rubenstein 1942) and by disturbances of personality apparently associated with the premenstrual phase (Parlee 1973). Our own objective is to evaluate evidence for premenstrual enhancement of anxiety.

Directly bearing on the question is a study by Ivey and Bardwick (1968) using college women as subjects. Twice in this cycle, at ovulation and again in the premenstrual phase, the subjects were asked to tell about a personal experience. The answers were scored by two judges using Gottschalk's Verbal Anxiety Scale; one of the judges was ignorant of the subject or her menstrual phase.

The results were clear: premenstrual anxiety, as measured, was definitely higher than at ovulation ($p < .0005$). Examples of the stories were impressive. One subject, near ovulation, told of an idyllic trip to Jamaica: "blue water . . . lush island . . . friendly natives." The same subject, premenstrual, recalled the death of her dog, and the loss of her grandparents in a plane crash.

Paige (1969) confirmed this finding in what might be called a controlled experiment. Using the same procedure she compared two groups of women; one with normal cycles, the other using a pill containing estrogen and progesterone that prevented cyclic changes. Only the normal group showed a significant cyclic difference in anxiety.

Not all such experiments have given positive results. It is not clear whether the measuring instruments are responsible. Two studies using adjective checklists yielded no significant cyclic variation in anxiety (Persky 1974; Little & Zahn 1974), but a third showed a clear premenstrual peak (Moos et al. 1969).

Can we conclude that anxiety in women is increased by the drop in ovarian hormones just before menstruation? There are other possibilities. An unknown number of cases might be caused by fear of pregnancy. It is important to know if the cyclic effect is restricted to anxiety or if other emotions are likewise sensitized.

Besides anxiety, both Ivey and Bardwick and Paige found evidence of a premenstrual increase of hostility in their subjects' stories. Moreover, in an experiment aimed directly at measuring aggression (Schonberg et al. 1976), female undergraduates were assigned to teach others a card-sorting task with shock for errors. Later, determination of menstrual periods revealed that subjects in the premenstrual phase had given the strongest shocks. These and other experiments (Silbergeld et al. 1971) suggest that the female hormonal cycle affects the general level of tension rather than any specific emotion.

References

Benedek, T., and Rubenstein, B.B. 1942. "The Sexual Cycle in Women." *Psychosomatic Medicine Monographs*, vol. 3, nos. 1 and 2.

Bernstein, D.A., and Allen, G.F. 1969. "Fear Survey Schedule: 11. Normative Data and Factor Analysis Based upon a Large College Sample." *Behavior Research and Therapy* 7:403-408.

Bronson, G.W. 1969. "Sex Differences in the Development of Fearfulness: A Replication." *Psychonomic Science* 17:367-368.

_____ . 1972. "Infants' Reactions to Unfamiliar Persons and Novel Objects." *Monographs of Society for Research in Child Development*, vol. 37, no. 3.

Castaneda, A.; McCandless, B.R.; and Palermo, D.S. 1956. "The Children's Form of the Manifest Anxiety Scale." *Child Development* 27:317-326.

Cohen, J.; Dearnaley, E.J.; and Hansel, C. 1955. "The Risk Taken in Crossing a Road." *Operational Research Quarterly* 6:120-127.

Ebbesen, E.B., and Haney, M. 1973. "Flirting with Death: Variables Affecting Risk-Taking at Intersections." *Journal of Applied Social Psychology* 3:303-324.

Ford, L.H. 1964. "A Forced-choice, Acquiescence-free, Social Desirability (Defensiveness) Scale." *Journal of Consulting Psychology* 28:475.

Geer, H. 1965. "The Development of a Scale to Measure Fear." *Behavior Research and Therapy* 3:45-53.

Hagen, R.E. 1975. "Sex Differences in Driving Performance." *Human Factors* 17:165-171.

Hersen, M. 1973. "Self-assessment of Fear." *Behavior Therapy* 4:241-257.

Hill, K.T., and Sarason, S.B. 1966. "The Relation of Test Anxiety and Defensiveness to Test and School Performance over the Elementary School Years: A Further Longitudinal Study." *Monographs of Society for Research in Child Development*, vol. 31, no. 2.

Ivey, M.E., and Bardwick, J.M. 1968. "Patterns of Affective Fluctuation in the Menstrual Cycle." *Psychosomatic Medicine* 30:336-345.

Jackson, T.T., and Gray, M. 1976. "Field Study of Risk-taking Behavior of Automobile Drivers." *Perceptual and Motor Skills* 43:471-474.

Jersild, A.T., and Holmes, F.B. 1935. *Children's Fears*. New York: Teachers College Bureau of Publications, Columbia University.

Kagan, J. 1972. "The Emergence of Sex Differences." *School Review* 80:217-227.

Katkin, E.S., and Hoffman, L.S. 1976. "Sex Differences and Self-report of Fear: A Psychophysical Assessment." *Journal of Abnormal and Social Psychology* 85:607-610.

Little, B.C., and Zahn, T.P. 1974. "Changes in Mood and Autonomic Functioning during the Menstrual Cycle." *Psychophysiology* 11:579-590.

Marks, I.M. 1969. *Fears and Phobias*. New York: Academic Press.

Martin, B. 1961. "The Assessment of Anxiety by Physiological Behavior Measures." *Psychological Bulletin* 58:234-255.

Mayo, P. 1976. "Sex Differences and Psychopathology." In B. Lloyd and J. Archer, eds. *Exploring Sex Differences*. New York: Academic Press.

Moos, R.H.; Kopell, B.S.; Melges, F.T.; Yalom, I.D.; Lunde, D.T.; Clayton, R.B.; and Hamburg, D.A. 1969. "Fluctuations in Symptoms and Moods during the Menstrual Cycle." *Journal of Psychosomatic Research* 13:37-44.

Paige, K.E. 1969. "The Effects of Oral Contraceptives on Affective Fluctuations Associated with the Menstrual Cycle." Doctoral dissertation, University of Michigan.

Parlee, M.B. 1973. "The Premenstrual Syndrome." *Psychological Bulletin* 80:454-465.

Persky, H. 1974. "Reproductive Hormones, Moods, and the Menstrual Cycle." In R.C. Friedman, R.M. Richart, and R.L. Vande Wiele, eds. *Sex Differences in Behavior*. New York: Wiley.

Rabinowitz, F.M.; Moelym, B.E.; Finkel, N.; and McClinton, S. 1975. "The Effects of Toy Novelty and Social Interaction on the Exploratory Behavior of Preschool Children." *Child Development* 46:286-289.

Sarason, S.B.; Lightall, F.F.; Davidson, K.S.; Waite, R.R.; and Ruebush, B.K. 1960. *Anxiety in Elementary School Children*. New York: Wiley.

Schonberg, W.B.; Costanzo, D.J.; and Carpenter, R.S. 1976. "Menstrual Cycle: Phases and Reaction to Frustration." *Psychological Record* 26:321-325.

Schwartz, M.S. 1972. "The Repression-Sensitization Scale: Normative Age and Sex Data on 30,000 Medical Patients." *Journal of Clinical Psychology* 28:72-73.

Schwartz, N.B. 1975. "New Concepts of Gonadotropin and Steroid Feedback Control Mechanisms." In J.J. Gold, ed. *Gynecologic Endocrinology* 2d ed. Hagerstown: Harper & Row.

Silbergeld, S.; Brast, N.; and Noble, E.P. 1971. "The Menstrual Cycle: A Double Blind Study of Symptoms, Mood and Behavior, and Biochemical Variations Using Enovid and Placebo." *Psychosomatic Medicine* 33:411-428.

Speltz, M. 1976. "A Note on the Effects of Anonymity, Response Consequence Information, and Sex on the Self-assessment of Fear." *Behavior Research and Therapy* 14:375-377.

Spence, K.W., and Farber, I.E. 1953. "Conditioning and Extinction as a Function of Anxiety." *Journal of Experimental Psychology* 45:116-119.

Spence, K.W., and Spence, J.T. 1966. "Sex and Anxiety Differences in Eyelid Conditioning." *Psychological Bulletin* 65:137-142.

Spence, K.W., and Taylor, J.A. 1951. "Anxiety and Strength of the UCS as Determiners of the Amount of Eyelid Conditioning." *Journal of Experimental Psychology* 42:183-188.

Stern, D.N., and Bender, E.P. 1974. "An Ethological Study of Children Approaching a Strange Adult: Sex Differences." In R.C. Friedman, R.M. Richart, and R.L. Vande Wiele, eds. *Sex Differences in Behavior*. New York: Wiley.

Taylor, J.A. 1953. "A Personality Scale of Manifest Anxiety." *Journal of Abnormal and Social Psychology* 48:285-290.

Wilcoxon, L.A.; Schrader, S.L.; and Sherif, C.W. 1976. "Daily Self-reports on Activities, Life Events, Moods, and Somatic Changes during the Menstrual Cycle." *Psychosomatic Medicine* 38:399-417.

Wilson, G.D. 1967. "Social Desirability and Sex Differences in Expressed Fear." *Behavior Research and Therapy* 5:136-137.

11 Compliance, Nurturance, and Affiliation

Compliance

Most people would probably agree that the male animal typically takes the lead in initiating courtship and copulation, while the receptive female yields to his demands. If, as we suggest, these deeply rooted tendencies generalize, we should expect females to be more compliant than males in some nonsexual activities as well.

There are signs pointing in this direction. Take the statistics of crime. The overwhelming majority of lawbreakers in the United States are men. On January 1, 1977, the population of New York's state prisons numbered 17,791. Only 479 of these were women (Sheehan 1977). Or take the ever maligned woman driver. Studies of male and female drivers have found men less willing to obey a stop sign (Feest 1968) and more willing to make an illegal turn on a red light (Sigelman & Sigelman 1976).

Portents of this asymmetry can be found in children just starting to school. One study (Werry & Quay 1971) involved over 900 boys and 800 girls, almost the entire public school population of Urbana, Illinois, from kindergarten through the second grade. Teachers rated these children on a checklist of fifty-five common behavior problems. Girls exceeded boys in five symptoms, such as shyness, jealousy, and hypersensitivity. Almost all the disruptive symptoms (tantrums, disobedience, destructiveness) were among the thirty-six symptoms in which boys exceeded girls.

Cross-cultural evidence also attests to the greater compliance of females. Barbara Whiting's Herculean analysis of six cultures, sampling Africa, India, Okinawa, Philippines, Mexico, and New England, included behavioral observations of children aged 3 to 11 (Whiting & Edwards 1973). Combining all six cultures the authors found older girls more passive, more obedient to their mothers than older boys. In this as in other respects they confirmed another well-known survey. Barry et al. (1957) had rated practices of socialization in a variety of cultures, mostly nonliterate. As to training for obedience, they had found some evidence that twenty-four of sixty-nine societies pressed girls harder than boys, while only two did the opposite. Note that this leaves forty-three cultures in which no distinction was made.

But all signs do not agree. Consider, for example, hypnosis. In human society compliance connotes yielding to suggestion, and hypnotism has been defined as a technique for enhancing suggestibility. Our hypothesis, therefore, implies that females should be more easily hypnotized than males. Early evidence offered some slight support for this deduction (Weitzenhoffer 1953). But more recent tests in Hilgard's laboratory have consistently failed to show any sex difference in susceptibility to hypnosis (Hilgard 1965).

Hypnosis is, after all, an abnormal state and may depend on special conditions. So let us look at another area: jury duty. Until the present century women in the United States were exempted, not because of prior responsibilities but because they were considered unfit. At first the alleged defect was intellectual, later they were supposedly too emotional and too passive and submissive (persuasible?). Few if any such restrictions remain in force, but it would be unsafe to assume that the prejudice is dead. What is the evidence?

In a recent study (Nemeth et al. 1976) over 400 male and 300 female undergraduates were asked to read copies of the testimony at a trial for first-degree murder and to vote guilty or not guilty. The sexes did not differ in their verdicts. The next step was to arrange for volunteers from the original subjects to meet in mixed-sex groups of six to deliberate on the same case. Videotapes of the deliberations showed that the men took a more active part, but that neither sex was more influential in arriving at the group verdict. In the third and final step more volunteers from the original group served as jurors in a lifelike situation, a practice trial in a real courtroom with a real judge, followed by deliberation. In this case there were no sex differences.

To explain the one difference found—more male participation in step 2—the authors ventured that familiarity with the case left more freedom for self-expression. The question is: were the women expressing compliance or were the men expressing a need for self-display? A comment by the authors is pertinent: "Whenever two protagonists entered into sustained disagreement, repeating themselves without compromise or the introduction of new points, they invariably were both males" (p. 303).

A point of incidental interest: at the end of steps 2 and 3, subjects were asked to rate one another on adjective scales. In both cases the men were judged more influential, rational, strong, independent, confident, and aggressive than the women. The hardihood of stereotypes is, indeed, legendary.

More directly concerned with persuasibility was an experiment on the effectiveness of group discussion (Steinbacher & Gilroy 1976). Undergraduates took a test of attitudes toward social topics; for example, "many problems facing blacks today are caused by blacks themselves." Eight weeks later some of them met in groups of four to discuss one of the topics. Groups consisted of three males and one female or vice versa, and were so chosen that in each group the two sexes were strongly opposed to each other on the topic in question. Right after the discussion they took the test of attitudes again.

The results are: isolated females produced a significant change of opinion in male majorities ($p<.05$); no other change was significant. Supplementary data suggested that the isolated female's advantage lay in her greater willingness to recognize and discuss an opposing viewpoint without abandoning her own. This is not compliance in the sense of conformity; it seems rather to fall on a dimension between cooperation and competitiveness.

Turning to Maccoby and Jacklin (1974), we find one encouraging note in a generally negative review of this area: among preschool children girls seem more willing than boys to obey adults. In later childhood results have been equivocal. Does this mean that a difference in compliance has disappeared, or that researchers have overlooked a crucial question: compliance with whom? Many studies of schoolchildren have measured resistance to pressure from peers rather than respect for established authority.

The difference is well illustrated by Bronfenbrenner's (1970) interesting study of moral attitudes in Soviet and American children. He presented his 12-year-old subjects with a series of hypothetical choices between adult-approved and peer-approved behavior; for example, going to a questionable movie, stealing fruit from a private orchard, neglecting homework for a game. Two differences were clear-cut: (1) the Soviet children conformed to adult standards much more closely than the American; and (2) girls were significantly more dutiful than boys in both countries, this despite the supposed equalizing of social roles in the Soviet Union.

We approach the bulk of experimental work on this issue with somewhat dampened hopes of establishing a general sex difference at a respectable level of significance. At this stage it may be more profitable to look at a few typical experiments to see what conditions favor or block the appearance of a sex difference.

One experimental approach to compliance with authority is to measure resistance to defying it. A favorite form of this approach, often used with young children, might be called the forbidden-toys technique. The experimenter shows the child an array of shiny new toys (appropriate for both sexes) within easy reach but not to be touched since they "belong to someone else." Later the experimenter "has to make a phone call," leaving the child alone in the locked room for several minutes; an observer behind a one-way mirror records the subject's reactions to the toys. As to sex differences, there are frequently none, but when one does occur it is almost always the girls who are more resistant to temptation. What factors are important here? An example may point the way to possible answers.

Ward and Furchak (1968) used the forbidden-toys method with twenty-four kindergarten and second-grade children. In both grades the boys broke the taboo on new toys sooner than the girls ($p < .02$), but more interesting was the difference in manner of breaking. Six of the ten "boy delinquents" tried to make the crime look accidental; the five girls who yielded did so directly, though with clear signs of conflict. It seemed as if the boys were concerned with avoiding external consequences; the girls, with internal guilt. This led the authors to speculate that girls may be taught self-control through love-oriented techniques, while boys are more likely to be punished.

Some light on this point was already at hand in an intensive study of the development of conscience. Sears et al. (1965) had tested 4-year-old children with a variety of temptations including forbidden toys. On the whole the boys yielded more than the girls; most of the differences were insignificant, but for all tests combined the difference had a chance probability of .001.

But the authors also interviewed both parents in detail about the parts they had played in bringing up their child. The results gave little support to Ward and Furchak's idea. Fathers seemed to have done much to stiffen their sons' moral fiber but not through punishment, rather by developing a close relationship and contrasting right from wrong. Girls were strengthened in impulse control by high standards of achievement set by both parents and by the father's expressed dissatisfaction with his daughter. If love techniques were involved in the process, they somehow escaped measurement.

Perhaps a direct experimental attack would succeed where interviews failed. How could love function as a disciplinary method anyhow? It would have to be made contingent on good behavior, that is, withdrawn when rules were broken and restored on return to virtue. No experiment that we know of has done precisely that, but a few attempts have been made to test the effect of withdrawing love on resistance to temptation.

Parke (1967) used the forbidden-toys procedure with children 6 to 7 years old as subjects. Half of them had a male experimenter; the other half, a female. In each case the ordeal-by-toys was preceded by a drawing session in which the experimenter either gave help and encouragement throughout or abruptly stopped doing so at the halfway point. Again the boys touched forbidden toys more often than the girls ($p < .05$). The "nurtured" children touched more often than the "abandoned" ones. But this difference was significant for the girls only, and then only if the experimenter was female, a finding that fits in well with Ward and Furchak's observations.

A second experiment (Burton et al. 1966) addressed the same problem but used a different measure of resistance to temptation. In the don't-cheat method the child is taught the rules of a game, then given a chance to cheat undetected in order to win a prize. (Results of this method are inconclusive with respect to a sex difference; they depend, for example, on how much the game [Medinnus 1966] or the prize [Keasey 1971] appeals to one sex or the other.)

In the Burton experiment 4-year-old children had to toss bean bags under certain restraining rules. The experimenter was either male or female and either continued or withdrew his attention. There was no overall sex difference in cheating. But the experimenter's sex did make a difference: boys cheated more when the experimenter was male; girls, when female.

Withdrawal of the experimenter's attention also made a difference, but here, contrary to Parke's finding, only the boys were affected; that is, those boys who had lost the attention of a male experimenter cheated more than those who had not.

Why should girls resist temptation more after losing adult support (Parke's experiment), while boys resist it less in similar circumstances (Burton et al.)? Burton et al. suggest, as a partial answer, that young girls may be trying to please a parent figure by complying with rules of conduct. Young boys, on the other hand, may cheat because they are trying to please a father figure by achieving a high level of performance. (But notice the sex difference here in choice of ways to please.) Admittedly, our search for a difference in compliance between human male and female has carried us into deep waters.

So far we have talked about children's conformity to adult standards. Turning to compliance with peers we find a field under active investigation. By far the most widely used method was introduced by Asch (1952). In essence the subject is called on to make a judgment (for example, which of three lines is the longest) in the presence of peers; he knows how the peers judged and that they agree with one another but not with him. The question is how much the subject's response will be influenced by this knowledge. Our question is whether female subjects are more susceptible to such influence than males.

Most of the relevant experiments have been done with high school and college students, though lower grades are also represented (see below). The reader will find an incisive review of this work in Maccoby and Jacklin (1974). As there summarized, a large majority of studies do not show a significant sex difference; of those that do, an equally large majority find girls and women more suggestible than boys and men.

How are we to reach an understanding of the sporadic nature of this difference? The answer is inescapable: analysis and more analysis of the conditions of its occurrence. Here are two revealing examples.

Sistrunk and McDavid (1971) tested the hypothesis that part of the apparent sex difference in conformity was due to characteristics of the measuring situation. The likeliest source of such an effect was the type of judgment the subjects were asked to make. Specifically, female subjects would be expected to yield in predominantly masculine territory (mathematics, engineering, law, football). But in the feminine domain (nursery, supermarket, cosmetics, theater) men should be easier to influence. Sistrunk and McDavid drew up a set of statements some of which were previously classified as masculine, others feminine, and still others neutral, and presented them for agreement or disagreement to students ranging from high school to university. Each statement was accompanied by the supposed majority response as the source of social influence.

The results gave impressive support to the authors' hypothesis. There was no overall sex difference in conformity. But four separate experiments showed a clear tendency for males to yield more than females on feminine items and for females to yield more on masculine ones.

Does the Sistrunk-McDavid study "explain away" the higher incidence of female compliance? There would seem to be quite a difference between checking a dissenting opinion beside a recorded majority vote and voicing it in the physical presence of one's peers. Other investigators (Deutsch & Gerard 1955) have recognized at least two motives at work in the Asch situation: a need to be correct and a need to be accepted by others. Sistrunk and McDavid presumably tapped the first of these needs, but the second hardly at all. Did they miss the essential ingredient?

For convenience, let us call the total effect of social influence in the Asch situation *conformity*, the part due to uncertainty *revision*, and the part due to social insecurity *appeasement*. Pasternack (1973) was concerned not merely with these two components of conformity but with their origins and development in childhood. His subjects were schoolchildren from first to eighth grade. Each came with five classmates ostensibly to take a test of visual judgment. Pasternack devised an ingenious procedure for getting separate measures of revision and appeasement. Briefly, each subject was tested under two conditions: he heard his classmates' judgments in both, but in one he had to speak his opinion publicly, in the other he wrote it privately.

In total *conformity* Pasternack found no sex difference in the early grades, but in the fourth to seventh grades girls yielded significantly more than boys. Scored for appeasement, yielding behavior showed no sex difference over all grades, but in the first five grades boys appeased more than girls, while in the sixth to eighth grades the difference was reversed.

Several questions arise. Why should girls in the fourth and fifth grades conform more than boys but appease less? As Pasternack pointed out, conformity was motivated partly by doubt of one's ability, while appeasement reflected doubt of one's status. In grade school the former motive might be more typically a girl's problem, the latter a boy's.

Again how are we to explain the sudden increase of appeasement that appeared in eighth-grade girls? Pasternack's suggestion of the onset of puberty is a provocative one, that should be extended to both sexes and followed into high school.

Nurturance

Nurturance is such a vague term, it requires definition. It has been used to cover all kinds of giving, sharing, and helping. Tests for sex differences in altruistic behaviors have usually found none. For our purpose nurturance means being concerned with and caring for young, small, helpless creatures. By our hypothesis, at least for mammals, such a trait should be more conspicuous in females than males.

Across Species. In rats we have experimental evidence that both virgin females and males would "mother" rat pups after being caged with them for six to seven days (Rosenblatt 1967). But under most conditions females have proved more assiduous than males (Quadagno et al. 1977). Experiments with hormones suggest a possible mechanism: androgens secreted before and shortly after birth in the male may act on a "parental behavior center" to prevent its full development (Bridges et al. 1973).

Experiments on nurturance in nonhuman primates are scarce. Field studies provide some clues. Among African langurs any newborn baby becomes a center of attention for all adult females of a troop. Adult males are quite indifferent. The divergence starts young. Juvenile males in their second year play only with one another, while their sisters join the mother's circle in welcoming new arrivals (Jay 1963). Young baboons show a similar tendency to segregate, but adult males, as self-appointed guardians of the troop, show considerable interest in the newly born (DeVore 1963).

An experiment with rhesus monkeys bears out these impressions (Chamove et al. 1967). Male-female pairs of preadolescents, reared without mothers, were tested with a month-old infant. These youngsters had never seen an infant monkey, and the hormonal changes of puberty were still ahead. Nevertheless the sexes reacted differently: compared with the males, the females were more positively attracted by the infant and less hostilely aroused.

Infancy Appeal. At the human level most people probably believe that women are innately more nurturant than men, but hard supporting evidence is scarce. Personally we find a mother's unexpectedly profound response to her firstborn child (Bardwick 1971, p. 34) as convincing as many a published study, but as scientific evidence it must be rated "soft." The same comment applies to Harlow's (1971, p. 61) report on audience reactions when he flashed a picture of a baby monkey on the screen. At a women's college 500 girls gasped in ecstasy, while all-male or mixed audiences made no response.

Harlow's experience, however, calls to mind Konrad Lorenz' (1943) concept of babyness. The term refers to physical features common to the infants of various species—protruding forehead, round cheeks, head large relative to body—that cause people to say "how cute!" and to feel like taking care of the infant. A few attempts have been made to test the validity of Lorenz' idea.

Fullard and Reiling (1976) presented pairs of photographic slides showing humans and animals, with instructions to check the slide preferred. Among them were twenty critical pairs consisting of an adult matched with an infant, ten human and ten animal. The subjects were twenty boys and twenty girls in each of six grades from the second to the twelfth, plus twenty graduate students of each sex.

Reversing an early preference for pictures of adults, upper-grade children of both sexes preferred infants, whether human or animal. For boys the shift of preference was gradual, not reaching significance until twelfth grade. In contrast, the girls' preference reversed abruptly between the sixth and eighth grades and stayed well above that of boys thereafter ($p <$ .001). The coincidence of these shifts with the onset of puberty, earlier in girls than boys, is worth noting, though it is not clear whether the effect is mediated by hormones or by social expectancies.

Must we wait till near puberty for signs of a nurturant impulse? A cursory search of literature at the preschool level produced little to encourage hope. The single exception was McGrew's (1972) observation of nursery school children. Concerning reactions to new children, he described girls as more attentive than boys, and boys as mostly indifferent. Four girls in particular were "maternal," that is, comforting, soothing, hugging, and trying to cheer up. Regrettably, we can take little comfort from this solitary note.

Across Cultures. Turning to anthropology, we comb Whiting and Whiting's (1975) report on children of six cultures for information on nurturant behavior. Their samples, as noted earlier, included villages of Okinawa, the Philippines, northern India, Kenya, a town in Mexico, and one in New England. Children from 3 to 11 years old were observed and their daily activities recorded. Nurturance was defined too broadly for our purpose, since it included any offer of help or support, whether to infant, peer, or parent; but 40 percent of the cases involved infants.

The results were predictable. Over all cultures combined there was no sex difference before age 7, but between 7 and 11 girls engaged in more nurturant activities than boys ($p<.001$). Similarly, in girls nurturance increased with age ($r = +.51$, $p<.001$), while in boys there was no relation.

Do these findings bear at all on the hypothesis of a biological disposition in females toward nurturing behavior? The authors argue that its late development in girls points to the impact of social training rather than instinct. They report that in all six cultures infant care was assigned more often to girls than to boys. Yet they are unwilling to attribute the entire sex difference to this practice. While not ruling out biology altogether, Whiting and Whiting believe it more important that girls have a better chance to imitate the mother's role. Girls simply spend more time interacting both with infants and with their own mothers than boys do.

A Clinical Anomaly. Evidence for a biologically determined sex difference in human nurturance still eludes us. For the closest approximation to a bona fide experiment we return to the work with the adrenogenital syndrome (AGS) cited in chapter 7 (Money & Ehrhardt 1972; Ehrhardt & Baker 1974). As noted there, AGS girls (exposed to androgens before birth) showed less interest in dolls and babies than their normal controls. For more than half of the AGS groups neither marriage nor motherhood figured in their daydreams. These results clearly imply that prenatal androgen in the human female prevents the normal development of a need to nurture. The crucial assumption is that this finding could not be ascribed to social pressure, since the subjects were brought up as girls.

In their critical review, Quadagno et al. (1977) question that assumption. They point out that since the parents knew their daughter's clitoris had originally resembled a penis, they might well have been looking for tomboyish traits, thus affecting their own reports and the girl's self-image. Of course it might be argued, with equal cogency, that the parents' awareness might move them to try all the harder to make their daughter a complete woman. In either case it seems that even the most promising quasi-experiment turns out to be inconclusive.

Affiliation

Affiliation, defined most simply as a tendency to form close ties with other persons, would seem to present no problems to the student of sex differences; the trait appears so clearly to lie at the core of femininity. We saw, for example, that Bakan selected communion as the counterpart of masculine agency. In our hypothetical scheme of biological sex differences, affiliation takes its place along with nurturance as a source of social stability, if only to offset the competitiveness of the male. In one way or another most reviewers in the 1950s and 1960s made the point that women in general are more interested in people; men, in things. The divergence appeared in the games they played, the books they read, the values they acknowledged. An impressive collection of studies fleshed out the basic split (Oetzel 1966).

Maccoby and Jacklin changed all that. Even if they had not, we should still face the twofold imperative: first, verify the alleged sex difference. Second, if such a difference seems probable, sift the available evidence to assess the relative importance of inheritance and experience in producing it. In the case of affiliation let us start with step 2.

One way, if not the only way, to avoid stereotypes is to look at infants as soon after birth as possible. Korner (1974), observing babies 2 to 4 days old, was struck by the more active role of the female mouth. She found the sexes about equal in total number of nervous discharges during sleep, but the males predominated in startle reflexes, the females in reflex smiles and rhythmic mouth movements. Korner did not suggest a possible connection between early mouthing and later babbling and speaking, though it would be interesting to know. But another investigator, Freedman (1972), confirmed her reported sex difference in smiling and held that sleep-smiling could be considered an adaptive trait, inherited as a mechanism for social attachment. Of course it might be just a transient reflex.

Much better known are the studies of visual attention in babies. In one experiment (Lewis et al. 1966) 6-month-old infants were shown pictures of human faces along with nonsocial objects such as a target or a nursing bottle. The girls stared longer at the faces than the objects; the boys made no distinction.

Another experiment (Lewis 1969) used several versions of a male face (for example, one eye only, scrambled features) as stimuli, and infants at four age levels in the first 13 months as subjects. Here the male infants stared longer, but the females vocalized more. Interestingly, the females again proved more discriminating than the males, this time with their smiles.

These results are hard to interpret. There is no dearth of measures, but little grasp of what they mean. Does a protracted stare indicate keen interest or slow intake? One recurrent objection to the use of young children as subjects in this field is that girls are known to mature, physically and mentally, ahead of boys (Tanner 1970).

In any case, to establish affiliation as more feminine than masculine we must find confirming evidence later in life. At this point we confront a baffling situation: the former years of plenty have given way to a period of drought. Here and there a small oasis appears: the accidental touch of a library clerk's hand affects female undergraduates' mood ratings more than males' (Fisher et al. 1976). Yet after a fairly exhaustive search of recent literature, Maccoby and Jacklin (1974) were unwilling to concede that women had more social capacity than men. Further evidence has done little to restore our own confidence in the hypothesis.

One gets the impression, however, that there are qualitative differences, if only we knew how to measure them. For one thing, there are hints that a woman may empathize more than a man; that is, she may share more fully an emotion felt by someone else. For another, a girl's "social space" seems to reflect more directly than a boy's how much she likes or dislikes those persons that make it up. For a third example, perhaps related to the second, girls of school age are more likely to pair off as best friends, while boys form larger social groups. These hints are intriguing enough to prompt a brief search for further clues. The rest of the section is devoted to these possibilities.

Empathy. To measure empathy, Feshbach & Roe (1968) showed sequences of slides individually to children aged 6 to 7. Each sequence illustrated a story about a boy or girl who was made to feel happy, sad, angry, or afraid. After seeing it the child was asked, "How do you feel?" Empathy was scored by the number of feelings correctly matched. Feshbach and Roe's female subjects scored higher than the males ($p<.05$). (A more lenient scoring method, preferred by the authors, eliminated this difference.) A second study (Feshbach & Feshbach 1969) used the same method with two age groups, 4 to 5 and 6 to 7. They found no sex difference in the older subjects, but in the younger group a difference favoring the girls was almost significant.

Recently an experiment using the Feshbach method was done by Hoffman and Levine (1976), this time with 4-year-olds. Again the girls scored slightly but not quite significantly higher in empathy than the boys ($p<.06$). (As Hoffman and Levine point out, the obtaining of $p<.06$ in two independent repetitions of an experiment has itself a likelihood given by $p<.025$.)

So elusive a difference might well be produced by four years of sex typing. It seems unlikely that a baby could tell us much about empathy. But what about the disputed claim that newly born infants will cry at the sound of another infant crying? In a series of well-controlled experiments on infants about 70 hours old, Simner (1971) showed that this was truly a social response, not just the baby's protest against a loud noise. (Of course, it could depend on circular, or feedback, conditioning to the sound of the baby's own voice and still qualify as a social response.)

More to our point, Simner also found, in three of four experiments, that females cried more than males when they heard a newborn cry. Sagi and Hoffman (1976) repeated his experiment with infants 34 hours old and found the same sex difference. In no single experiment did the difference reach statistical significance; the two studies combined, however, are quite impressive. Sagi and Hoffman credited their young subjects with empathic distress, implying that an infant's cry could arouse in them an emotion similar to its own. We might add, tentatively, especially in females.

Social Space. We use this term in a broad sense to refer to the distances separating people: the physical ones, measured in feet or meters; the psychological ones, regulated by looking toward one another or away. We assume that such measures can be used to indicate the strength of attraction between persons; in a word, affiliation.

Many studies are available for comparing preferred distances of males and females from peers or adults of the same or opposite sex. Of twenty-four such studies cited by Maccoby and Jacklin (1974) a bare majority found females favoring shorter distances than males, two placed males closer, and the rest found no significant difference.

An impressive experiment was reported by Tennis and Dabbs (1975). They tested equal numbers of boys and girls in same-sex pairs drawn from first grade to college sophomore. Within each pair subject A approached B until B said "stop": this marked B's preferred conversational distance. Averaged by grade and sex, these distances produced the curves shown in Figure 11-1. Males preferred more social distance than females, the difference increasing throughout childhood and youth.

Other experimenters have observed pairs of boys or girls in conversation and measured "eye contact"; that is, how often and how long they looked at each other. Results were on the whole similar to those on distance, with females in visual contact more than males (Ashear & Snortum 1971; Levine & Sutton-Smith 1973). But all too often the expected sex difference failed to reach significance. Why should this be? One possibility is that the conditions of some experiments were too artificial to release affiliation. (Tennis and Dabbs, for example, found no relation between their direct measure of social distance and an indirect paper-and-pencil method.) If so, any way of accentuating the influence of liking or disliking on the subject's responses should widen the gap between females and males.

There is some evidence in this direction. Exline et al. (1965) had college students of both sexes interviewed by a male or female graduate student. An unseen observer timed the subject's glances at the interviewer, who looked steadily in the other's eyes. Each subject also filled out rating scales (Schutz 1958) designed to measure need to give and receive "inclusion" and affection.

Of this study's provocative results the most pertinent are these: (1) on the Schutz scales female subjects scored above males on inclusion and affection ($p < .01$); (2) females scored more eye-to-eye contact than males while speaking or during informal discussion ($p < .05$); (3) high scorers on the Schutz scales made closer visual contact than low scorers ($p < .01$).

It would be interesting to know how early such differences appear. Russo (1975) looked for them in same-sexed pairs of boys and girls from kindergarten to the sixth grade. Half of the pairs were composed of self-selected friends, the other half were considered neutral. During conversation girls averaged longer mutual glances than boys ($p < .001$), and friends looked at each other longer than neutrals ($p < .05$); the last difference, moreover, was significantly larger for girls than boys ($p < .05$).

Finally, Post and Hetherington (1974) tried a different approach with 4-year-olds and 6-year-olds. A child was shown four cards containing two figures, male and female, either near together or farther apart, and either facing toward each other or away. The child was asked, "Which like each other best?" Six-year-old girls, but not boys, did better than 4-year-olds in judging affiliation. When 4-year-olds were given special training, only the girls improved. These studies, and more that might be mentioned, have one

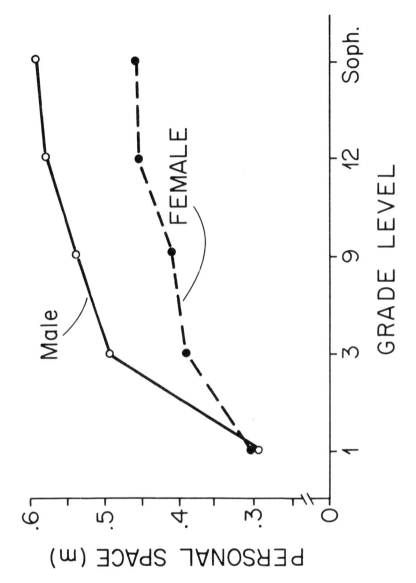

Figure 11-1. Preferred conversational distance.

Source: G.H. Tennis and J.M. Dabbs, "Sex, Setting, and Personal Space: First Grade through College," *Sociometry*, 38 (1975):385-394. Copyright 1975 by the American Sociological Association. Reproduced by permission.

thing in common: they can be more easily explained if we assume that even as early as 4 years of age affiliation is more important to females than to males.

Intensity versus Extensity. A person's social life may be concentrated in a few close attachments or diffused over many superficial ones; it may vary, in other words, along a scale of intimacy. The favored view is that on such a scale females will be found closer to the intensive end, males toward the extensive end.

Supporting evidence comes from observations of children in kindergarten (Laosa and Brophy 1972), where more girls than boys played in pairs, while more boys than girls played in larger groups. The same trend was seen on playgrounds among children from kindergarten to third grade: "girls move in groups of two or three, boys in 'swarms'" (Omark & Edelman, cited by Maccoby & Jacklin 1974, p. 553). Damico (1975) studied social interactions of 8-to-10-year-olds in an informal classroom. Here, too, boys interacted with more classmates than girls did; girls, more often than boys, had only one companion ($p<.05$). Damico observed that the boys circulated freely among the tables, with occasional chats, while the girls sat quietly in corners, working.

Closely related to the intensive-extensive dimension is the one May Seagoe (1970) explored with her Play Report, a questionnaire ("What do you spend most of your time playing . . .?") devised to show how far a child's play has been socialized. The scale, standardized on over 1,200 American children from 5 to 11 years of age, runs all the way from unstructured playing by oneself to cooperative-competitive play on a team. In general, socialization increases with age, and Seagoe took her instrument overseas and brought back some interesting international comparisons. But for us her important discovery was the marked sex difference she found throughout preadolescence, with the boys moving ahead to meet the complex social demands of team play, while the girls persisted in simpler forms of individual competition.

We have introduced Seagoe's Play Report as closely related to the intensity-extensity of social relations. We can hear the careful reader's question: how closely? At present we cannot be sure. He may also object that the sex difference Seagoe found was largely the product of school management rather than spontaneous expression. Both points seem to us cogent. The reader would be well advised not to think of the Play Report as directly measuring intimacy of affiliation. On the other hand, the suggested relationship does deserve further attention.

The most persuasive evidence for a sex difference in intimacy is a study by Waldrop and Halverson (1975). Their subjects, thirty-five males and twenty-seven females, were observed and rated for social adaptation at 2½ and again at 7½ years of age. Twelve measures of their behavior toward peers at 7½ were factor-analyzed separately for males and females. A striking relationship emerged: the first, and most important, factor for boys had loadings in measures of extensiveness; for example, hours with more than one peer, number of peers seen. For girls the corresponding factor had loadings in measures of intensiveness; for example, hours with one peer. When the two ages were compared, it turned out that social adaptation at 2½ was significantly correlated ($p < .01$), five years later, with extensiveness in boys and with intensiveness in girls. That is, a boy who was involved, friendly, and able to cope with his peers in the nursery would probably thrive in group activities at school. An equally sociable preschool girl, however, would be likely to seek out one or more close friends. Moreover, extensive boys and intensive girls were equally sociable by other measures.

How is this remarkable divergence to be explained? The authors suggest several possibilities, such as different interests in play, needs for activity, and socializing pressures. Aside from the indirect influence of activity level, we know of no solid evidence that intensiveness or extensiveness of affiliation is inborn.

In view of these findings, however, a postscript may be of added interest. Powers & Bultana (1976) interviewed 234 persons 70 years old and over about their present social contacts, exclusive of spouse and children. Men reported being in regular contact with a larger number of familiars than did women. But in answer to the question, "Is there any person you feel particularly close to—not 'just a friend'?", women acknowledged more frequent contacts with intimate friends than did men.

References

Asch, S.E. 1952. *Social Psychology*. New York: Prentice-Hall.

Ashear, D.V., and Snortum, J.R. 1971. "Eye Contact in Children as a Function of Age, Sex, Social, and Intellectual Variables." *Developmental Psychology* 4:479.

Bardwick, J.M. 1971. *Psychology of Women*. New York: Harper & Row.

Barry, H., III; Bacon, M.K.; and Child, I.L. 1957. "A Cross-cultural Survey of Some Sex Differences in Socialization." *Journal of Abnormal and Social Psychology* 55:327-332.

Bridges, R.S.; Zarrow, M.X.; and Denenberg, V.H. 1973. "The Role of Neonatal Androgen in the Expression of Hormonally Induced Maternal Responsiveness in the Adult Rat." *Hormones and Behavior* 4:315-322.

Bronfenbrenner, U. 1970. "Reaction to Social Pressure from Adults versus Peers among Soviet Day School and Boarding School Pupils in the Perspective of an American Sample." *Journal of Personality and Social Psychology* 15:179-189.

Burton, R.V.; Allinsmith, W.; and Maccoby, E.E. 1966. "Resistance to Temptation in Relation to Sex of Child, Sex of Experimenter, and Withdrawal of Attention." *Journal of Personality and Social Psychology* 3:253-258.

Chamove, A.; Harlow, H.F.; and Mitchell, G. 1967. "Sex Differences in the Infant-directed Behavior of Preadolescent Rhesus Monkeys." *Child Development* 38:329-335.

Damico, S.B. 1975. "Sexual Differences in the Responses of Elementary Pupils to Their Classroom." *Psychology in the Schools* 12:462-467.

Deutsch, M., and Gerard, H.B. 1955. "A Study of Normative and Informational Social Influences upon Individual Judgment." *Journal of Abnormal and Social Psychology* 51:629-636.

DeVore, I. 1963. "Mother-Infant Relations in Free-ranging Baboons." In H.L. Rheingold, ed. *Maternal Behavior in Mammals.* New York: Wiley, pp. 305-335.

Ehrhardt, A.A., and Baker, S.W. 1974. "Fetal Androgens, Human Central Nervous System Differentiation, and Behavior Sex Differences." In R.C. Friedman, R.M. Richart, and R.L. Vande Wiele, eds. *Sex Differences in Behavior.* New York: Wiley.

Exline, R.; Gray, D.; and Schuette, D. 1965. "Visual Behavior in a Dyad as Affected by Interview Content and Sex of the Respondent." *Journal of Personaiity and Social Psychology* 1:201-209.

Feest, J. 1968. "Compliance with Legal Regulations: Observations of Stop Sign Behavior." *Law and Society Review* 2:447-461.

Feshbach, N.D., and Feshbach, S. 1969. "The Relationship between Empathy and Aggression in Two Age Groups." *Developmental Psychology* 1:102-107.

Feshbach, N.D., and Roe, K. 1968. "Empathy in Six- and Seven-Year-Olds." *Child Development* 39:133-145.

Fisher, J.D.; Rytting, M.; and Heslin, R. 1976. "Hands Touching Hands: Affective and Evaluative Effects of an Interpersonal Touch." *Sociometry* 39:416-421.

Freedman, D.G. 1972. "Genetic Variations on the Hominid Theme: Individual, Sex, and Ethnic Differences." In F.J. Mönks, W.W. Hartup, and J. Dewit, eds. *Determinants of Behavioral Development.* New York: Academic Press.

Fullard, W., and Reiling, A.M. 1976. "An Investigation of Lorenz' babyness." *Child Development* 47:1191-1193.

Harlow, H.F. 1971. *Learning to Love.* San Francisco: Albion.

Hilgard, E.R. 1965. *Hypnotic Susceptibility.* New York: Harcourt, Brace.

Hoffman, M.L., and Levine, L.E. 1976. "Early Sex Differences in Empathy." *Developmental Psychology* 12:557-558.

Jay, P. 1963. "Mother-Infant Relations in Langurs." In H.L. Rheingold, ed. *Maternal Behavior in Mammals*. New York: Wiley, pp. 282-304.

Keasey, C.B. 1971. "Sex Differences in Yielding to Temptation: A Function of the Situation." *Journal of Genetic Psychology* 118:25-28.

Korner, A.F. 1974. "Methodological Considerations in Studying Sex Differences in the Behavioral Functioning of Newborns." In R.C. Friedman, R.M. Richart, and R.L. Vande Wiele, eds. *Sex Differences in Behavior*. New York: Wiley.

Laosa, L.M., and Brophy, J.E. 1972. "Effects of Sex and Birth Order in Sex Role Development and Intelligence among Kindergarten Children." *Developmental Psychology* 6:409-415.

Levine, M., and Sutton-Smith, B. 1973. "Effects of Age, Sex, and Task on Visual Behavior during Dyadic Interaction." *Developmental Psychology* 9:400-405.

Lewis, M. 1969. "Infants' Responses to Facial Stimuli during the First Year of Life." *Developmental Psychology* 1:75-86.

Lewis, M.; Kagan, J.; and Kalafat, J. 1966. "Patterns of Fixation in the Young Infant." *Child Development* 37:331-341.

Lorenz, K.Z. 1943. "Die angeborenen Formen möglicher Erfahrung." *Zeitschrift für Tierpsychologie* 5:235-409.

Maccoby, E.E., and Jacklin, C.N. 1974. *The Psychology of Sex Differences*. Stanford, Calif.: Stanford University Press.

McGrew, W.C. 1972. *An Ethological Study of Children's Behavior*. New York: Academic Press.

Medinnus, G.R. 1966. "Age and Sex Differences in Conscience Development." *Journal of Genetic Psychology* 109:117-118.

Money, J., and Ehrhardt, A.A. 1972. *Man and Woman, Boy and Girl*. Baltimore: Johns Hopkins University Press.

Nemeth, C.; Endicott, J.; and Wachtler, J. 1976. "From the Fifties to the Seventies: Women in Jury Deliberations. *Sociometry* 39:293-304.

Oetzel, R.M. 1966. "Annotated Bibliography and Classified Summary of Research in Sex Differences." In E.E. Maccoby, ed. *The Development of Sex Differences*. Stanford, Calif.: Stanford University Press.

Parke, R.D. 1967. "Nurturance, Nurturance Withdrawal, and Resistance to Deviation." *Child Development* 18:1101-1110.

Pasternack, T.L. 1973. "Qualitative Differences in Development of Yielding Behavior by Elementary School Children." *Psychological Reports* 32:883-896.

Post, B., and Hetherington, E.M. 1974. "Sex Differences in the Use of Proximity and Eye Contact in Judgments of Affiliation in Preschool Children." *Developmental Psychology* 10:881-889.

Powers, E.A., and Bultana, G.L. 1976. "Sex Differences in Intimate Friendships of Old Age." *Journal of Marriage and the Family* 38:739-747.

Quadagno, D.M.; Briscoe, R.; and Quadagno, J.S. 1977. "Effect of Prenatal Gonadal Hormones on Selected Nonsexual Behavior Patterns: A Critical Assessment of the Nonhuman and Human Literature." *Psychological Bulletin* 84:62-80.

Rosenblatt, J.S. 1967. "Nonhormonal Basis of Maternal Behavior in the Rat." *Science* 156:1512-1513.

Russo, N.F. 1975. "Eye Contact, Interpersonal Distance, and the Equilibrium Theory." *Journal of Personality and Social Psychology* 31:497-502.

Sagi, A., and Hoffman, M.L. 1976. "Empathic Distress in the Newborn." *Developmental Psychology* 12:175-176.

Schutz, W.C. 1958. *FIRO: A Three-dimensional Theory of Interpersonal Behavior*. New York: Rinehart.

Seagoe, M.V. 1970. "An Instrument for the Analysis of Children's Play as an Index of Degree of Socialization." *Journal of School Psychology* 8:129-144.

Sears, R.R.; Rau, L.; and Alpert, R. 1965. *Identification and Child Rearing*. Stanford, Calif.: Stanford University Press.

Sheehan, S. 1977. "Annals of Crime: A Prison and a Prisoner." *The New Yorker*, October 24, p. 48.

Sigelman, C.K., and Sigelman, L. 1976. "Authority and Conformity: Violation of a Traffic Regulation." *Journal of Social Psychology* 100:35-43.

Simner, M.L. 1971. "Newborn's Response to the Cry of Another Infant." *Developmental Psychology* 5:136-150.

Sistrunk, F., and McDavid, J.W. 1971. "Sex Variations in Conforming Behavior." *Journal of Personality and Social Psychology* 17:200-207.

Steinbacher, R., and Gilroy, F.D. 1976. "Persuasibility and Persuasiveness as a Function of Sex." *Journal of Social Psychology* 100:299-306.

Tanner, J.M. 1970. "Physical Growth." In P.H. Mussen, ed. *Carmichael's Manual of Child Psychology*. 3d ed., vol. 1. New York: Wiley.

Tennis, G.H., and Dabbs, J.M. 1975. "Sex, Setting, and Personal Space: First Grade through College." *Sociometry* 38:385-394.

Waldrop, M.F., and Halverson, C.F. 1975. "Intensive and Extensive Peer Behavior: Longitudinal and Cross-sectional Analyses." *Child Development* 46:19-26.

Ward, W.D., and Furchak, A.F. 1968. "Resistance to Temptation among Boys and Girls." *Psychological Reports* 23:511-514.

Weitzenhoffer, A.M. 1953. *Hypnotism: An Objective Study in Suggestibility*. New York: Wiley.

Werry, J.S., and Quay, H.C. 1971. "The Prevalence of Behavior Symptoms in Younger Elementary School Children." *American Journal of Orthopsychiatry* 4:136-143.

Whiting, B., and Edwards, C.P. 1973. "A Cross-cultural Analysis of Sex Differences in the Behavior of Children Aged 3 to 11." *Journal of Social Psychology* 91:171-188.

Whiting, B.B., and Whiting, J.W.M. 1975. *Children of 6 Cultures: A Psychocultural Analysis*. Cambridge, Mass.: Harvard University Press.

12

Need to Achieve

Power, Glory, and the Need to Achieve

A common practice among writers on sex differences is to point out the vast discrepancy between the accomplishments of men and women in such fields as art, music, science, medicine, architecture, and literature. There is no argument here for a sex difference in motivation; differences in opportunity, backed by long-standing tradition and deep-seated prejudice, are too obvious. Yet a hankering doubt remains. If all cultural barriers to women's eminence were removed, would the gap be quite closed?

Our working hypothesis is that in evolution most adult female mammals were preoccupied with bearing and rearing young. Males, aside from rivalry with other males, were freer to explore the environment, cope with its dangers, and make use of its benefits; the most successful in these pursuits were the most likely to survive. For *Homo sapiens* this assumption leaves open the possibility of an inborn difference between male and female in the reinforcing value of solving problems, overcoming obstacles, reaching goals—in a word, achievement. As usual, let us first examine evidence, then consider how best to account for it.

Until fairly recently most of the experimental work on the need to achieve (nAch) was done with male subjects. The reason sometimes given was that attempts to measure the motive and relate it to other traits were more fruitful when males were used rather than females. It could be inferred that nAch was somehow more central to the masculine makeup. Alternatively, the experimenters' choice of activities might be responsible; if they had assigned tasks more typical of the female role, women might have yielded more rewarding results.

An example from early work with the projective method comes to mind. Publication of *The Achievement Motive* by McClelland et al. (1953) was a landmark in the study of motivation in general and nAch in particular. In that book a small section can be found devoted to comparing results on men and women. McClelland's method was to have the subject tell stories suggested by pictures under two conditions: relaxed and achievement-oriented, that is, facing a test of intelligence or leadership. The score for nAch was the difference in number of achievement-related responses between the two conditions.

In two experiments by Veroff and Wilcox high school girls and college women made more achievement-related responses to pictures of males than to females, but no more in the arousing condition than relaxed. In a third experiment, however, Field tried a different method of arousal. He led his subjects to believe that each had been socially accepted or rejected by a committee of peers. This method increased nAch in college women but not men. McClelland was persuaded that achievement for females was a matter of social acceptance, while for men it concerned individual competence.

Two later studies tested this hypothesis by comparing nAch in two groups of college women: those with intellectual interests and those oriented toward the traditional women's role. Both studies used a projective method to measure nAch under two arousing conditions: one involving a test of verbal ability (scrambled words), the other, a test of social skills. French and Lesser (1964) confirmed McClelland's hypothesis by showing that motivation was higher when arousing conditions matched the subject's values. Friedrich (1976) did much the same experiment but devised a separate scoring procedure for "women's-role nAch." She did not confirm the earlier findings, but she did find women's-role nAch a better predictor of other performances than "intellectual nAch," for intellectual and traditional subjects alike.

Friedrich took special pains to eliminate other motives, such as affiliation, in scoring women's-role nAch. Still a question arises whether perfection of social skills, aside from affiliation and nurturance, plays as important a part in female values as individual excellence plays in male. Enough doubt exists to justify a search for further evidence, including other ways of measuring nAch.

A clearer idea is needed of what processes make up achievement motivation. Weiner's (1972) attributional theory should prove helpful. Figure 12-1 shows what supposedly goes on in a person's mind between confronting a task and responding to it. Whether he attempts or evades it depends on how important it is to succeed and how likely it is that he will. These mediators in turn

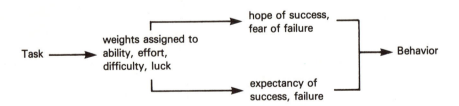

Source: Adapted from figure 6-1, p. 355, B. Weiner, *Theories of Motivation*, Chicago: Rand McNally College Publishing Company, Copyright 1972. Reproduced by permission.

Figure 12-1. Attributional model of achievement motivation.

depend on the weights he assigns to internal factors (his own ability and effort) and external ones (luck and difficulty). Artificial as these constructs may appear, they have stimulated a great deal of trenchant investigation.

Is Success for Men Only? Starting with hope of success and fear of failure, we are brought face to face with the unorthodox notion of fear of success (FOS). We cannot avoid it in any case, since Matina Horner (1972) introducd the concept as crucial to understanding sex differences in achievement. Like McClelland et al., she had used a projective technique, asking male and female college students to write stories suggested by several verbal cues. One of the cues was: "After the first-term finals Anne (John) finds herself (himself) at the top of her (his) medical school class." (Males received the words in parentheses.) Scored for pleasant or unpleasant content, 66 percent of the women's stories, but only 9 percent of the men's, contained negative features. Female subjects, explained Horner, felt that Anne's success threatened her acceptance by her male classmates; she would lose her feminine identity. In evidence Horner compared her subjects' skill at anagrams in a large mixed group and alone. The men did better in the group than alone and so did most women low in FOS. But most high-FOS women did better alone.

Horner's evidence seemed quite compelling and her thesis tempted ready acceptance. It was timely, credible, and seemed to provide a likely interpretation of common experience. But, inevitably, questions were raised, resulting in a flood of doctoral dissertations and a more circumspect appraisal.

1. Can Horner's fantasy-based finding be replicated? In a critical review of work on FOS, Zuckerman and Wheeler (1975) reported results of fifteen later attempts using mainly high school and college students of both sexes. The percentage of subjects showing FOS was higher for females than males in six samples, almost the same in six, and higher for males in three.

Among these studies was one by Hoffman (1974) done, like Horner's, at the University of Michigan but six years later. The incidence of FOS among coeds remained at about 65 percent, but that of men jumped from 9 percent to 76 percent. Could the women's liberation movement have somehow misfired? Before deciding, we should take account of another of Hoffman's findings. Success meant something different to men and women. According to the stories they told, women thought of academic success as threatening to friendships, while men questioned the value of academic and professional success itself.

2. Did Horner's projective method reveal a true feminine characteristic or simply deviation from a stereotype? Some of the replications did more than repeat Horner's work; they gave the John and Anne cues to subjects of both sexes. In five out of six such studies men responded with more FOS to

Anne than to John; women did so in only two studies out of the six. It would seem that men projected more FOS into women than did women themselves.

3. Does FOS really interfere with female achievement? As noted above, Horner did an experiment that appeared to validate her thesis in a competitive situation. But later investigators reexamined her data and took issue with her conclusions (Zuckerman & Wheeler 1975; Tresemer 1976). These two critiques raise doubts that FOS played any part in the result.

These doubts are not allayed by Romer's (1977) developmental study of FOS in schoolchildren from fifth through eleventh grades. Along with Horner-type measures of FOS she gave all her subjects scrambled words to decipher under five different degrees of competition. She found no overall sex difference in amount of FOS imagery or in changes with age. As to scrambled words, girls with FOS did better than those without and better than boys with or without FOS; all three of these inferior groups performed about the same. True, Horner did say that the best performers should be most vulnerable to FOS. But analysis of the data on competition produced few convincing signs that FOS had any detrimental effect.

Does this mean that FOS exists only in the stories subjects tell and that it has no effect on how they behave? The answer is, not quite. Morgan and Mausner (1973) tested 200 high school students for FOS, using the John/Anne cues, and also gave them the first half of a Hidden Figures Test. For the second half of the test, boy-girl pairs were selected consisting either of a high-scoring girl with a low-scoring boy or the reverse, and told to work together as a team. In the Horner test boys told more FOS stories than girls. But in the second session of Hidden Figures something quite inconsistent happened. Among the fourteen pairs with the girls superior, half of the girls performed more poorly than their partners; of the fourteen superior boys, only one dropped below his partner. These results suggest that it is easier to talk about changing the roles of women than to put it into practice.

Elusive as FOS has proved to be, it shows itself in tantalizing ways that defy dismissal. Krauss (1977) studied effects of competition in high school seniors. On masculine tasks (assembling a doorbell, changing nuts and bolts) females did better competing against a male than against another female or alone. Yet there were signs of not going "all out." One girl tightened the last bolt twenty times before announcing she was done just after her male competitor's announcement. Krauss closed her discussion with a pithy comment on the current scene: "it may be that females are invited to compete but are still not expected to win" (p. 479).

Winner or Loser? Let us turn now to the lower branch of the diagram for achievement, where we find expectancies of success and failure. Do males and females differ in estimating their own abilities? Recent investigators have sought the answer at various ages from nursery school to college. A review of this work (Parsons et al. 1976) finds little if any difference in confidence in ages up to 5, but from 6 on boys seem surer of success than girls even though, in some cases, girls do better.

Several questions arise. First, how general is this difference between the sexes in self-confidence? Not all studies agree in finding it. Lenney (1977) pointed this out and suggested that lower confidence is characteristic, not of females as such, but of females in certain situations. Among these she specified masculine-typed activites (Deaux & Farris 1977; Stein et al. 1971) and a still broader class, that is, situations stressing social evaluation. Competition is an example of the latter.

House (1974) tested male and female undergraduates in solving anagrams, a task in which, as we have seen, women more than hold their own. He compared three conditions: alone and competing against a partner of the same or opposite sex. Before they started the subjects had to record how many words they expected to unscramble within the time limit. Females and males working alone made closely similar estimates, but on entering competition female expectancy dropped below male. This shift might suggest FOS, except that the lowest estimates of all were made by females competing against females. House preferred to attribute his findings to the social stereotype of the woman as noncompetitive.

A second, more basic question is how the reported sex differences in expectancy arise. Perhaps the most enlightening attempt to answer it can be found in the work of Virginia Crandall (1969). In three separate experiments, at the elementary, eighth grade, and college levels, she found that boys expected higher scores than girls in tests of mental abilities, though their IQs or course grades were essentially the same. Along the way she tested, and rejected, several hypotheses: (1) that the subjects were trying to please the examiner; (2) that their expectancies were related to M-F; (3) that boys valued intellectual prowess more highly than girls did; and (4) that males and females reacted differently to positive or negative reinforcements, that is, rewards or punishments for good or bad performance. But the difference in confidence remained to be accounted for.

Crandall's experiment with eighth-grade adolescents permitted one more analysis. She was able to reclassify each subject according to two criteria: the ability level of his classroom group and his standing within the class. The clearest sex difference in expectancy appeared in those children whose placements were inconsistent, that is, high in group-ability level but low within the class, or vice versa. Crandall suggested that when a child receives contradictory cues to his ability in a long-term, real-life situation, a girl tends to respond to negative cues, a boy to positive ones. Why that should be is left an open question.

Fitness or Fate? Still searching for clues to the nature of achievement motivation in males and females, we turn once more to Weiner's diagram (figure 12-1). Recall that according to his theory a person facing a task takes into account, consciously or unconsciously, the relative importance of certain internal and external factors in determining the outcome. We are concerned with whether or not males and females differ in the weights they assign to two of these factors, ability and luck.

Why should this matter? A possible objection—that attributions must be measured after the task rather than before—can be easily removed. The answer is that the attribution is learned. Our diagram is only a segment of a complete motivational sequence. In the whole sequence attribution would appear twice: once after an initial experience, again in anticipation of a similar event. The theory assumes that on its second occurrence the attributive process strengthens or weakens the motive to achieve.

But have we any assurance that this assumption is sound? It is not easy to prove. Weiner and his associates have presented a good deal of experimental evidence that achievement motivation and certain attributions are correlated. For example, high achievers are likely to ascribe their successes to ability, while low achievers tend to account for their failures by inability (Weiner 1972, p.371). Of course, a correlation does not tell us which variable is cause and which is effect. But it does give more point to the question of a possible sex difference in this area.

Nicholls (1975) tested 9-year-old girls and boys individually on an angle-matching task. By arbitrary feedback half of each sex was made to fail, the other half, permitted to succeed. (Failed subjects were allowed to succeed before being dismissed.) Attributions to ability, effort, difficulty, and luck were secured by an ingenious device. After the last trial the child was handed a disc with four adjustable sectors labeled, for success and failure respectively, as follows: "I am smart (not smart) at this," "I tried (didn't try) hard," "The test was easy (hard)," "I had good (bad) luck." He was told to adjust the sectors to show how much each one had to do with his score.

Boys and girls were equal in the degrees they assigned to effort and difficulty. But they felt differently about luck and ability. Boys were much readier than girls to blame failure on bad luck. As to ability, girls were more willing to account for their failures by lack of skill than to claim credit for their successes. For boys this was not the case.

Confirmatory results soon followed (Etaugh & Ropp 1976). The subjects were 8 and 10 years old and the game was to see how many marbles a child could throw into a can held by Mr. Munchie, a toy clown (there was also a Mrs. Munchie, for sex typing). To induce success or failure, the experimenter told the subject that he (she) had done much better or worse than most of the boys (girls) in his grade. Causal attributions were made by drawing four cards, appropriately labeled, in order of importance.

The boys in this experiment, but not the girls, thought skill more important than good luck in explaining their success. Compared with the girls they were loth to admit that their failure might be due to lack of skill. As in Nicholls' experiment, only the girls assigned more weight to ability or the lack of it in failure than success. These results held good whether Mr. or Mrs. Munchie received the marbles.

At the college level the picture is still recognizable, though with some inconsistency and one notable change. Both of these qualifications apply to experiments by Feather and Simon. Feather (1969) gave mixed classes of undergraduates ten anagrams to finish in five minutes, of which they would have to solve five to pass the test. He then asked them to explain their success (or failure) by checking a scale running from mainly due to ability (lack of ability) to mainly due to good (bad) luck. The result was: whether they passed or failed, females checked closer than males to the lucky (unlucky) end of the scale.

When Feather and Simon (1971) did a similar experiment, again using college students, they found no significant difference in explaining failure. This time the subjects worked in same-sex pairs, and the authors ascribed their negative result to the reduced incentive to compete. But a later study of the same problem (Deaux & Farris 1977) confirmed the original findings; in this case the subjects came in small mixed groups but worked in individual cubicles, hardly conducive to rivalry. On bipolar scales the males favored skill, the females luck. Separate scales were also used for rating all four causal factors. In rating luck, females gave it more clout than males for both success and failure. In the case of ability a new qualifying condition emerged. Half of the subjects of each sex were given reasons to believe that males were better at solving anagrams than females; the other half heard just the opposite. Only the masculine-typed task produced a sex difference: compared with men, women weighted ability more heavily in failure, less heavily in success.

As we have seen, children in the early grades reacted differently to failure. There it was found that failing girls were less inclined than boys to call themselves unlucky (Nicholls 1975), more inclined to admit lack of skill (Etaugh & Ropp 1976). Now we find that college women, though still ready to confess lack of skill in a masculine specialty, are more likely than college men to invoke chance in accounting for their own performances, good or bad. This is the apparent change with age previously noted. It consists of an increase in female awareness, or at least acknowledgment, of dependence on external, chance factors. We cannot be sure that the samples at the two age levels are comparable; indeed, it would be surprising if they were. The generality of these conclusions is therefore open to question.

Mastery or Community?

Early in this chapter a theory about sex differences in the need to achieve was mentioned. It held that nAch in human males and females was the same in strength but different in direction; that is, men seek individual excellence, superiority, mastery in profession, business, sport, artistic creation, or scientific discovery; women strive for proficiency in gaining social approval, improving social relations, harmonizing group activities. This theory, advanced in essence by McClelland (1953) and strongly endorsed by Stein and Bailey (1973), could accommodate evidence reviewed here by attributing the results to the masculine activities sampled. If socially oriented tasks had been used, the sex differences might have been reversed.

An alternative position, shared by us, may be stated as follows: the quality of a motive is not separate from its object but is partially shaped by its goal. Thus the aim to achieve mastery is assertive, competitive, selfish, and ruthless. The aim to achieve community is group-centered, cooperative, generous, and sympathetic. To direct masculine nAch to feminine goals is either impossible or self-defeating. It calls to mind images of the wily manipulator, turning on her charms to win people's confidence, while scheming to use their trust to her own advantage.

Just as motives acquire their character partly from objects that arouse them, so they are open to influence from other motives. We suggest that males and females are innately disposed to respond differently to certain social situations. The same circumstances may evoke in the male motives to compete, dominate, excel; in the female, motives to cooperate, comply, share, comfort. These two sets are mutually inhibitory; arousal of a motive in one set will tend to prevent or weaken those of the other.

Parents and educators are intensely interested in the question of how children can be motivated to strive for various goals. What makes nAch so elusive is that it seems autogenic, as if it emerged somehow from the activity itself. More generally recognized, perhaps because it is easier to control, is the need for approval by one's elders or peers. A plausible hypothesis is that a need to achieve may be more readily kindled in young males, a need for social approval, in young females. A look at a few typical experiments will make the nature of the evidence more concrete and also reveal some of the difficulties of interpretation.

Senior and Brophy (1973), for example, had kindergarten and second-grade children engage in a boring activity (canceling circles and putting pegs in a pegboard) to see which would induce them to keep at it longer—praise from the experimenter or competition with another group. Competition turned out to be a stronger incentive than praise, and more so for boys than for girls. When a more challenging task was used (building a tower of blocks as high as possible), only the older boys worked longer when urged to help their group win. The chief question of interpretation here is whether group rivalry qualifies as a stimulus to nAch. It could be objected that the experiment actually compares adult approval with peer approval as incentives.

Susan Harter (1975) also chose persistence as a measure but dealt more directly with mastery motivation, comparing it with need for approval in 11-year-old girls and boys. The task was a game called Push the Lights, in which the child had to learn which color to push, red or green, so as to release a marble on every trial. Two light patterns were used, one relatively easy to solve, the other impossible; the idea being that only a mastery-minded child would work longer on the insoluble problem. To measure need for approval half of the subjects were tested with the experimenter absent, the other half with the experimenter assuring them from time to time that they were doing well. Harter found that the boys, but not the girls, persisted longer at the insoluble game than at the easier one. On the other hand, the girls played longer with the experimenter's encouragement than without the experimenter, while the boys, at least after finding the solution, did the opposite.

Harter's primary aim was not to discover a sex difference but to compare high and low scorers on a Children's Social Desirability (CSD) Scale. (Though the sexes were equally represented at both levels, she found much the same differences between high and low scorers as between girls and boys.) The background of this scale contains one or two points worth noting.

Its forty-five true-false items (Crandall et al. 1965) were designed to measure a child's need to appear socially desirable ("I am always glad to cooperate with others," "I sometimes feel angry when I don't get my way"). It was standardized on close to 1,000 children from third to twelfth grades. Throughout the entire sample girls gave more of the approved responses than boys.

For us the most interesting discovery came when the scale was given to twenty-five boys and girls under observation at the Fels Institute summer camp (Crandall 1966). Significant correlations between CSD scores and free-play behaviors fell into two distinct groups according to sex with no overlapping. For the girls they had to do with social interactions (such as withdrawal from aggression and from associative play); for the boys they involved achievement-related behaviors (time spent, effort, and persistence). Scores on CSD were also correlated with those on a test for expectancy of success in four areas of achievement. All four coefficients were significantly negative for the boys, insignificant for the girls.

It is easier to find experiments on social rewards than on the achievement motive per se. Hill and Dusek (1969) worked with somewhat younger children than Harter's, 8 to 9 years old, and used a different measure—expectancy of success, a response related, as we have seen, to motivation. The task they assigned their subjects was to match angles according to size; each subject, before and after his stint, was asked to rate his expected level of performance. In one group, as the subject worked the experimenter gave continual words of encouragement; in the other he gave no sign.

From our standpoint the most striking outcome of this experiment was the change of expected scores from before to after performance of the task. An upward shift occurred only in the groups with social reinforcement. In these there was a significant sex difference, with the girls' confidence rising more sharply than the boys' ($p < .05$).

The authors apparently found the latter result surprising. This is understandable when we think of expectancy as a potent factor in nAch. But here we are talking about a *change* of expectancy produced by adult encouragement, and this seems to us to express more directly a need for social approval.

Rather than try the reader's patience by citing more experiments it might be more fruitful to refer him to a provocative article by Paula Caplan (1975). In it she proposes to account for the common belief that boys are more antisocial than girls, at least insofar as it rests on laboratory findings. She contends that the belief is upheld only under certain conditions, and she specifies two of the most important ones: the presence of an adult, and an experience of failure. Here we come to the relevant part of Caplan's argument. The adult presence is important because it appeals to the need for social approval, in which girls exceed boys. Failure is important because it frustrates nAch, in which boys exceed girls. Caplan goes on to assemble an impressive body of experiments to support her position.

We are about ready to conclude our brief sampling of the evidence, but not without mentioning one unusual approach to sex differences in late adolescence. Lerner et al. (1976) gave several hundred undergraduates three scales to fill out about themselves. On one they rated the attractiveness of twenty-four of their own bodily parts or features (ears, arms, ankles). On another they rated the same twenty-four properties for effectiveness in daily functioning. On the third scale they checked sixteen dimensions of personality (mature-immature, capable-not capable) to show how they perceived themselves.

The investigators asked how these three scales were related within each sex. They found that the perceived attractiveness of the twenty-four bodily components corresponded more closely with their effectiveness in males than in females. Using the multiple-correlation technique they also found that for females the twenty-four ratings for attractiveness predicted self-concept scores more closely than did those for effectiveness. Among males the difference was in the opposite direction.

The Lerner group saw their results as stemming from a more interpersonal orientation in young adult females as compared with a more self-sufficient attitude in males. We see them as altogether compatible with the view favored here: the sexes differ in the balance between the goals of community and mastery, between the need for social approval and the need to achieve.

Origins

There can be no quarrel with the statement that nAch is largely learned. The same applies to whatever difference may exist between the sexes. An impressive literature has piled up demonstrating the importance of cultural tradition, social class, parental attitudes, models, and the like in shaping the divergent aspirations of young males and females (Crandall 1963; Hoffman 1972; Manley 1977; Stein & Bailey 1973). The question we ask at this point is whether society is totally responsible for the divergence.

What sort of evidence would suggest that biology had anything to do with it? One attack would be to look for a difference when in all pertinent respects the sexes had been treated precisely the same. Such a condition narrows our search to children at the earliest age when behavior of interest can be measured. For example, in one experiment (Hoffman 1972) Lahtinen used a "talking animal" to arouse either fear of rejection or fear of failure in kindergarten children, testing its effect on task performance and story completion. Her results suggested that the little girls were more sensitive to the threat of rejection, the boys to lowering of self-esteem. But the experiment falls far short of a crucial test: the children were already too old to have escaped the undoubted impact of sex typing.

The reader may recall another attempt, cited in chapter 8, to find rudimentary differences in the behavior of male and female infants. We refer in particular to the work of Goldberg and Lewis (1969), who observed toddlers at 13 months with their mothers. In the course of that study, when the infant was separated by a barrier from mother and toys, girls stayed longer at the middle of the fence, crying; boys spent more time at the ends, apparently trying to get through. We are tempted to attribute the observed behaviors to the early emergence of a sex difference in nAch. Unfortunately the venture may prove abortive, since several experimenters have failed to confirm the finding (Maccoby & Jacklin 1974).

A second strategy offers a possible way out. Instead of trying to equalize the treatment of boys and girls from the beginning, one might take advantage of the existing inequalities of treatment within as well as between the sexes. That is, one could take a mixed sample of children, measure the varying amounts of a selected factor—say, training for independence—they had had, and give a test of nAch. Then one could see how the two variables were related in girls as compared with boys. If the sexes were equally predisposed, the correlation coefficients, though they might differ in size, should at least be on the same side of zero.

Data for such comparisons are available from a number of published studies. One source is the long-term study of development carried on at the Fels Research Institute, where close to a hundred subjects of both sexes were observed, tested, and interviewed from birth to early adulthood. Of special interest to us is a frequently cited finding reported by Kagan and Moss (1962). Mothers of the Fels subjects were rated on four dimensions of child rearing: protection (prevention of independence), restriction (adherence to imposed standards), hostility (critical attitude), and acceleration (concern with rate of development). These ratings were correlated with achievement-related behavior at intervals during childhood.

Maternal acceleration was positively correlated with achievement in both sexes from 3 years of age to the 20s. But protection appeared to have opposite effects on males and females, and so did hostility. Mothers protective of their 2-year-olds were likely to have ambitious sons and apathetic daughters. When the children of "hostile" mothers grew up, the daughters proved to be striving, the sons sluggish.

What do these unexpected results mean? Do they point to a genetic interpretation? We might speculate that females are innately more amenable to social pressure, while males are more resistant to it. There is even some evidence to support the assumption (Crandall et al. 1964). But "innately" is unwarranted and the reasoning ad hoc. The authors' view is more plausible. They suggest that the overprotected, achieving males might be striving to please their mothers; the overcriticized, achieving females were possibly following the model of their mothers' strong-mindedness. At this tantalizing point in our quest for origins we are forced to leave a more dependable verdict to future research.

References

Caplan, P.J. 1975. "Sex Differences in Antisocial Behavior: Does Research Methodology Produce or Abolish Them?" *Human Development* 18:444-460.

Crandall, V.C. 1966. "Personality Characteristics and Social and Achievement Behaviors Associated with Children's Social Desirability Response Tendencies." *Journal of Personality and Social Psychology* 4:477-486.

_____. 1969. "Sex Differences in Expectancy of Intellectual and Academic Reinforcement." In C.P. Smith, ed. *Achievement-related Motives in Children*. New York: Russell Sage Foundation.

Crandall, V.C.; Crandall, V.J.; and Katkovsky, W. 1965. "A Children's Social Desirability Questionnaire." *Journal of Consulting Psychology* 29:27-36.

Crandall, V.J. 1963. "Achievement." In H.W. Stevenson, ed. *Child Psychology: 62d Yearbook of the National Society for the Study of Education*. Chicago: University of Chicago Press, pp. 416-459.

Crandall, V.J.; Dewey, R.; Katkovsky, W.; and Preston, A. 1964. "Parents' Attitudes and Behaviors and Grade School Children's Academic Achievement." *Journal of Genetic Psychology* 104:53-66.

Deaux, K., and Farris, E. 1977. "Attributing Causes for One's Own Performance: The Effects of Sex, Norms, and Outcome." *Journal of Research in Personality* 11:59-72.

Etaugh, C., and Ropp, J. 1976. "Children's Self-evaluation of Performance as a Function of Sex, Age, Feedback, and Sex-typed Task Label." *Journal of Psychology* 94:115-122.

Feather, N.T. 1969. "Attribution of Responsibility and Valence of Success and Failure in Relation to Initial Confidence and Task Performance." *Journal of Personality and Social Psychology* 13:129-144.

Feather, N.T., and Simon, J.G. 1971. "Attribution of Responsibility and Valence of Outcome in Relation to Initial Confidence and Success and Failure of Self and Others." *Journal of Personality and Social Psychology* 18:173-188.

French, E.G., and Lesser, G.S. 1964. "Some Characteristics of the Achievement Motive in Women." *Journal of Abnormal and Social Psychology* 68:119-128.

Friedrich, L.K. 1976. "Achievement Motivation in College Women Revisited: Implications for Women, Men, and the Gathering of Coconuts." *Sex Roles* 2:47-61.

Goldberg, S., and Lewis, M. 1969. "Play Behavior in the Year-Old Infant: Early Sex Differences." *Child Development* 40:21-31.

Harter, S. 1975. "Mastery Motivation and the Need for Approval in Older Children and Their Relationship to Social Desirability Response Tendencies." *Developmental Psychology* 11:186-196.

Hill, K.T., and Dusek, J.B. 1969. "Children's Achievement Expectations as a Function of Social Reinforcement, Sex of Subject, and Test Anxiety." *Child Development* 40:547-557.

Hoffman, L.W. 1972. "Early Childhood Experience and Women's Achievement Motives." *Journal of Social Issues* 28:129-155.

_____. 1974. "Fear of Success in Males and Females: 1965 and 1972." *Journal of Consulting and Clinical Psychology* 42:353-358.

Horner, M.S. 1972. "Toward an Understanding of Achievement-related Conflicts in Women." *Journal of Social Issues* 28:157-175.

House, W.C. 1974. "Actual and Perceived Differences in Male and Female Expectancies and Minimal Goal Levels as a Function of Competition." *Journal of Personality* 42:493-509.

Kagan, J., and Moss, H.A. 1962. *Birth to Maturity*. New York: Wiley.

Krauss, I.K. 1977. "Some Situational Determinants of Competitive Performance on Sex-stereotyped Tasks." *Developmental Psychology* 13:473-480.

Lenney, E. 1977. "Women's Self-confidence in Achievement Settings." *Psychological Bulletin* 84:1-13.

Lerner, R.M.; Orlos, J.B.; and Knapp, J.R. 1976. "Physical Attractiveness, Physical Effectiveness, and Self-concept in Late Adolescents." *Adolescence* 11:313-326.

Maccoby, E.E., and Jacklin, C.N. 1974. *The Psychology of Sex Differences.* Stanford, Calif.: Stanford University Press.

Manley, R.O. 1977. "Parental Warmth and Hostility as Related to Sex Difference in Children's Achievement Orientation." *Psychology of Women Quarterly* 1:229-246.

McClelland, D.C.; Atkinson, J.W.; Clark, R.A.; and Lowell, E.L. 1953. *The Achievement Motive.* New York: Appleton-Century-Crofts.

Morgan, S.W., and Mausner, B. 1973. "Behavioral and Fantasized Indicators of Avoidance of Success in Men and Women." *Journal of Personality* 41:457-470.

Nicholls, J.G. 1975. "Causal Attribution and Other Achievement-related Cognitions: Effects of Task Outcome, Attainment Value, and Sex." *Journal of Personality and Social Psychology* 31:379-389.

Parsons, J.E.; Ruble, D.N.; Hodges, K.L; and Small, A.W. 1976. "Cognitive-Developmental Factors in Emerging Sex Differences in Achievement-related Expectancies." *Journal of Social Issues* 32:47-61.

Romer, N. 1977. "Sex-related Differences in the Development of the Motive to Avoid Success, Sex Role Identity, and Performance in Competitive and Noncompetitive Conditions." *Psychology of Women Quarterly* 1:260-272.

Senior, K., and Brophy, J. 1973. "Praise and Group Competition as Motivating Incentives for Children." *Psychological Reports* 32:951-958.

Stein, A.H., and Bailey, M.M. 1973. "The Socialization of Achievement Orientation in Females." *Psychological Bulletin* 80:345-366.

Stein, A.H.; Pohly, S.R.; and Mueller, E. 1971. "The Influence of Masculine, Feminine, and Neutral Tasks on Children's Achievement Behavior, Expectancies of Success, and Attainment Values." *Child Development* 42:195-207.

Tresemer, D. 1976. "Do Women Fear Success?" *Signs* 1:863-874.

Weiner, B. 1972. *Theories of Motivation.* Chicago: Rand McNally College Publishing Company.

Zuckerman, M., and Wheeler, L. 1975. "To Dispel Fantasies about the Fantasy-based Measure of Fear of Success." *Psychological Bulletin* 82:932-946.

13 Society's Options

In this volume we have marshaled evidence bearing on critical issues in sex differences from nonhuman species, primitive peoples, and selected variants of Western culture. We have also followed the course of normal and deviant development in males and females reared in this culture, and examined differences between them in abilities and dynamics in an effort to determine their sources. It is appropriate at this time to bring the evidence together in brief review. We shall then look at the options open to society for dealing with the critical problems in sex differences revealed by our study.

A Backward Glance

Mental Abilities. Efforts to measure intelligence have given no consistent evidence that either girls or boys are superior. But the sexes do seem to specialize in different directions. In all things verbal, whether spoken, written, or read, girls seem to take precedence over boys. Signs of this flair appear before the first word. But the best evidence of innateness is negative; that is, that girls are less susceptible than boys to the probably hereditary disorder of dyslexia.

Spatial ability promises to restore the balance. Here there is evidence, as yet inconclusive, for sex-linked inheritance and a possible role of androgenic hormones. Work in perception and problem solving has suggested that males not only do better with spatial matters but have a different cognitive style; that is, an analytic as contrasted with females' more global approach.

Cerebral Asymmetry. New discoveries about the hemispheres of the human brain prove to be more exciting than studies of cultural influences. While the major (usually left) hemisphere has long been recognized as the seat of language, the "silent" (usually right) hemisphere is now given a vital role in visualizing spatial relations.

Just how these fresh insights will deepen our understanding of sex differences in cognition is not clear, but the question is being actively pursued. Two hypotheses are front-runners; one (Buffery and Gray) stressing left-sided specialization of the female brain, the other (Levy) claiming divergent specialization of the male hemispheres. It is still too early to predict the outcome.

Masculinity and Femininity. In chapter 5 we explored the meaning, or rather meanings, of masculinity (M) and femininity (F). The twin concepts appear in several forms, varying with the method of discovery:

1. As the essential cores of maleness and femaleness in some social philosophies; for example, Bakan's agency and communion.

2. As stereotypes, the typical woman and typical man of social mythology, brought out in the open through questionnaires and checklists. These contain no surprises: males are seen as frank, rational, and bold; females are believed to be tactful, touchy, and affectionate.

3. As averaged answers of many individuals attempting to describe themselves. Real men and women resemble their mythical counterparts, but they differ from each other in fewer ways. It appears that women are *not* more neurotic or moral or suspicious than men after all.

To uncover the basic ingredients of M and F is a task for factor analysis. Results so far suggest that toughness and self-assertion in the male, sensitivity and social need in the female are stable tendencies.

Activity. One test of resistance in newborn babies and a good many studies of general activity in children from the second year to puberty testify that males expend more energy than females. A clinical syndrome of hyperactivity occurs much more frequently and lasts longer in boys than girls.

Do parents produce this difference in output of energy by rewarding strenuous activity in boys more than in girls? Or does the same damping treatment produce resistance in boys but compliance in girls? Or do male toddlers simply exert themselves more than their sisters from the beginning? Observational data are still inconclusive. Also inconclusive, but suggestive, are some statistical data pointing to biological factors in hyperactivity.

Aggressiveness. It is readily acknowledged, even by psychologists, that human males are on the whole more aggressive than females. Field studies bear out the dictum; that is, behind the steering wheel, but not at the supermarket. It is also widely held, at least by psychologists, that social learning is importantly involved in making them so. But just what the rewards and punishments are and how they operate are still obscure. A complicating factor is that both sexes share the same impulses but in different proportions. Recent experiments suggest that boys may fight more than girls because girls are readier to withdraw, or sympathize, or share. Questions multiply and there are no easy answers.

A strong case can be made for a biological origin of male aggressiveness if we admit evidence from other animals. In most vertebrate species males dominante females and fight other males. That aggressiveness is inherited is shown by the difference between a wirehaired fox terrier and a cocker spaniel; more convincingly by selective breeding of poultry and mice.

At the human level the most startling clue to a possible genetic origin of aggression was a 1965 report of too many cases of a double-Y chromosome in a criminal population. But fifteen years of investigation have failed to establish a connection between the XYY pattern and violence.

A chemical correlate of dominance and aggressiveness has been found in the male hormone testosterone. In the mouse castration diminishes fighting and implants of testosterone restore it. In monkeys the androgen appears to be related to dominance, both as cause and effect. In both species there is evidence that male hormone given to females near the time of birth organizes brain mechanisms for later aggression: play fighting in monkeys, serious combat in mice.

In humans the effect of androgens on aggressiveness is harder to document. Our belief is that the relation is there, deeply buried under a "psychological blanket." But a belief without firm evidence is, of course, merely a challenge to seek further.

Fear. Even if human males were proved to be more pugnacious, it would not necessarily follow that females are more timid. Studies of preschool children contain a few indications of a sex difference in timidity, but these are neither consistent nor on the whole easy to interpret. Tests of anxiety given to schoolchildren either failed to separate the sexes or found girls more anxious, but there was reason to suspect the boys of concealment.

Evidence at the college level is more compelling. Not only do women confess more fears, but a variety of experiments has shown the men not guilty of suppressing theirs. Finally, in traffic conditions women have been found to take fewer risks than men whether driving or walking across a busy intersection.

Compliance. Compliance fits the traditional role of the female in our culture and in many others. Yet as a trait it shows unexpected gaps; for example, women are no easier to hypnotize than men. Experiments with children serve to probe the dynamics of conformity.

Obedience to adult rules is measured by techniques such as Forbidden Toys and Don't Cheat. Boys usually break the rules more than girls, but their motives may be different; girls seem more concerned with being loved, boys with avoiding punishment or winning. A different type of conformity is tested by a person's reluctance to disagree publicly with his peers. If girls are more reluctant than boys, experiments detect it only occasionally, but some of the occasions are too interesting to be ignored.

Nurturance. Whether we talk of rats or monkeys, juvenile or adult, females are more concerned with infants of the species than are males. Human attitudes are not so accessible. But according to one experiment, upper-grade children liked pictures of infants better than pictures of adults, and the preference was earlier and stronger in girls than boys.

Cross-cultural studies are of little use in trying to tease out a biological root, since girls are so uniformly given precedence in baby care. Better, though less than solid, evidence comes from female patients with adrenogenital syndrome. Exposed to prenatal androgens, then reared as girls, they seemed quite indifferent to the joys of motherhood.

Affiliation. If affiliation is the basic ingredient of which little girls are made, early signs should be eagerly sought and interpreted with caution. It may or may not be significant that female infants as compared with males (1) do more sleep smiling; (2) attend to pictures of faces rather than things; and (3) cry more at the sound of another infant's cry. Somewhat more weight should probably be given to the finding that 4-year-old girls show more empathy than boys, and that girls of all ages prefer less distance and more eye contact while conversing.

There is also evidence from studies of children and interviews with senior citizens that females cultivate fewer but more intimate friendships than males.

Need to Achieve. A lingering doubt persists. Behind the specific traits we have considered, is there a basic difference in motivation between males and females? Is Bakan's idea of two principles, agency and communion, essentially sound? A favored view today is that men and women have the same need for achievement (nAch), differing only in direction: men striving for excellence in prestigious pursuits, women for success in forging social relationships. Experiments using McClelland's projective method supported this view. Using Weiner's attributional theory of motivation, we can ask several questions about sex differences in nAch.

1. Are boys more confident of success than girls? A suggested answer is probably, but especially in masculine domains and competitive conditions. (Fear of success is no longer confined to women; it may, however, arise out of conflict with affiliative needs.)

2. Are boys more likely than girls to take credit for their successes and blame their failures on bad luck? Results suggest in grade school, yes; in college, women are more inclined than men to attribute both good and poor performance to luck.

In our view a more trenchant question is whether achievement is as important to females as to males. We have cited experiments with children showing that boys put forth greater effort just to solve a problem or complete a task, while girls do so to gain adult approval. Not to mention one study of college students' attitudes toward their own bodies, showing that females were chiefly concerned with the body's attractiveness, males with its effective functioning.

In either sex a need to achieve must be largely learned. The only question we ask, here as elsewhere, is: given equal opportunities, would males or females learn nAch with equal ease? The catch is, of course, that opportunities are never equal. Longitudinal studies of development have brought out striking sex differences in response to parental treatment, but have so far fallen short of answering our question. Much the same can be said of attempts to push comparisons as close to birth as possible. The search continues, sustained by its own rewards.

Looking Ahead

Stereotyping Gender Differences. In light of the evidence on gender differences assembled in this volume, a few speculations may be in order as to how they might best be handled. Most commonly throughout the history of the culture males and females have been dichotomized into separate categories or stereotypes, with a masculinity axis around agency-instrumentalism; and femininity clustering around expressive-communion traits. This dichotomy follows a sex cleavage in basic abilities and in behavioral dynamics, with a female verbal advantage correlated with a predominant need for social affiliation and emotional warmth. The parallel male advantage in handling space has been correlated with a predominant need for aggression and competitive achievement. These stereotypic models have been reinforced by child training throughout much of the Western world.

The trouble with stereotypes, of course, is that they do not fit all individuals, thus imposing severe restrictions on many. In the case of women, sex typing has been seen as a power struggle between the stronger male and weaker female under the prevailing conditions of patriarchism. Protest movements have been mounted on behalf of the female sex minority as in cases of ethnic minorities, and even endangered animal species, to ensure for them a fair deal and access to the good life or at least survival.

Commendable as resistance to the arbitrary stereotyping may be, there is risk of neglecting the minority-within-minority of individuals whose resistance is directed against emancipation from the stereotypes, and who, as in the case of the kibbutzniks, have moved away from radical feminist equality, back to the earlier, prerevolutionary gender differentiation. In other words, to force everyone into the new mold may violate the individual as much as to force them into the older stereotypes. As we shall point out later, freedom to choose according to individual need would seem to be the preferred way of dealing with the complex problem of man/woman roles.

In the case of men, the destructive effects of role stereotypes in preventing them from realizing their full potential as human beings have until recently been overlooked presumably because of their higher social status. Now such popular books on Fasteau's (1974) *The Male Machine*, and a spate of research studies bearing on the problem, have heightened public and scientific awareness of the male plight. Even as a little boy, the need for finding an occupational goal is borne in upon him at home, at school, and through the media. No alternatives are offered and if he doesn't like it, he is expected to keep his negative attitudes to himself. His model is a clockwork executive who must always appear rational and keep a tight rein on emotional expression (Balswick & Peek 1971). Social sanctions are especially strict regarding any show of dependency, passivity, or tenderness, which are usually associated with femininity. Human concerns or achievement unrelated to power are also suspect (Wong et al. 1976). Even though the raw truculence that was a male asset in a cruder age has been smoothed in the modern bureaucracy into subtle manipulation geared to the attainment of more complex goals, aggression is still a power tool in the race to the top.

Eliminating Gender Differences

Frustration over failure to free themselves from male dominantion has led an extremist branch of the current women's liberation movement to propose cutting the Gordian knot by eliminating gender role altogether. According to these radical feminists, sex roles which have been defined on the basis of biological differences are as discriminatory and oppressive as the widely disseminated notions of race differences. They hold that the very core of sexism is the dependence of a woman's identity on her relationship to some man rather than on her own personal resources (Hole & Levine 1971). In their opinion the solution cannot be accomplished through the existing establishment, as the more moderate National Organization of Women advocates, but demands nothing short of the total dissolution of patriarchal social structure (Pollock 1972).

Along with this iconoclastic program goes the refusal to credit the body of scientific evidence on sex differences or the established relationships between physiological mechanisms and behavior. All sex differences are categorically attributed to social conditioning. By ruling out biologically based differences women can make themselves over in the image of men and consequently be free to reject men, marriage, and motherhood (Rossi 1973).

Support for this extreme environmentalist position is found in Kessler and McKenna's (1978) so-called ethnomethodological approach. According to this viewpoint gender roles would be ruled out on the ground that, except for the occasional sperm- and ova-bearing functions of males and females respectively, differentiation between the sexes results solely from cultural influences.

Synthesizing the Genders

Blending. Rather than forcing the issue by futile attempts to eliminate gender roles altogether, a more realistic approach to the problem may be sought in the cultural redefinition of gender roles that has been going on ever since World War II. Although stereotyping is still apparent in American student opinion (Der-Karabetian & Smith 1977), a gradual blurring of gender differences has been facilitated by sociocultural influences during recent years, which have loosened the rigidity of the traditional feminine role and softened male sexual assertiveness (Gagnon & Simon 1973). As evidence of this trend we may cite McKee and Sherriffs' (1960) early study showing that women's images of the ideal man contained many feminine as well as masculine qualities, including more emotional expressiveness and interest in interpersonal relations than was stereotypical (see chapter 5). In a later study, male and female students perceived the ideal for both as possessing characteristics valued in the opposite sex, so that a woman could be competent without risk to her femininity, and a man could be kind without jeopardizing his masculinity (Elman et al. 1970). In other college populations this overlap of roles is expressed in greater concern by males with family relationships and in greater female pride in achievement (Lunneborg & Rosewood 1972). Actually, an integration of needs for achievements and affiliation should yield more satisfaction to the person of either sex than either need alone.

During the past decade, Anne Steinmann and her coworkers have carried out an extensive cross-national research program on sex-role perception (Steinmann & Fox 1974). This work involved gathering data on thousands of men and women ranging from late teens to the 70s; from many nations of Europe, North America, South America, Near and Far East; and from subcultures within many of these cultures. To implement their study the authors devised an Inventory of Female Values, designed to elicit women's concepts of self, ideal self, and their notions of men's ideal woman. Analogously they obtained men's concepts of self, ideal self, and their ideas of woman's ideal man.

Although the standardization of the inventories has been criticized (Gump 1975), certain clear and consistent trends were established. Over and above minor cultural differences, a major difference stood out in the way the subjects perceived their opposite sex's ideal. While women saw their own values as balanced between self and family orientations, they believed that men wanted a more traditional woman whose role as wife and mother would take precedence over her own need for achievement. This stereotyped feminine ideal was attributed to men by female respondents everywhere within the limits of the surveys.

Parallel male data revealed the same kind of communication failure: the men's self-perceptions as well as their closely related masculine ideals, like those found for the women, expressed a good balance between self-achievement motivation and family devotion, while their concepts of the women's ideal man leaned strongly toward family centeredness.

Paradoxically, though both men and women had much the same ideal images of their own sex, neither seemed to have an accurate picture of what the other wanted. In conflict and confusion, men have feared that they were not as family-centered or as socially submissive as women expected them to be while, conversely, women have been convinced that they were more self-assertive and self-oriented than men wanted them to be.

Of course these interpretations are based on the assumption that the respondents were telling the truth. It must be admitted, however, that the women may have been projecting a more passive role than they actually wanted and wanted the men to accept for them. On their part, the men may have been talking a liberal line which they did not really mean.

Taken at face value, the results suggest that each sex is moving away from the stereotyped conceptions of masculinity-femininity (M-F) toward more flexible, integrative ones, but with the misgiving that the other sex may still be adhering to the old attitudes and unable to meet on the mutual, new ground.

Changes in M-F concepts are reflected in the recent views of the ideal man and ideal woman of 28,000 college-educated male and female readers of *Psychology Today* (Tavris 1977). Interestingly, no single trait was applied exclusively to either gender. A large proportion of men as well as of women believed that the ideal man should be warm, gentle, and able to love. At the same time, work success was seen by both male and female respondents as an asset to the ideal man, and also valued in the ideal woman. Moreover, competitiveness, aggressiveness, and risk taking no longer seemed to play a major part in the ideals of either masculinity or feminity.

Adrogyny. Recognition of the need for synthesis of separate masculine and feminine elements within the individual is an integral part of Jungian theory according to which *Heilsweg* or wholeness of self is attained through the balance between various dualities including M-F (Singer 1976).

This theme has been further elaborated in the androgyny movement (Heilbrun 1973). According to this thinking, masculine and feminine qualities need to be combined not only for individual integrity, but also to provide an essential synthesis for civilization. Androgyny has presumably characterized the high periods in Western culture when the feminine principle of woman, the nourisher, modulated the aggressive, controlling masculine principle of man, the maker. The Shakespearian plays expressed the idea of men and women as complementary and, as such, necessary to the full expression of humanity. The androgynous ideal was perhaps nowhere else acted out so completely as in the Bloomsbury Group of turn-of-the-century England, where a group of avant-garde intellectuals—Virginia Woolf, Bertrand Russell, Roger Fry, and others—created quite a stir by setting themselves up as the trustees of civilization, rejecting Victorian gender stereotypes in favor of androgynous fusion of reason and passion, respectively representing masculine and feminine.

A recent attempt to take into account the androgynous mixture of personality traits, is the Bem Sex Role Inventory (BSRI; Bem 1974). The test, based on separate masculinity and femininity scales, yields measures of a subject's adherence to prevailing sex stereotypes. Applying the inventory to college students, Bem (1975) found that androgynous individuals of both sexes displayed high levels of masculine independence when under pressure to conform, and high levels of feminine playfulness when given a kitten to interact with. Stereotypical (M) men, however, showed independence but not playfulness, while stereotypical (F) women showed neither independence nor playfulness. In general, high M scores in males and high F scores in females correlated with high anxiety, low self-esteem, a low degree of social acceptance, and poor emotional adjustment. Strict adherence to the sex stereotypes thus limits the range of behavior available to a person, while androgynous behavior permits the individual to respond to any situation in a manner that best meets one's personal needs and the situational demands, regardless of sex (Kaplan & Bean 1976).

Transcendence. Another formulation for dealing with the gender-role problem is sex-role transcendence (Rebecca et al. 1976). While androgyny in a sense attempts to meld together sex differences in order to achieve an ambisex society, transcendence accepts and utilizes them. In Kohlberg and Ullian's (1974) version of this view, as we noted in chapter 6, the child in growing up is directly taught the gender role considered appropriate for his sex, and at the same time he indirectly learns the opposite-sex role that he is expected to avoid. Rigid stereotyping is only a first stage, however, on the way to the ultimate attainment of a dynamic and flexible orientation to life which transcends the roles of either sex. Maturity is marked by the freedom to express human qualities for which gender is irrelevant. According to this theory, though a person would retain his core-gender identity, he would be able to transcend specific gender characteristics according to the demands of specific situations.

Personal Expression. A child from a healthy home can be expected to develop a good ego identity which allows easy expression of his individual qualities in the context of flexible gender roles. Since he is accepted for himself, whether boy or girl, he can accept himself whether boy or girl, without being locked into a fixed social mold. No longer required to adhere to specific role prescriptions, such an individual is free to express attitudes and attributes that "come naturally" (O'Leary & Donoghue 1978). Under these favorable circumstances, differences between the sexes do not need to be defensively eschewed, but may even be affirmed and positively cultivated, as in McClelland's (1965) image of femininism which glories in the sex differences that point up feminine interpersonal skills on which social cohesion depends.

By denying the gross differences in structure and function that separate the sexes and demanding identical roles in an effort to ensure status equality, women have done themselves the injustice of suppressing their distinctively female sources of satisfaction. The problem of status equality has overshadowed the subtler question of role equivalence. Since many of the activities in the traditional feminine role have been associated with inferior status, the struggle of women has naturally been directed toward achieving the status symbols of economic and social power that society has so long kept for its men and from its women. In light of this trend it is not surprising to find in a recent large student sampling a correlation between adjustment and masculinity in both males and females (Jones et al. 1978). In general, adaptability appeared as a function of a mix of traits dominated by assertiveness, decisiveness, and intellectuality rather than by nurturance, responsibility, and emotionality, or by an androgynous blend of both dimensions.

The implications of these findings go beyond the limits of this book. If adjustment to the prevailing competitive, capitalistic, self-serving philosophy is the societal goal, the social planner would simply reinforce instrumentalism over nurturance in both boys and girls to ensure their internalizing the traits most likely to succeed. If, however, realizing the richest human potentials is the societal goal, the individual regardless of gender will be encouraged to develop unique personal characteristics.

In the case of women, only after attaining full status equality will they be free to express their primary femininity (Stoller 1976) without fear of downgrading, and to evolve their own equivalent role models. A woman's femininity may come out in her style of performing any type of job. Engineering, for example, may be done in a feminine "embracing" way in contrast to a masculine "conquering" way (Chien-Shiung Wu 1965). Commenting on this situation, Erikson (1968) points out: "It is as yet unpredictable what the tasks and roles, opportunities and job specifications will be once women are not merely adapted to male jobs in economics and politics but learn to adapt jobs to themselves . . . since a woman is never not-a-woman, she can see her long-range goals only in those modes of activity which include and integrate her natural dispositions" (p. 290).

Although role stereotyping has been no less restrictive for men than it has for women, in an atmosphere of freedom for individual self-expression regardless of gender men will be able to come out of their closets and be themselves as persons. Permission to express the softer feelings is bound to relieve the role strain to which instrumentalism has long condemned them. As they learn to give up the image of being a big wheel and of giving the other fellow hell, their relationships with men will have a chance to become more meaningful and allow the development of closer friendships more like those between girlfriends (Goldberg 1975; Lewis 1978).

Changes in the concept of masculinity are reflected in the changes in male sexuality, which is broadening its scope (Gross 1978). Although naturally penis-centered, a man's virtuosity is now expected to combine the basic biological virility with the sensuous nuances demanded by the sophisticated contemporary woman whose needs encompass more fondling and tenderness in a prolonged foreplay as well as climactic satisfaction (Farrell 1974).

Within the home men are moving away from their overconcern with the job toward greater family orientation. In line with this trend are the recent proposals to give fathers and mothers equally the option of child-care leaves of absence (Romer & Secor 1971). If given the opportunity, it has been suggested that fathers might prove as nurturant child rearers as mothers (Lott 1973). Greater involvement of men in their children's care and companionship would have the double advantage of enriching their own personalities and of laying the foundation for more secure identities in their sons and daughters (Pleck & Sawyer 1974). There can never be full recognition of the worth of parenthood as long as it is defined in terms of an exclusive relationship between mother and children, instead of a concern of caring adults of both sexes with the growth of society's most precious resource.

As the role stereotypes give way to flexibility and personal choice, sex labeling of jobs will also become obsolescent. The man who chooses child-care work as his career, by his example can expose the fallacy that men have to act in some special manly way rather than to behave as their individuality dictates (Seifert 1974). Social casework presents a similar challenge to young men entering this "feminine" field. Teachers alerted to the risk of sex-role conflict may help the trainees develop a more acceptable image of their occupation (Lee & Haskell 1976).

We may end our analysis of sex differences on the hopeful note that the current climate of liberation will continue to generate discussions in which men and women can air their views concerning conflict areas between them and their suggestions for resolving them (Abramowitz et al. 1977). From the battle of the sexes, new exciting forms of creative social synthesis between them may be expected to emerge in the future.

In Margaret Mead's (1977) very nearly last words to her colleagues: "We may eventually develop a culture in which specific traits are not viewed as belonging to one gender."

References

Abramowitz, S.I.; Abramowitz, C.V.; and Moore, D. 1977. "Masculine, Male, and Human: Implementing and Evaluating a Men's Conference." *Professional Psychology* 8:185-191.

Balswick, J.O., and Peek, C.W. 1971. "The Inexpressive Male: A Tragedy of American Society." *The Family Coordinator* 20:363-368.

Bem, S.L. 1974. "The Measurement of Psychological Androgyny." *Journal of Consulting and Clinical Psychology* 42:155-162.

_____. 1975. "Sex-Role Adaptability: One Consequence of Psychological Androgyny." *Journal of Personality and Social Psychology* 31:634-643.

Chien-Shiung Wu. 1965. "Panelist Discussion." In J.A. Mattfeld and C.G. Van Aken, eds. *Women and the Scientific Professions.* Cambridge, Mass.: MIT Press, pp. 44-48.

Der-Karabetian, A., and Smith, A. 1977. "Sex-Role Stereotyping in the United States: Is It Changing?" *Sex Roles* 3:193-198.

Elman, J.; Press, A.; and Rosenkrantz, P. 1970. "Sex Roles and Self-concepts: Real and Ideal." *Proceedings of the 78th Annual Convention of the American Psychological Association* 5:455-456.

Erikson, E.H. 1968. *Identity: Youth and Crisis.* New York: Norton.

Farrell, W. 1974. *The Liberated Man: Freeing Men and Their Relationships with Women.* New York: Random House.

Fasteau, M.F. 1974. *The Male Machine.* New York: McGraw-Hill.

Gagnon, J.H., and Simon, W. 1973. *Sexual Conduct: The Social Sources of Human Sexuality.* Chicago: Aldine, pp. 283-307.

Goldberg, H. 1975. "The Psychological Pressures on the American Male." In K.C.W. Kammeyer, ed. *Confronting the Issues: Sex Roles, Marriage, and the Family.* Boston: Allyn & Bacon, pp. 431-435.

Gross, A.E. 1978. "The Male Role and Heterosexual Behavior." *Journal of Social Issues* 34:87-107.

Gump, J. 1975. "A Promise-Yield Dilemma." Review of *The Male Dilemma: How to Survive the Sexual Revolution* by A. Steinmann and D.J. Fox. *Contemporary Psychology* 20:515.

Heilburn, C.G. 1973. *Toward a Recognition of Androgyny*. New York: Knopf.

Hole, J., and Levine, E. 1971. *Rebirth of Feminism*. New York: Quadrangel Books.

Jones, W.H.; Chemovetz, M.E.; and Hansson, R.O. 1978. "The Engima of Androgyny: Differential Implications for Males and Females?" *Journal of Consulting and Clinical Psychology* 46:298-313.

Kaplan, A.G., and Bean, J.P., eds. 1976. *Beyond Sex-Role Stereotypes: Readings toward a Psychology of Androgyny*. Boston: Little, Brown.

Kessler, S.J., and McKenna, W. 1978. *Gender: An Ethnomethodological Approach*. New York: Wiley-Interscience.

Kohlberg, L., and Ullian, D. 1974. "Stages in the Development of Psychosexual Concepts and Attitudes." In R.C. Friedman, R.M. Richart, and R.L. Vande Wiele, eds. *Sex Differences in Behavior*. New York: Wiley.

Lee, V.R., and Haskell, M.H. 1976. "Casework Training and the Masculine Ethic." *Newsletter for Research in Mental Health and Behavioral Sciences* 18:17-20.

Lewis, R.A. 1978. "Emotional Intimacy among Men." *Journal of Social Issues* 34:108-121.

Lott, B.E. 1973. "Who Wants Children?" *American Psychologist* 28:573-582.

Lunneborg, P.W., and Rosewood, L.M. 1972. "Need Affiliation and Achievement: Declining Sex Differences." *Psychological Reports* 3:795-798.

McClelland, D. 1965. "Wanted: A New Self-image for Women." In R.J. Lifton, ed. *The Woman in America*. Boston: Houghton, Mifflin, pp. 173-192.

McKee, J.P., and Sherriffs, A.C. 1960. "Men's and Women's Beliefs, Ideals, and Self-concepts." In J.M. Seidman, ed. *The Adolescent: A Book of Readings*, rev. ed. New York: Holt, Rinehart, & Winston, pp. 282-293.

Mead, M. 1977. "Twenty-fourth Annual Karen Horney Lecture: Temperamental Differences and Sexual Dimorphism." *American Journal of Psychoanalysis* 37:179-192.

O'Leary, V.E., and Donoghue, J.M. 1978. "Latitudes of Masculinity: Reactions to Sex Role Deviance in Men." *Journal of Social Issues* 34:17-28.

Pleck, J.H., and Sawyer, J., eds. 1974. *Men and Masculinity*. Englewood Cliffs, N.J.: Prentice-Hall.

Pollock, M.J. 1972. "Changing the Role of Women." In H. Wortis and C. Rabinowitz, eds. *The Women's Movement: Social Psychological Perspectives*. New York: Halsted Press, pp. 10-20.

Rebecca, M.; Hefner, R.; and Oleshansky, B. 1976. "A Model of Sex-Role Transcendence." *Journal of Social Issues* 32:197-206.

Romer, K.T., and Secor, C. 1971. "The Time Is Here for Women's Liberation." *Annals of the American Academy of Political and Social Science* 397:129-139.

Rossi, A.S. 1973. "Maternalism, Sexuality, and the New Feminism." In J. Zubin and J. Money, eds. *Contemporary Sexual Behavior: Critical Issues in the 1970s*. Baltimore: Johns Hopkins University Press, pp. 145-173.

Seifert, J. 1974. "Some Problems of Men in Child Care Center Work." In J.H. Pleck and J. Sawyer, eds. *Men and Masculinity*. Englewood Cliffs, N.J.: Prentice-Hall, pp. 69-73.

Singer, J. 1976. *Androgyny: Toward a New Theory of Sexuality*. Garden City, N.Y.: Anchor Press/Doubleday.

Steinmann, A., and Fox, D.J. 1974. *The Male Dilemma: How to Survive the Sexual Revolution*. New York: Aronson.

Stoller, R.J. 1976. "Primary Femininity." *American Psychoanalytic Association Journal* 24:59-78.

Tavris, C. 1977. "Men and Women Report Their Views of Masculinity." *Psychology Today* 10:35-42, 82

Wong, M.R.; Davey, J.; and Conroe, R.M. 1976. "Expanding Masculinity: Counseling the Male in Transition." *Counseling Psychologist* 6:58-61.

Index

Index

Achievement. *See* Need to achieve

Activity level: heritability, 124-125; hyperactivity, 122-123; infancy and childhood, 121-122, 123-124; pathology, 125; social factors, 123-124

Acuity: auditory, visual, 31

Adrenogenital syndrome (AGS), 50, 111-113, 143, 171

Affiliation: empathy, 172-173; intensive-extensive, 176-177; signs in infancy, 171-172, 173; social distance, 173-176; socialization of play, 176

Aggressiveness, biological factors: breeding experiments, 135-137; hormones in humans, 142-144; hormones in monkeys, 140-142; hormones in rodents, 139-140; XYY syndrome, 137-138

Aggressiveness, social factors: adult intervention, 130; empathy, 131; field experiments, 133-134; models, 131-132; moods, 131; peer acceptance, 130-131; stereotypes, 132-133

Aggressiveness and dominance, 129-130; in animals, 134-135, 140-141

Agricultural revolution, 6-7

Androgen: and animal aggressiveness, 138-142; and human aggressiveness, 142-144. *See also* Hermaphrodites

Androgyny, 204-205

Anxiety. *See* Fear

Cerebral asymmetry: clinical evidence, 59; cognitive style, 66-69; experimental evidence, 59-60; functions involved, 59-60; split brain, 60

Cerebral asymmetry, sex difference in: cognitive style and, 66-71; dyslexia and, 65; experimental evidence, 62-65; maturation rate and, 65-66; theories of, 61-62, 64-65

Cognitive style: as field-dependence, 37-39; in problem solving, 39-40; and spatial ability, 39, 40; tests of, 37. *See also* Cerebral asymmetry

Compliance: with authority, 165-167; behavior problems, 163; cross-cultural evidence, 163, 165; in group discussion, 164-165; hypnosis, 163-164; in jury duty, 164; with peers, 167-168

Compliance, tests of: Asch situation, 167-168; Don't Cheat, 166-167; Forbidden Toys, 165-166

Confidence, 186-187, 191-192

Crime, 163

Dominance. *See* Aggressiveness

Dyslexia, developmental, 47-48

Empathy, 171-172

Estrogen: and aggressiveness in humans, 142, 142-144; in mice, 140; premenstrual anxiety, 156-158

Factor analysis: of abilities, 33-35, 46; definition, 32; of M-F, 82-85

Fear: in children, 151-153; concealment of, 152-154; in eyelid con-

Fear: in children (cont.)
   ditioning, 154-155; relation to
   menstrual cycle, 156-158; risk in
   traffic, 155-156; in young
   adults, 153-155
Fear of success, 185-186
Feminine boys, 109

Gay. *See* Homosexuals
Gender development: cognitive
   developmental theory, 93-95;
   psychoanalytic theory, 92-93;
   social learning theory, 93
Gender identity: confusions in,
   103; developmental changes,
   90-92; modeling, 95-98; relation
   to sex, 89-90; theories of, 92-95;
   toy preferences and, 90
Gender roles: flexibility in, 206-
   207; measures of, 205; perception of, 203-204; social changes,
   12-13; social class differences,
   8-9, 11, 99; synthesis of,
   203-206
Gender roles across cultures:
   ancient Rome, 8-9; Celtic
   Europe, 10; classical Athens,
   7-8; Cuba, 24-25; Germany,
   14-15; Israeli Kibbutz, 20-22;
   Latin America, 22-25; Middle
   Ages, 10-11; Minoan Crete, 7;
   mother-focussed cultures, 7;
   prehistoric societies, 5-7;
   Renaissance Europe, 11-12;
   Scandinavia, 18-20; Soviet
   Union, 16-18

Heredity-environment problem, 1-3
Hermaphrodites, 110-113: femin-
   ized genetic males, 113;
   masculinized genetic females
   (AGS), 111-113
Homosexuals, female: compared

with male homosexuals, 105;
   development, 106; family patterns, 106; measurement of
   M-F, 85-86
Homosexuals, male: compared
   with normals, 105; genetic and
   hormonal effects, 107; measurement of M-F, 85-86; parental
   relations, 104-105;
   psychoanalytic studies, 104-105;
   relations to transsexuals,
   108-109; twin studies, 114-116
Hormones, gonadal. *See*
   Androgen, Estrogen, Progesterone
Hypnosis, 163-164

Intelligence: inheritance of, 45-46;
   Wechsler scales, 32
Intimacy, 176-177

Kibbutz, 20-22

Lesbians. *See* Homosexuals,
   female

Masculinity-femininity (M-F):
   adjustment and M-F scores,
   206; changes in concepts of,
   204; essence of, 75-76. *See also*
   Androgyny, Feminine boys,
   Homosexuals, Transsexuals
Menstrual cycle, 156-158
M-F, measurement of: bipolar
   hypothesis, 77-78; factor
   analysis, 81-85; in homosexuals,
   85-86; self-descriptions, 78-81,
   83-85; stereotypes, 76-78, 80-81,
   82-83

Need to achieve: attributional
   theory of, 184, 187-189; *versus*
   need for approval, 190-192;

origins, 193-194; projective
method, 183-184; relation to sex
role, 272-273, 283
Numerical ability: across cultures,
42; biological factors, 46-47;
development of, 34-35; father
model, 43; sex roles, 42
Nurturance: across cultures, 170;
adrenogenital syndrome, 171;
"babyness," 169-170; in
monkeys, 169; in rats, 169

Patriarchism: ancient Rome, 8-9;
classical Athens, 7-8; Germany,
14-15; Latin America, 22-24;
origins, 6
Progesterone: aggressiveness in
humans, 143-144; premenstrual
anxiety, 156-158
Psychoanalysis. See Gender development

Sex-change surgery, 107-110
Sex-linked inheritance: of
numerical ability, 46-47; of
spatial ability, 48-49
Sex stereotypes: effects on men,
202, 207; role of media, 96-98;
and sex differences, 201. See

also Gender roles; M-F,
measurement of
Spatial ability: across cultures, 43-
44; hormones, 49-50; nature of,
35-37; sex-linked inheritance,
48-49; sex roles, 44; Turner's
syndrome, 49. See also Cerebral
asymmetry

Testosterone. See Androgen
Transsexuals: determinants of,
110; female-to-male, 109-110;
male-to-female, 107-109; relation to feminine boys, 109
Transvestites. See Transsexuals
Turner's syndrome, 49
Twin studies: activity level, 125;
dyslexia, 48; intelligence, 45; sex
and gender, 114-116; special
abilities, 46

Verbal ability: biological factors,
47-48; development of, 33-34;
nature of, 34; social factors,
41-42. See also Cerebral asymmetry

Wechsler scales, 32

About the Authors

John Seward received the A.B. from Cornell University and the Ph.D. in psychology from Columbia University. He has taught psychology at Columbia University, Connecticut College, Boston University, and the University of California at Los Angeles, where he is now professor emeritus. His central interest is research in motivation and learning, in which he has published extensively.

Georgene Seward, is emerita professor of psychology at the University of Southern California. A graduate of Barnard College, she received the doctorate from Columbia University, where she and her husband taught for several years before accepting a joint post at Connecticut College. In 1946 they moved to California.

Dr. Seward is the author of *Sex and the Social Order* and *Psychotherapy and Culture Conflict*. In 1958 she edited *Clinical Studies in Culture Conflict* and, with John Seward, edited a *Festschrift* for R.S. Woodworth's 90th birthday, *Current Psychological Issues*. In 1970 she and Robert C. Williamson coedited *Sex Roles in Changing Society*.